D0928133

DANIEL PATRICK
MOYNIHAN

3-97-M.

DANIEL PATRICK MOYNIHAN

THE INTELLECTUAL IN PUBLIC LIFE

EDITED BY
ROBERT A. KATZMANN

THE WOODROW WILSON CENTER PRESS
WASHINGTON, D.C.

THE JOHNS HOPKINS UNIVERSITY PRESS
BALTIMORE AND LONDON

EDITORIAL OFFICES

The Woodrow Wilson Center Press
370 L'Enfant Promenade, S.W., Suite 704
Washington, D.C. 20024-2518
Telephone 202-287-3000, ext. 218
wwics.si.edu

ORDER FROM

The Johns Hopkins University Press
Hampden Station
Baltimore, Maryland 21211
Telephone 1-800-537-5487
www.press.jhu.edu

Printed in the United States of America on acid-free paper ♾

2 4 6 8 9 7 5 3 1

Library of Congress Cataloging-in-Publication Data

Daniel Patrick Moynihan : the intellectual in public life / edited by Robert A. Katzmann.
p. cm.
Based on a conference held at the Wilson Center on March 17, 1997 in honor of Moynihan's seventieth birthday.
Includes bibliographical references.
ISBN 0-8018-6071-7 (acid-free paper)
1. Moynihan, Daniel P. (Daniel Patrick), 1927– —Congresses. 2. Moynihan, Daniel P. (Daniel Patrick), 1927– —Political and social views—Congresses. 3. Legislators—United States—Biography—Congresses. 4. Ambassadors—United States—Biography—Congresses. 5. Intellectuals—United States—Biography—Congresses.
I. Katzmann, Robert A.
E840.8.M68D36 1998
973.92'092—dc21
[b] 98-24914
CIP

THE WOODROW WILSON INTERNATIONAL CENTER FOR SCHOLARS

The Center is the living memorial of the United States of America to the nation's twenty-eighth president, Woodrow Wilson. Congress established the Woodrow Wilson Center in 1968 as an international institute for advanced study, "symbolizing and strengthening the fruitful relationship between the world of learning and the world of public affairs." The Center opened in 1970 under its own board of trustees.

In all its activities the Woodrow Wilson Center is a nonprofit, nonpartisan organization, supported financially by annual appropriations from the Congress, and by the contributions of foundations, corporations, and individuals. Conclusions or opinions expressed in Center publications and programs are those of the authors and speakers and do not necessarily reflect the views of the Center staff, fellows, trustees, advisory groups, or any individuals or organizations that provide financial support to the Center.

For Senator Daniel Patrick Moynihan
and Elizabeth B. Moynihan

CONTENTS

FOREWORD

In March 1997, Saint Patrick's Day at the Wilson Center was also Daniel Patrick Moynihan Day. To mark the senator's seventieth birthday, a select group of academics, government officials, and journalists gathered here to assess, and in most cases to celebrate, the many contributions this extraordinary man has made to our national life over the past four decades.

The Wilson Center, instructed by its founding legislation to strengthen relations between the world of learning and the world of public affairs, was the natural setting for such an event. As the daylong conference on "The Intellectual as Public Servant" underscored, the two worlds are united in Senator Moynihan. Robert Katzmann crafted the program and selected the participants with the greatest skill and imagination.

Because I have been a friend of Pat Moynihan's since we worked together on the creation of the Wilson Center—in addition to being a founding father, he was its first vice chairman—and because I have read 17 books he has written and many of his other writings, I did not expect to learn much about him that I did not already know. As the day unfolded, however, it turned out that I was quite mistaken.

The analogy that comes to mind is a retrospective exhibition of the works of a well-known artist. Some artists are diminished by this exposure, as it reveals the thinness or repetitiousness of their oeuvre. Others are suddenly revealed, as Pat Moynihan was, as greater than we had imagined.

In the course of that day, a number of characteristic Moynihan qualities became clearer to me than they had ever been. I mention just three.

The first is Moynihan's almost uncanny ability to fix upon issues that are not yet widely noticed or discussed, but that soon come to occupy center stage in our national consciousness. Examples of this gift abound, but I will cite only one: the report on *The Negro Family: The Case for National Action,* which he wrote while at the Department of Labor in 1966, earned him considerable vilification at the time, but it is now nearly universally recognized as the bedrock upon which all current discussions of social pathology must rest.

The second characteristic is Moynihan's consistency over the years. Although he is more than occasionally criticized by former allies on the left and on the right for having abandoned or betrayed their common cause, the examination of his entire career showed that he has never ceased to use the best data he can find to illuminate the issues. If the data fail to support positions he has previously espoused, he will follow the data; when the data confirm his earlier views, he will inform us of that fact with unrivaled credibility and eloquence; if the data are insufficient, he will counsel caution. Today, confronted with seemingly insoluble problems and with politicians and pundits guided more by ideology or polls than by hard realities, perhaps his favorite saying is the ancient medical precept, "Above all, do no harm."

The third characteristic, and to me the one most underappreciated before, is his ability to transform the very nature of a familiar, even somewhat shopworn debate by looking at a problem in an entirely new way. Two utterly disparate examples must suffice here. The first was traffic safety, which he addressed in an article in *The Public Interest* in the spring of 1966 entitled "Traffic Safety and the Body Politic." His seminal insight here was that traffic accidents were in fact not accidental and would not be abated by a regime of state troopers and legal sanctions. Rather, they should be viewed from the point of view of epidemiology, to which, "the primary units of concern are groups of persons, not individuals." As he wrote, "Just as classical forms of disease were in general treated by magic until perhaps two centuries ago, accidents have until this moment been thought of as somehow 'wild' occurrences which do not conform to the sequential chain of causal events that define the way things in general take place."

The most recent instance of Moynihan's transformation of an age-old problem is his insight that secrecy as practiced by governments is a form of regulation, indeed regulation of the most precious commodity in any polity: information. There is little question that the report of a bipartisan congressional commission on secrecy that he chaired will radically and beneficially change the way in which our government classifies and declassifies "secret" documents.

Much more could be said in praise of Pat Moynihan, but Michael Barone, coauthor of *The Almanac of American Politics* and a participant in our conference, put it well: "No American politician since Thomas Jefferson has contributed as much to scholarship and no American scholar since Woodrow Wilson has contributed as much to politics."

Charles Blitzer
Director Emeritus of the Woodrow Wilson International Center for Scholars

ACKNOWLEDGMENTS

We are especially indebted to Daniel and Joanna Rose for their generous support for this volume. Joseph Brinley and Carol Walker of the Woodrow Wilson Center Press skillfully shepherded the work through its various editorial stages. Tara Adams Ragone brought her watchful eye to the manuscript and saved us from many errors.

Richard Bland, deputy chief of staff to Senator Daniel Patrick Moynihan, ably and indefatigably answered all queries. Vicki Bear Dodson, George Wagner, and Moira Egan of the Woodrow Wilson Center were invaluable as plans for the Moynihan symposium unfolded. William Schneider, Michael Lacey, and Charles Blitzer moderated the panels of the Moynihan symposium.

From the outset and at every stage, Elizabeth B. Moynihan took time to provide needed counsel. For all that, I am most grateful to her.

Robert A. Katzmann

CHAPTER ONE

INTRODUCTION
THE INTELLECTUAL IN PUBLIC LIFE
A TRIBUTE TO DANIEL PATRICK MOYNIHAN

ROBERT A. KATZMANN

In the course of the American experience, gifted individuals have moved back and forth between academia and government. But entering one realm, they tend to leave the other behind. The pressures of time and circumstance seem to impose a separation between scholarship and the claims of politics. More fundamental perhaps, intellectuals tend to be most comfortable questioning the existing political order free of the responsibilities of governing. As Richard Hofstadter observed more than a generation ago, intellectuals struggle between "alienation and conformity."[1] On the one hand, they seek acceptance of their ideas; on the other hand, they believe that fierce critical detachment, indeed alienation, is necessary for the exercise of their creative juices. For the intellectual in politics, life is lived on a slippery tightrope, on which balance is difficult to maintain for very long.

In the tradition of the intellectual in public service, Senator Daniel Patrick Moynihan stands apart. Unlike the "in and outer," he has for more than a generation occupied space simultaneously in the world of ideas and politics, nourishing both. Centrally involved in every major issue of our age, Moynihan has been a distinct and unique voice in this century—often prescient, independent in his convictions, a scholar, teacher, statesman, and politician, skilled in the art of the possible.

That singular role is acknowledged across the political and philosophical spectrum. John Kenneth Galbraith wrote that "Daniel Patrick Moynihan is, quite possibly, the most diversely interesting and influential political figure in our time."[2] George Will commented that Moynihan "is at the top of the short—the very short—list of indispensable senators. They are indispensable in part because they do important things that would not get done if they were not there. . . . And in a town that is, in matters of the mind, constantly inventing the wheel, he supplies an unrivaled sense of intellectual and institutional history."[3] And David Broder observed: "He's sometimes over our heads, and often light years ahead of us. But we know he's something special."[4]

Senator Moynihan's public service is well-known (Appendix A). A member of the cabinet or sub-cabinet of Presidents Kennedy, Johnson, Nixon, and Ford, he served as assistant secretary of labor for policy planning, counselor to the president, and U.S. representative to the United Nations. He was also assistant to the secretary of labor and the U.S. ambassador to India. Senator Moynihan is the only person in American history to serve in the cabinet or sub-cabinet of four successive administrations. As the senior U.S. senator from New York, he has been elected four times and now is seventeenth in tenure.

In academia, Daniel Patrick Moynihan was director of the Joint Center for Urban Studies at MIT and Harvard University, a professor of government at Harvard University, a fellow at the Center for Advanced Study at Wesleyan University, and assistant professor of government at Syracuse University.

In a career melding ideas and public service, Senator Moynihan has authored or edited sixteen books, written countless articles, and delivered scores of lectures (noted in Appendix B, historian Michael Lacey's selected annotated bibliography). With an original mind, he has sparked new debates and recast old ones through fresh and often provocative approaches. A pioneer of ethnicity on the domestic and international scene, he was virtually alone in predicting the collapse of the Soviet Union due to ethnic conflict. A student of epidemiology, he understood, even before Ralph Nader entered the public arena, the link between the interior design of automobiles and safety. A scholar of social policy, Moynihan crafted a family assistance plan and, later, the Family Support Act. As this text goes to print, his proposals to preserve social security are the focus of a national discussion. Devoted to international law, Moynihan has championed the rule of law and human rights, in his writings, in the United Nations, and in the Senate. A keen analyst of federalism, he shepherded through the Senate the revolutionary Intermodal Surface Transportation Efficiency Act, which provided large sums for transportation and gave states discretion to use money for highways or mass transit.

A critic of art and architecture, Moynihan would over a generation oversee the transformation of Pennsylvania Avenue in the nation's capital. And finally, as a student of bureaucracy and regulation, he would redefine the debate about government secrecy in the quest to make government more accessible.

In blending ideas and politics, Georgetown University president Rev. Leo J. O'Donovan, S.J., commented: "Senator Moynihan is always a moral voice, the voice of our collective conscience."[5] Father O'Donovan continued:

> Throughout his accomplished career . . . the Senator has challenged himself and, indeed, all of us to recognize our obligations to one another in the human community, to be careful and reflective in our decisions as we meet those obligations, to do not what is easy, not what is popular, but what is right. For more than three decades the Senator has championed the cause of children in our country. . . . The Senator also challenged us to remember our obligations to the generations that have come before us. . . . [H]e stood on the Senate floor and challenged both sides of the aisle not to forsake the poorest among us, not to leave countless children with nowhere to turn. He was a voice of reason and a voice of conscience.[6]

Political analyst William Schneider, who once served as a Council of Foreign Relations fellow in the office of Senator Moynihan, remarked that in an age in which a pervasive sense of cynicism poisons American politics: "Moynihan is an example to be cherished for those who would believe that [being] a professional politician is a respectable, decent career. A real calling. A distinguished calling."[7]

On the occasion of Senator Moynihan's seventieth birthday, celebrants across the political spectrum—those who have worked with and for him, and observed his career—joined to offer a tribute to a life dedicated to ideas and public service.[8] A festschrift such as this one is an occasion to capture the perceptions and give voice to the affection of those who have shared time and space with the honoree. In the years ahead, Senator Moynihan's career will no doubt be the subject of many in-depth studies. Following his ideas and politics offers a unique perspective on the last four decades, and with his career at full force, on the future as well. Is there any other figure on the American scene about whom that could be said?

In the case of Senator Moynihan, ideas and office are inseparable. But for purposes of organization, we focus first on the ideas, and then on how Senator Moynihan used his public positions to further those intellectual concerns. As to the former, we examine ethnicity, social policy, epidemiology, public works, and secrecy. With regard to the latter, we explore Moynihan as federal executive, ambassador, U.S. senator, and protector of the third branch. The volume concludes with reflections on Moynihan the man, with a sampling of the Moynihan wit and wisdom, and with very personal observations of a Senate colleague and a tribute from a longtime friend.

I. IDEAS

Ethnicity

Three decades, writes Nathan Glazer, separate Daniel Patrick Moynihan's examination of the Irish in *Beyond the Melting Pot* and his exploration of ethnicity in international politics in *Pandaemonium*. Moynihan "has moved from using the ethnic factor as a searchlight to examine our own society and its problems to extending it to illuminate obscure issues all over the world, at a time when ethnicity it seems is exploding everywhere." Glazer traces Moynihan's contributions to the study of ethnicity, beginning with the origins of their collaboration. He finds three periods in Moynihan's work: an early phase, marked by his analysis of the Irish; a middle phase, characterized by a persistence in the importance of ethnicity in totalitarian societies; and the latest phase, focused on the study of ethnicity as a factor in international politics. Moynihan's greatest achievement as a student of ethnicity, Glazer believes, was his steady claim that the ethnic factor would rip the Union of Soviet Socialist Republics apart: "It is hard to believe that any other academic, observing the customary academic cautions, with the usual 'on the one hand this is possible, but on the other hand so is this,' could have been as bold."

Social Policy

Reviewing his writings in social policy, Seymour Martin Lipset concludes that Moynihan has been prescient, frequently anticipating important developments and trends. Before others would do so, Moynihan recognized the importance of family stability; the family has been central to his analyses of American social problems. His Family Assistance Plan, for example, proposed during the Nixon administration, would have established a national guaranteed income. Although that plan failed to secure legislative passage, Lipset notes that the effort provided the impetus for passage of the Supplemental Security Income, which produced a guaranteed income for the aged, the blind, and the disabled. Moynihan's Family Support Act, enacted in 1988, contained vigorous child-support enforcement mechanisms; required states to implement work, education, and training programs for welfare mothers; required states to provide welfare benefits to poor two-parent families; and offered extended child-care and medical benefits to families in which parents left the welfare rolls for employment. Moynihan's concern for the family, and for children, was at the heart of his opposition to the 1996 law ending the federal entitlement to welfare.

Lipset observes that Moynihan believes that the role of social science lies not in the formation of social policy, but in the measurement of its results. Moynihan is prescient, Lipset concludes, "because he has known from the start that there is no first cause, not in politics, not in social science. . . . What Pat teaches is that not only are there no utopias, there are no solutions, not in the state or in the completely uncontrolled market. There are only approximations, only the continuing struggle for decency, for morality, for equality of opportunity and respect."

Epidemiology

Moynihan's writings, comments Nicholas Eberstadt, show him to be a formidable student of epidemiology—the "study of the distribution and determinants of health-related states or events in specific populations, and the application of this study to control of health problems." Traffic safety, illicit drug use, and violent crime are three areas that have been the objects of Moynihan's attention. In the 1950s, while working on the staff of Governor Averell Harriman of New York, he began (along with William Haddon) to think about road safety as an area of policy inquiry. When viewed in the aggregate, there was a regular structure to, or "etiology" of, motor vehicle injury. Moynihan proposed that a juridical paradigm for auto injury control—with its emphasis on law enforcement and legal sanctions—be replaced with an epidemiological approach, one that would explore specific auto safety improvements. In the "spread and gradual inculcation of epidemiological reasoning," which was "partly responsible for the specific auto safety improvements that were actually achieved," Eberstadt concludes that "Daniel Patrick Moynihan was a prominent vector in the process."

On the subject of crime, Moynihan examined the question of how society coped with rising rates of violence. We have done so, he observed "by defining deviancy down." He proposed "that over the past generation...the amount of deviant behavior in American society has increased beyond the levels the community can 'afford to recognize' and that accordingly we have been redefining deviancy so as to exempt much conduct previously stigmatized, and also quietly raising the 'normal' level in categories where behavior is abnormal by any earlier standard."

On the matter of drugs, Eberstadt points to Moynihan's essay "Iatrogenic Government"—a reference to the medical term having to do with illnesses induced or exacerbated by the physician's own interventions. The problem of illicit use of drugs, Moynihan asserts, is the direct, unambiguous consequence of federal law prohibiting their licit use.

Eberstadt concludes that "America's foremost political epidemiologist [in his writings on auto safety, crime, and drugs] has never been one to shrink from the hard questions, or to neglect their moral dimension. That is a legacy to be ignored only at considerable risk."

Public Works

Robert Peck offers the view that Moynihan has transformed the debate on public works: "On public buildings, urban design, highways, transit, waterways, and water supply he has brought to bear his trademark qualities: an eclectic historical memory, a rapier tongue and typewriter, a nose for demography and geography, a sixth sense for data, and an immunity to ideological blinkering." Moynihan understood that public works underlie most economic development, and accordingly, he set about to create a new Gallatin plan.

One example among many that Peck provides of Moynihan's vision is the 1991 Intermodal Surface Transportation Efficiency Act (ISTEA). That legislation, which revolutionized the federal highway and transit programs, encourages states to use federal funds for modes of transportation other than limited-access highways. It calls for planning before spending. Concerned about the absence of reliable data on the declining investment in public works, Moynihan pushed for the gathering of information that would allow measurement and corrective action.

Peck writes that Moynihan's "reinvention of a noble, humanist public architecture" has been a quest of thirty-five years, beginning with his authorship in 1962 of "Guiding Principles for Federal Architecture." In New York, he championed the renovation of the Prudential Building in Buffalo, the Custom House at Bowling Green and Pennsylvania Station in Manhattan and the building of the new Foley Square federal courthouse and federal office building. Peck recounts that in Washington, D.C., Moynihan was the one person most responsible for the rebirth of Pennsylvania Avenue. He helped save the Old Post Office Building, preserved the aesthetic values of the Capitol, authored the legislation that transformed the dilapidated Pension Building into the National Building Museum, was a forceful proponent of renovating Union Station, and saw through the construction of the Thurgood Marshall Judiciary Building. As Moynihan once declared: "the American polity—the experience as well as the sense of community and shared convictions—has...atrophied in our time because of the retreat from architecture and public buildings as a conscious element of public policy and a purposeful instrument for the expression of public purposes...If we are to save our cities and restore to American public life the sense of shared experience, trust and common purpose that seems to be draining out of it, the quality of public design has got to be made a public issue because it is a political fact."

Secrecy

As I describe in my own chapter, Moynihan has been at the forefront of efforts to reduce unnecessary government secrecy. He spearheaded legislation creating a national Commission on Protecting and Reducing Government Secrecy and chaired that body. By a unanimous vote across the political spectrum, the commission determined: "It is time for a new way of thinking about secrecy.... The best way to ensure that secrecy is respected, and that the most important secrets *remain* secret, is for secrecy to be returned to its limited but necessary role. Secrets can be protected more effectively if secrecy is reduced overall." The central theoretical insight of the commission report is Senator Moynihan's concept that "secrecy is a mode of regulation"—indeed, "it is the ultimate mode, for the citizen does not even know that he or she is being regulated." Drawing upon organizational theory, Moynihan argues that we have created not one, but two regulatory regimes. The first, "public regulation," provides for all kinds of disclosure, discovery, and due process, and is under constant scrutiny. The second regulatory regime—the secrecy regime—is concealed within a vast bureaucratic information. For Moynihan, secrecy "can be a source of dangerous ignorance." It interferes with the free flow of information upon which sound analysis depends; thus the American government overestimated the capacity of the Soviet economy with consequent effects for our foreign policy. The culture of secrecy prevented the nation from learning the degree of Communist subversion in the 1930s and 1940s; at the same time, it fed the paranoia of the McCarthy era. It also, in Moynihan's view, "abetted a form of threat analysis which led to all manner of misadventure"—the most costly being the Vietnam War.

Moynihan's concept of "secrecy as regulation" proved a powerful organizing concept around which to form a consensus. In a time in which conservatives and liberals alike attack overregulation, Senator Moynihan proposed deregulation. Declassification also had the potential of releasing information of interest to those who believed that it would confirm their view of the extent of Communist subversion. For still others, dismantling of secrecy promised to improve decision making and analysis, and to restore the public's right to know.

II. OFFICE

Federal Executive

Stephen Hess reflects upon Moynihan as federal executive, first in the Labor Department during the Kennedy and Johnson administrations, and then on the White House staff of President Nixon. He shows how Moynihan skillfully used his position to pursue policy objectives in such diverse areas as traffic safety, architecture, and family policy. In one example, charged by Secretary of Labor Arthur Goldberg with drafting a *Report to the President by the Ad Hoc Committee on Federal Office Space*, Moynihan took the opportunity to craft a statement to guide architectural policy and to propose the redevelopment of Washington's Pennsylvania Avenue. As an adviser to President Nixon, Moynihan crafted the Family Assistance Plan. He raised creating an agenda to an art form, putting to full use his intellect, staff, and sense of bureaucratic politics. Hess concludes that Moynihan is "our generation's greatest spotter of ideas that might make our society somehow better. This is a remarkable talent. But what turns it into a national treasure is a finely attuned antenna for knowing when an idea is ready for the public arena, the skill to be in positions to make his ideas matter, and the flair to make others notice."

Ambassador

As ambassador to India and to the United Nations, Moynihan, in the words of Suzanne Garment, "helps us understand why it is hard to be a superior diplomat nowadays without possessing a distinctly undiplomatic mind." During his India stint, Moynihan renegotiated the rupee debt and sold the compromise to Congress, "a feat that a less politically well-connected diplomat would have found hard to accomplish." At the United Nations, he denounced Idi Amin, president of Uganda, for his assault on the United States in the General Assembly, and the UN majority for its hostility toward Israel (equating Zionism with racism), and strongly defended the cause of human rights. In much of that work, the official U.S. foreign policy apparatus "did not offer such wholehearted support"; indeed, with "every action he took, there was a nontrivial possibility that some U.S. colleague would openly countermand Moynihan or secretly foment antagonism toward him or try to make him look like a fool." Moynihan was able to influence U.S. politics and policy at the UN, Garment writes, because larger movements of public opinion were with him. When we hear the criticism that ambassadorial appointments are going to outsiders who lack "'ambassadorial temperament,' . . . we should remember that making reasonable room for outsiders is necessary if we are to have room for the Moynihans, and that having one Moynihan around at a crucial foreign policy–making juncture makes it worthwhile to put up with entire troops of lesser nonprofessionals in the ambassadorial ranks."

United States Senator

For Michael Barone, Moynihan's career could be seen as a "work of art"—"he proceeded through reflection and calculation to make a Senate career congruent with the preoccupations of his mind and quite unlike any other that has been seen for a very long time." Elected four times, with his wife, Elizabeth, as his key political adviser, Senator Moynihan understood from the start how best to use his position to serve New York and the nation. Thus, he secured appointment to the Finance Committee "because that's where the money is." Barone details how in that committee, Moynihan was critical to the maintenance of the Social Security system, in crafting welfare legislation. On the Committee on Environment and Public Works, the senator was key to the passage of ISTEA. As a member of the Committee on Foreign Relations and the Select Committee on Intelligence, Moynihan foresaw, long before others, that the danger from the Soviet Union would come not from its expansion but from its disintegration—and that the defense buildup was largely unnecessary. Always a vigilant, tireless defender of the interests of New York, he began to issue a series of reports on New York State and the Federal Fisc, which showed that the state sent more money to Washington than it got back; he has used that information in dozens of amendments and formula fights. He strongly supported the Free Trade Agreement with Canada (Buffalo is only a two-hour drive from Toronto, Montreal is less than an hour from Plattsburgh); opposed the North American Free Trade Agreement with Mexico; and worked to maintain the deductibility of state and local taxes. Assessing his role, Barone finds that "Daniel Patrick Moynihan is the nation's best thinker among politicians since Lincoln and its best politician among thinkers since Jefferson."

The Third Branch

In office, Senator Moynihan has been dedicated to the preservation of an independent judiciary and a nonpartisan process to choose federal district judges and U.S. attorneys. Richard K. Eaton, chair of the Moynihan advisory screening committee for judicial and U.S. attorney vacancies, describes the groundbreaking procedure the senator instituted to ensure merit, nonpartisan appointments. In two decades, Moynihan has proposed thirty district judges, the largest number of all senators in the history of the country. As Eaton points out, Moynihan "has become something of a protector of . . . the 'least dangerous branch,'" vigorously opposing measures to strip the courts of jurisdiction. A student of the Constitution, he has stood against the curtailing of habeas corpus and has been a sharp critic of the balanced budget amendment and the line-item veto.

III. THE MAN

Wit and Wisdom: Moynihan and *Meet the Press*

Perhaps nowhere else in the public mind is the fusion of Moynihan the intellectual and Moynihan the public servant more apparent than in his television appearances. It is through such forums that the public also catches a glimpse of the Moynihan personality and wit. To make the point, Tim Russert, moderator of *Meet the Press* and Washington bureau chief of NBC News, presents excerpts of Moynihan's interviews on the Sunday-morning show. Moynihan has been "a guest an extraordinary twenty-four times, and his appearances span thirty-one years." The subjects are wide-ranging, including the family, the Family Assistance Plan, J. Edgar Hoover, the Carter White House, Iran-Contra, taxes, and welfare repeal. Russert concludes that "Senator Moynihan taught the nation and me that politics is much more than a competitive sport, that ideas do matter, that elections have consequences, and that it is your duty and your honor, if elected, to influence, shape, and make public policy."

A Colleague's Perspective

For eighteen years a fellow senator, Bill Bradley comments that Senator Moynihan "has always remained a giant to me." Moynihan has "consistently foreseen the near future." He "sees great truths where others are lost in a fog of politics, and he sees mothers and children, and people struggling for meaning in their lives, where others see only abstract policy choices." As a senator, Moynihan well understands that "success . . . is a function of substance, procedure, and personality, but substance is the most important, not only because when people of substance speak, other people listen, but also because when people of substance speak, often they control the debate." Bradley then offers vignettes of Moynihan in committee, on the floor, and in caucus, as well as observations about Moynihan and presidents.

A Concluding Tribute

In his remarks, James Q. Wilson explains that Moynihan has been a Democrat for the same reason as are people who had the Great Depression and the Second World War as their defining experience: "If you see one-fourth of a nation unemployed, you take the provision of jobs quite seriously. If you watch the elderly expect nothing but uncertain charity, you become preoccupied with ways of systematically supplying a retirement benefit." He is, in Wilson's view, the ideal public servant, "not because we always agree but because he will follow the facts." If the Senate had a hundred Moynihans, "speeches would be a lot better, and the government would be driven by hard facts rather than by empty ideology." Wilson noted that "Lord Palmerston once suggested that politicians have no permanent friends, only permanent interests. He did not know Pat. This world is filled with people who are his permanent friends, even though many of us have interests—or at least beliefs—that differ from his." Like Saint Patrick of Ireland, "Senator Pat is also a missionary," Wilson concludes, "and has brought to his task many of the same qualities of his illustrious predecessor: luminous intellect, personal conviction, deep historical knowledge, the eye of an artist and the pen of an angel, and above all, an incorruptible devotion to the common good."

NOTES

1. Richard Hofstadter, *Anti-Intellectualism in American Life* (New York: Vintage Books, 1963), 393.

2. Galbraith's words were in the form of an endorsement of Senator Moynihan's *Miles to Go: A Personal History of Social Policy* (Cambridge: Harvard University Press, 1996).

3. George F. Will, "The Presence of Malice," *Newsweek*, 7 December 1987, 106.

4. David Broder, "The Moynihan Imprint," *Washington Post*, 16 March 1997, C7.

5. Rev. Leo J. O'Donovan, S.J., "Introductory Remarks," in *The Marver H. Bernstein Symposium: Secrecy as Government Regulation—A Lecture by Senator Daniel Patrick Moynihan*, Georgetown University Series on Governmental Reform (Washington, D.C.: Georgetown University, 1998), 8.

6. Ibid.

7. William Schneider, remarks at Woodrow Wilson International Center for Scholars conference "The Intellectual as Public Servant: A Tribute to Senator Daniel Patrick Moynihan at Seventy," 17 March 1997.

8. C-SPAN captured the event on videotape, and the Public Broadcasting Service television show *Think Tank*, hosted by Ben Wattenberg, drew from it. In Washington, D.C., *The Hill* newspaper devoted a full page to a day-long celebration at the Woodrow Wilson Center: "Daniel Patrick Moynihan: The Senate's Renaissance Man Turns 70," *The Hill*, 19 March 1997, 18.

PART ONE

IDEAS

CHAPTER TWO

DANIEL P. MOYNIHAN ON ETHNICITY

NATHAN GLAZER

Thirty years separate Senator Moynihan's first large foray into writing about ethnicity—his examination of the Irish in *Beyond the Melting Pot*[1]—and his last major statement, *Pandaemonium.*[2] Of course, his views and interests have evolved in that time, as they would have had to, as he moved through the remarkable stages of his career, from the assistant professor he was when he was writing his essay on the Irish, to senator, with the well-known diverse stops in between as high government official, Harvard professor, adviser to presidents, and ambassador to India and to the United Nations. He has moved from using the ethnic factor as a searchlight to examine our own society and its problems to extending it to illuminate obscure issues all over the world, at a time when ethnicity, it seems, is exploding everywhere. Reading about the current troubles in Albania, I have been searching to see if any reporter would note that Albanians—as I have learned from *Pandaemonium* and as anyone else could from its first few pages—are divided between the Gegs of the north and the Tosks of the south. Is it possible that this may have something to do with the fact that it is the *south* that has risen in rebellion against the government over the collapse of the pyramid schemes? I do not know, of course, but I suspect this ethnic division may well explain why the rebellion has gained such power in one region.

Between these two dates of *Beyond the Melting Pot* and *Pandaemonium*, there is Pat's greatest achievement as a student of ethnicity, his steady insistence that it would be the ethnic factor that could tear the Union of Soviet Socialist Republics apart and end the Cold War. This point was repeated again and again in the 1980s with breathtaking daring. It is hard to believe that any other academic, observing the customary academic cautions, with the usual "on the one hand this is possible, but on the other hand so is this," could have been as bold, though a few academics saw the possibility and at least one, Hélène Carrère d'Encausse—who was given proper credit by Pat—explored it.

My thoughts on Pat and ethnicity will concentrate on these three moments. One might call them the early phase, the middle phase, the latest phase: the study of the Irish; the concentration on the persistence of ethnicity in totalitarian societies against those who insisted it was no longer a matter of consequence; and the wide-ranging study of ethnicity as a factor in international politics.

THE EARLY PHASE: THE STUDY OF THE IRISH

Of course, Pat's involvement with the ethnic factor in society and politics does not begin with his 1960s study of the New York Irish, or with any "study" at all. That is only the beginning of his *academic* writing on the subject. Growing up in New York City, involved in the politics of New York City and New York State, how could he not have been aware of the significance of the ethnic factor? But I believe I can pride myself on having inveigled him into looking at ethnicity more broadly, and not only from the point of view of working politics, which imposes on all involved the necessity of being aware of and knowledgeable about the role of ethnic factors in New York.

Here a few words on how Pat became involved in the research that became *Beyond the Melting Pot* would be in order. It was Irving Kristol who first told me about Pat. He had written a remarkable article, "Epidemic on the Highways," published in *The Reporter*, which Irving was then editing.[3] While still on the staff of Governor Averell Harriman, Pat had studied the problem of highway accidents, and considered how we might develop a new approach to reducing their awful cost in lives and disability and money. How he became involved with this topic I do not know. What Pat did was to approach highway safety as an epidemic and apply some of the insights from epidemiology to it.

I was then, in 1959 or so, organizing a study of the ethnic groups of New York City. Surprisingly, this was not a subject of great attention at the time.

There was the great historian of immigration, Oscar Handlin—but his students had not yet begun to publish their major works. The European ethnic groups were well on their way to assimilation, which reduced popular interest in them. Negroes, as they were then called, and Puerto Ricans had only recently become large and important groups in New York City, and were not generally considered under the rubric of immigration and ethnic studies. It was Daniel Bell who suggested to James Wechsler, then editing the *New York Post*, that a study of what had happened to ethnic groups as they moved from being immigrant groups to second- and third-generation ethnic groups could provide articles for the *Post* on a subject of interest to its readers. The age of immigrant literature was already receding into the distance. In those days, no one expected America would ever become an immigrant society again. It was already twenty years since Leo Rosten, who sadly has just recently left us, had written his wonderful books on Hyman Kaplan in evening English classes, and that was about where writing on immigrant and ethnic groups then stood. But what was their condition now, as their second and third generations rose to become predominant?

It seemed like a good idea, and it was a good project for me. I had already written a book on American Jews, had written another book, *The Social Basis of American Communism*,[4] which placed great emphasis on ethnic factors in explaining who did and did not respond to Communism's appeal, and had edited a book on race and segregation in American cities, so it seemed I was the right person for the topic. The New York Post Foundation—there was such a thing at the time—arranged a small grant. About that time, the Joint Center for Urban Studies at Harvard and MIT was being established, and it was headed by a friend of mine, Martin Meyerson. It seemed reasonable that I should affiliate myself with it to have an academic connection. (In time, Pat was to head the Joint Center for Urban Studies.)

But how does one go about such a study with a small—a very small—grant? I had been greatly influenced by the work of Robert E. Park of the University of Chicago, the father of American ethnic and urban studies, and one thing I knew about him—from David Riesman—was that Park would send his students back to study what they knew best. What they knew best was their community, or their group, where they came from. And so we had Louis Wirth studying the ghetto (in those days, the ghetto meant a Jewish urban place), Franklin Frazier studying the Negro family, and many others in Park's orbit returning to their origins.[5] David Riesman did the same thing with his students in his famous course at Harvard—they wrote on what they knew best. Riesman himself, after his magisterial study, *The Lonely Crowd*,[6] and his major essays on American society, decided what he knew best was the college and university, and devoted the rest of his career to studying and writing about just that. So it was my thought to find people who combined the knowledge that came from origins and involvement with the distance and objectivity that could come from training in the social sciences, and each would be responsible for a study of his or her ethnic group.

Perhaps with undue hubris, I felt I was such a person, and could manage the Jews well enough, but my plan was to find an African American, a Puerto Rican, an Italian-American, and an Irish-American social scientist to conduct the study of his or her group. At the time, it turned out to be harder to find such people than I had expected. There were in each group knowledgeable advocates who could tell me a great deal, and from whom I could learn a great deal, but they were advocates. There were, of course, the filiopietists, but they did not have sufficient distance and objectivity. (In his Irish study, Pat has perhaps best characterized filiopietism in a passage on the American Irish Historical Society: "Its journal . . . inclined to articles by aspiring judges beginning, 'While we know that an Irishman was in Columbus's crew on his first voyage to the New World . . .' ").[7] Filiopietists could not help me. There were those who could have done the job, but wouldn't. It was, after all, a very small grant. And then there was Pat, with the proper mix, I believed, of intuition and knowledge on the one hand and objective distance on the other. In the end, I could find no one else, and I added the African Americans, the Italians, and the Puerto Ricans to my own brief. Pat became my only collaborator.

I don't think there was anything in his past—except his experience—that qualified him to write the brilliant essay he did. I was vaguely aware that Pat had written a doctoral thesis on the International Labor Organization.[8] That did qualify him somewhat to understand the distinctive role of the New York Irish labor leader in the American labor movement and in its international involvements. He was also then working on a book on the administration of Governor Averell Harriman. (That and his thesis are only two of his unpublished books.) And he was active in Democratic politics in New York State, and for that, ethnicity is crucial.

The politics of New York State Democrats was going through a revolution while Pat was working on his essay. The revolution is reflected in it, and in our discussion of politics elsewhere in *Beyond the Melting Pot.* No one has explained better than Pat the nature of this revolution. The Irish in New York had shaped their own two great institutions—the Democratic Party, in its urban aspect, and the Roman Catholic Church. Pat explored the social and cultural features the Irish brought to both institutions. Both were great hierarchies, with carefully defined grades, which expected people to do their assigned job and wait their turn for the moment when, having paid their dues in lesser jobs such as block leader or parish priest, they could move up. Pat traced these characteristics back to the Irish peasant, who learned to become remarkably patient by waiting for Da to abdicate or pass on. Then the son could take over the farm, marry, and have children. His patience in waiting was punctuated by visits to the pub, all along combined with a remarkable celibacy, extended even to his forties. This was all good training for both the party machine and the Church.

It is, of course, a complex passage from the Irish countryside to the tenements of New York City, and Pat is properly cautious and tentative in making the connections. He explored why this social structure was not very good on the whole in training for high achievement and daring ambition. At the time Catholic (and Irish-American) scholars were wondering why, after all the enormous effort expended in establishing schools and colleges and universities, Catholic intellectual achievement in the United States was, well, limited. It also seemed that this mode of adaptation made Irish social mobility a plodding affair, but it did establish a solid middle class. The Irish could dominate the machine and the police force, become police chief and mayor, but it seemed they did not become statesmen, or weren't seen as such. (That all changed with John F. Kennedy, but Pat was devoting more attention in his essay to the career of Al Smith.) There are wonderfully apt and illuminating passages in this essay, and I quote one:

> In the era of security clearances [he is speaking of the McCarthy period], to be an Irish Catholic became *prima facie* evidence of loyalty. Harvard men were to be checked; Fordham men would do the checking. The disadvantage of this is that it put the Irish back on the [police] force. It encouraged their tendency to be regular rather than creative. . . . They remained with the FBI while Harvard men continued to run foreign policy—with an increasingly evident assist from the sons of Lower East Side radicals.[9]

That sums up in a nutshell a number of important ethnic relationships.

But to return to the revolution that was reshaping the politics of New York City and the state: The reform Democrats, following in the wake of Adlai Stevenson, were no longer willing to accept the forms and procedures of hierarchy. They had, after all, gone to Harvard and similar places, and their parents had the money to put them into politics, if that was what they wanted. So they could insouciantly ignore the stages and posts that the regulars of the party felt they should first serve in before aspiring to become, for example, congressmen. The weapon of the reform Democrats in circumventing the rules was to denounce the bosses and the machine. In any event, they destroyed the old Democratic Party. This was, as Pat saw, an ethnic revolution—it was Jews and WASPs who did not believe in the old forms and, using the strengths available to them because of their education, their connections, and their access to the press, transformed the politics of New York City and State. (Of course, it was not only Jews and WASPs who could benefit from these resources in the absence of a powerful party machine. Pat's own political career is not a model of rising through the ranks of party loyalists, though he once did contest a New York City primary for the nomination for president of the city council).

He was shortly to move to the national and international stage as assistant secretary of labor and in other posts. He brought to his observations as he found himself in places where he could not know much—but he always surprises one with the arcane things he does know—the experience of what had happened to the Democrats of New York State. Perhaps the beginning of his transition to considering how the template of ethnicity might provide a different view of a totalitarian society may be dated to his participation in a UN seminar on multinational societies. He tells the story of his first foray into the international stage in *Pandaemonium*:

> The Yugoslavian government offered to play host to the gathering, choosing the magical setting Ljubljana in Slovenia. Typically, governments sent delegations headed by minorities. The British dispatched a Jewish peer and a Welsh M.P. The American State Department was not much interested.[10]

It was owing to this lack of interest that it was Pat, then an assistant secretary of labor, who went. He continued: "I returned to Washington to report that regardless of what we were told, the Serbs and Croats were going to fight one day."[11] I recall that when he returned he announced, "I have seen the Austro-Hungarian Empire and it works." He was, of course, modifying Lincoln Steffens's famous report on his wide-eyed visit to the young Soviet Union, "I have seen the future and it works." Pat had two things in mind when he referred to a past that worked: One was that there were beautiful cities in the Austro-Hungarian Empire, but the second was that we might well envy the condition of relative peace and harmony that existed among the ethnic groups of that empire.

But, of course, the great question of the day, and many days to follow, was the Soviet Union and the Cold War. Pat had never been attracted to Marxism, and it was no part of his past, as it was of the pasts of Irving Kristol, Daniel Bell, myself, and other friends of his in the 1960s and 1970s. There was no need for him to break with its enchantment. Others had to discover that the prospect of workers joining together across ancient or even not-so-ancient national and ethnic boundaries to advance common class interests was generally a chimera. My friends and I discovered this quite early, I as a result of my early attachment to the idea of a binational state in Palestine, based on the common economic interests of the majority of Arabs and Jews. By the late 1940s, I pretty much knew this was an illusion. We always knew that all the claims, assertions, and even facts the Soviet Union propagated about itself were lies, and among these lies was the assertion that Communism had overcome antisemitism. It was clear shortly after the destruction of Nazism that the Soviet Union had become the greatest promoter of antisemitism in the world, and that antisemitism in the Soviet Union was no simple residue from czarist Russia but was actively propagated and practiced by government. It stood to reason that other ethnic and racial antagonisms and conflicts were at best papered over and, if one knew enough, could be observed. But how virulent were they, and what could be expected from them? One had to be cautious.

THE MIDDLE PHASE: ETHNICITY IN TOTALITARIAN SOCIETIES

In the 1970s, Pat and I collaborated on a conference on ethnicity, which led to the 1975 book *Ethnicity: Theory and Experience.*[12] Among our contributors were Richard Pipes, writing on Soviet Russia, and Lucian Pye, writing on China. In that enterprise we were alerted to many things that were then not much on people's minds, among them the ethnic divisions that persisted in Soviet Russia. We also learned, for example, that much of the land area of China, particularly near its borders, is inhabited by peoples who are minorities, see themselves as such, and are seen as such and that this should be taken into account in considering China's future. In the jointly written introduction to that work is a passage by Pat that shows how attuned he was to these issues. Societies, he asserted, could be divided more, and more urgently, by ethnicity than by property. Or the struggles over property and economic interest could be structured by ethnicity. He referred to some of the ethnic struggles of the time, and in listing them wrote: "Great Russians prattle on about the equality of ethnic groups in the Soviet Union, while Ukrainians in Washington rally in protest at the *Russian* embassy."[13] Pat notices such things.

He was convinced such conflicts would in the end undo the Soviet Union. We therefore had to think more than we did about the possibility that the Cold War could come to an end. Pat was meticulous in recording his repeated warnings of the possible end of the Soviet Union in *Pandaemonium*, along with his fears of the instability this might create as the central control of atomic arms was suddenly superseded by a variety of hands, with different interests, on the buttons.[14] Adam Roberts, of Balliol College, Oxford—where *Pandaemonium* had its origins as a lecture—writes in his introduction to the book:

> When in early 1992 [Pat] presented a doubting Henry Kissinger with evidence that some people at least had seen what was coming in the Soviet Union, he received what is probably the shortest, and certainly the humblest, letter from his former Harvard and government colleague: "Dear Pat: I stand corrected. Your crystal ball was better than mine."[15]

THE PRESENT: ETHNICITY IN INTERNATIONAL POLITICS

But now we come to the present, and what are we to do about such conflicts, in the former Yugoslavia, the former Soviet Union, in Northern Ireland and the Middle East, in Rwanda and Burundi, and on and on? Here the senator's books *On the Law of Nations* and *Pandaemonium* are relevant. At least we should understand these conflicts, study them, be aware of them. There should be no excuse for ignorance. Pat is a great admirer of Woodrow Wilson, but not without reservations. Wilson did not think through the implications of his call for self-determination for all peoples. He did not consider how many peoples were eligible, what made a people, how such a principle could be realized without opening Pandora's box. There are six or seven thousand languages in the world. We are now up to almost two hundred nations—there were fifty or less in Wilson's day. How many nations? What peoples qualified? What about the minorities left behind regardless of how we draw the boundaries? (There are only a half-dozen really homogeneous nations without minorities in the world, and after we list Iceland we already begin to run into trouble.)

The problems in addressing these conflicts are not simple, but there are some guidelines in process and developing. There is the charter of the United Nations, which, as Pat points out, embraces both the principle of self-determination and the principle of the integrity of every existing state and its borders. These two principles are not easy to reconcile. His book *On the Law of Nations* points out these problems.[16] It is an eloquent and learned plea for international law, arguing that whatever its difficulties, it gives us the only way, aside from the imposition of the will of the stronger, for dealing with these complicated problems. There is, as we all know, a good deal of fatuousness in talk of international law. But international law does exist. It is even recognized by our hardheaded Constitution. Treaties, we are told there, are "the supreme law of the land," and the United States has entered into many international treaties, including the Charter of the United Nations, which make up by now the larger body of international law. I recommend the book. It does not give answers, as even laws do not give answers, but it is an earnest and serious consideration of how international law, and its further development, can guide us in dealing with the difficult problems ethnicity raises in international relations.

Pat knows everything about American ethnicity, but he has chosen to make his greatest contribution as a writer and scholar to the understanding of the role of ethnicity in world affairs and international relations.

I think I understand this choice of emphasis. When one is active in politics, one must be careful about what one writes about ethnic groups and even more about racial groups, which we can subsume under the general heading of ethnicity. Almost anything can be taken amiss, and one can be attacked, having said or written anything, for having asserted the exact opposite of what one has really said and written. Pat has had that experience.

Yet ethnicity is a reality, and race lies at the base of just about all of our major domestic problems. So how does a statesman avoid this minefield and make a contribution? What Pat has done has been to leave aside the most controversial issues of race as a legislator, such as affirmative action or revisions of the civil rights laws, and has attempted rather to heal our divisions through the advocacy of social policies targeted to categories defined by misfortune, not by race or ethnicity. And so we have his deep involvement—going back a long way—with family policy, with policies for children, with welfare policy, with urban policy, with formulas directing more money to cities with large numbers of unfortunates, with transportation policy to improve life in the cities and make access to jobs easier for those who use public transportation. Undoubtedly, better policy in all these areas would do much to ameliorate our racial problems. One can take on our racial problems frontally, as our civil rights and voting rights laws do. But all good domestic policy makes a contribution, whether it deals with work, family, education, or whatnot.

That makes sense to me. There was a time, some decades ago when we were working on *Beyond the Melting Pot*, when ethnicity was not much addressed publicly. The *New York Times* would regularly take politicians to task for trying to organize a "balanced ticket." Why not the best man, asked the *Times*, regardless of ethnic group or religion? Without making any public fuss about it, the politicians nevertheless went ahead balancing their tickets, trying to make sure each major constituency was addressed. They talked less about it publicly, but did not handle matters any less effectively for all that. There was something to be learned there. I believe that lesson from long ago guides to some extent Pat's approach to how we may best handle our difficult racial problems.

NOTES

1. Nathan Glazer and Daniel P. Moynihan, *Beyond the Melting Pot: The Negroes, Puerto Ricans, Jews, Italians, and Irish in New York City* (Cambridge: MIT Press, 1963).

2. Daniel P. Moynihan, *Pandaemonium: Ethnicity in International Politics* (New York: Oxford University Press, 1993).

3. Daniel P. Moynihan, "Epidemic on the Highways," *The Reporter* 20, no. 9 (30 April 1959): 16.

4. Nathan Glazer, *The Social Basis of American Communism* (New York: Harcourt, Brace & World, 1961).

5. Louis Wirth, *The Ghetto* (Chicago: University of Chicago Press, 1928); E. Franklin Frazier, *The Negro Family in the United States* (Chicago: University of Chicago Press, 1939).

6. David Riesman, in collaboration with Reuel Denney and Nathan Glazer, *The Lonely Crowd* (New Haven, Conn.: Yale University Press, 1950).

7. Glazer and Moynihan, *Beyond the Melting Pot*, 253.

8. Daniel P. Moynihan, "The United States and the International Labor Organization, 1889–1934" (Ph.D. diss., Fletcher School of Law and Diplomacy, Tufts University, 1960).

9. Glazer and Moynihan, *Beyond the Melting Pot,* 271.

10. Moynihan, *Pandaemonium,* 56–57.

11. Ibid.

12. Nathan Glazer and Daniel P. Moynihan, with the assistance of Corinne Saposs Schelling, eds., *Ethnicity: Theory and Experience* (Cambridge: Harvard University Press, 1975).

13. Ibid., 17.

14. Moynihan, *Pandaemonium,* 41–44.

15. Adam Roberts, "Foreword," in Moynihan, *Pandaemonium,* x–xi.

16. Daniel P. Moynihan, *On the Law of Nations* (Cambridge: Harvard University Press, 1990).

CHAPTER THREE

THE PRESCIENT POLITICIAN

SEYMOUR MARTIN LIPSET

In preparing for this chapter, I believe I have read almost all of Daniel Patrick Moynihan's voluminous writings. Having known him for over three decades, I was not surprised to find evidence that he frequently anticipated important developments and trends. But given his linkages at different times to Democrats and Republicans and to neoconservatives and liberals, I did not expect to find that he has exhibited a strong strain of consistency in his positions on both international and domestic issues.

Although Moynihan's involvements in international affairs are outside my jurisdiction here, I would like to briefly touch on them. Much like Scoop Jackson and Hubert Humphrey, he has always opposed totalitarianism, whether of the fascist or communist variety. Some years ago, a Hungarian social scientist, Gyorgy Bence, and I sought to find out the extent to which American scholars and commentators on the Soviet Union had anticipated its downfall. As we assumed, almost all of the professional Sovietologists had not expected its collapse. Zbigniew Brzezinski and Richard Pipes were among the exceptions to this generalization. To our surprise, nonprofessionals, such as journalists and some politicians, turned out to be much more on the ball. The most accurate commentator was Senator Daniel Patrick Moynihan.

As noted in the article "Anticipations of the Failure of Communism,"

> Daniel Patrick Moynihan, in a series of prescient statements, made from the late seventies on, gave even more emphasis to the terrible weakness of the Soviet Union. Asked to predict what would happen in the 1980s, he stated in 1979 that the Soviet system "could blow up." He pointed to the economic downturn, the "*rise* in mortality rates . . . the nationality strains." In a speech in the Senate in January 1980, Moynihan noted: "The indices of economic stagnation and even decline are extraordinary. The indices of social disorder—social pathology is not too strong a term—are even more so. The defining event of the decade might well be the breakup of the Soviet Empire." In a commencement address at New York University in 1984, he pointed to the absence of legitimacy, "that the Soviet idea is spent . . . it summons no loyalty." Again in that year he commented, "the Soviet Union is weak and getting weaker," and in October 1984, before Gorbachev took office, Moynihan proclaimed: "The Cold War is over, the West won. . . . The Soviet Union . . . has collapsed. As a society it just doesn't work. Nobody believes in it anymore." Moynihan's . . . strategy "for dealing with the Soviets is to wait them out." They will collapse.[1]

I will refrain from evaluating Moynihan's role in foreign policy generally, although his ambassadorships to India and the United Nations constitute major parts of his career. I cannot resist noting his article published in *Commentary* in 1975 entitled "The U.S. in Opposition." As the title indicates, he believed that the United States should act as an opposition party within the United Nations to the then antidemocratic majority composed of Third World and Communist countries. His appointment to the UN position in 1975 allowed him to act out this role for this country. His activities and speeches sometimes put him in direct opposition to Henry Kissinger, who had a balance of power policy in mind and disliked the "rhetoric of confrontationalism."

Moynihan assumed that confrontationalism would result in many on the other side(s) backing down. He was proven right in confronting the supporters of the "Zionism Is Racism" resolution. Yet, throughout his UN career, he was criticized by the professional diplomats for his language—for example, his statement that "the abomination of anti-Semitism has been given the appearance of international sanction."[2]

History suggests that Moynihan was correct in his belief that toughness on the part of the United States would lead our European allies to support us and that many of our Third World critics would eventually give up their opposition. He was soon able to write a celebratory memorandum, "The Blocs Are Breaking Up."[3] I will not deal further with Moynihan in foreign policy.

To turn now to the domestic agenda, I would again report that the record shows convincingly that Moynihan has also been one of the most prescient analysts of American domestic problems and policies. His concerns have been diverse. My focus is on his lifelong involvement with the ways socially deprived environments affect the families of the underprivileged. What started him in June 1963 was a report to Congress and President Kennedy by the director of selective service. This report documented that literally half of all young men called up had to be disqualified for medical conditions. Moynihan argued that this finding required dealing extensively with youth unemployment. Then and later he believed that the best, perhaps the only, solution to the dysfunctional effects of poverty is jobs and that in the absence of sufficient openings in the private sector, government has the obligation to provide and require job training and, if necessary, to be an employer of last resort in lieu of supplying financial aid.

These concerns resulted in Moynihan's becoming the key staff person on a Kennedy-designated presidential task force dealing with manpower conservation, a large part of whose work would necessarily involve poverty. The task force continued after the assassination, and Moynihan completed the report by the end of 1963. It proposed that those potential draftees who failed to qualify physically or intellectually be provided with training and medical services that would enable them to function better in civilian life. The report, published under the heading *One-Third of a Nation,* was an early contribution to the emerging interest in a poverty program.[4] Moynihan was also to serve on the task force that drew up the first explicit antipoverty program.

Reflecting on the report over a quarter-century later in his most recent book, *Miles to Go,* Moynihan writes that growing up in poverty is not the principal source of the failure "to be an effective citizen and self-supporting individual," as he had once believed. He now recognizes that the poverty-stricken are not one group; rates of mental retardation and health problems differ greatly among subgroups and political jurisdictions—for example, 6.4 percent of Vermont draftees, 14.3 percent of Rhode Islanders, and 34.2 percent of New Yorkers failed the mental test. And he comments self-despairingly in 1996, "Why did I write [failing] was the result of poverty?" What he had not realized was though unequal economic circumstances "accounted for a lot of behavior," the varying outcomes "were in turn dependent variables of a yet more powerful agent," culture.[5]

Yet, the most noteworthy outcome of the 1963–64 discussions was not analyses of the sources of poverty but a proposal for "maximum feasible participation" (MFP). The term refers to the efforts to involve the poor themselves in the actual design and operation of programs intended to reduce the numbers living in poverty. The new emphasis was on extensive support for community organizations, to be funded by monies allocated to the poverty program. Moynihan opposed the policy, arguing that it would provide good incomes to middle-class professionals, with money that might be used for jobs for the poor. His position put him on the losing side of a quarrel with "liberals."

The record indicates that Moynihan was right, at least in his pessimism about MFP, which in fact did little to alleviate poverty. MFP contributed greatly to political radicalization, particularly in black communities, but also to some extent in Latino areas as well. The program put the federal government into the business of funding activism. As Moynihan notes in his book *Maximum Feasible Misunderstanding*, community control issues became "the center of the political controversy" in New York City and other large metropolises. When the local organizations of the poor turned on the hand that fed them—the government—the politicians turned on them. Many conservatives concluded that poverty-inspired social welfare programs should be eliminated. In any case, Moynihan saw MFP as a product of "a private ideology," that of white middle-class liberals, who then dominated the upper echelons of the bureaucracy of the Office of Economic Opportunity (OEO). Moynihan rejected the conclusions of liberal social scientists who claimed that their research and theory justified the MFP approach. He argued that social science rarely comes up with sufficient evidence to provide a scientific underpinning for broad policy changes, whether presented by liberals or conservatives. Research generally sustains the null hypothesis—that is, not proven. He, therefore, laid down the dictum, which has become highly controversial, that "the role of social science lies not in the formation of social policy, but in the measurement of its results." Then and later he argued that while social science "can call attention to some probable consequences of certain types of actions," it cannot and should not formulate policy.[6]

The issues of poverty, which continue to concern Moynihan to this day, can best be understood in the context of his interest in the structure of the family. For him, as for most others, family stability is a key requirement for socializing new members of society, to enable them to survive and perform adequately. While the conditions for family stability are obviously multivariate, the key factors revolve around socialization. It clearly is sensitive to family income and employment, both of which have a strong bearing on the principal intervening variable, the presence of two parents.

Thus, when Moynihan discussed policy for a war on poverty in a 1965 report to President Johnson, *The Negro Family: The Case for National Action*, now commonly known as the Moynihan Report, he emphasized family structure as the key element.[7] While family instability occurs among all social groups—that is, class, race, and ethnic—it has been most prevalent among the poorer black population in post–World War II America. The report called attention to the many children affected by family incapacities. At the time, one-quarter of urban black marriages were breaking up, while the same percentage of births were illegitimate, eight times the ratio among whites. Many black children were being raised in families that received welfare, either at that time or in the past. The data indicated not only that white families were more likely to be more stable (two parents present) than black ones but also that the disparity was growing. This emphasis on the dysfunctional nature of the lower-class black family created a firestorm of criticism from most black leaders as well as from many liberal activists and academics. The document was denounced as racist for seemingly placing the responsibility for dysfunction and failure on the blacks themselves—that is, on the victims.

Anyone now reading the Moynihan Report will wonder what all the shouting was about. He did stress the higher rates of family instability and illegitimacy among African Americans, which, he emphasized, contributed strongly to the inability of many black youth to perform well in school and in the labor market. But, as noted, family conditions are intervening variables. The causes of disproportionate instability in black communities lay, according to Moynihan, in external social factors and economic conditions, in particular those stemming from slavery and Reconstruction, as well as from the social disorganization consequent on the later great migration from southern rural environments to northern urban slums. Moynihan drew from the works of the leading black sociologist of the day, E. Franklin Frazier, to back his findings. Unemployment and low income were the major sources of weakened family structure, reducing the status and even the presence of fathers and forcing mothers to take jobs outside the home. Blacks, he reiterated, experienced much higher unemployment rates and lower wages then whites.

Antebellum slavery and depressed post-slavery conditions were followed by a pattern of inadequate education and job training in a highly segregated society. This made for low achievement orientations among black male putative heads of families. Mothers were better able to act out their parental role than fathers. These conditions produced matriarchal families within the black community. As Moynihan pointed out in the report, there was a resultant "tangle of pathology." Clearly he was not blaming the victim; he was blaming the society, the white society.

Criticism of the Moynihan Report was clearly wrong. Developments from the time it was written to the present have served to enhance Moynihan's reputation as a policy prophet, as prescient. The dysfunctional family conditions he emphasized in the mid-1960s have grown worse. The proportion of black children born out of wedlock today is near 70 percent. Yet, the economic situation of the African-American community as a whole has vastly improved. There is now a large middle class, as well as a significant stable working class. But the statistics continue to look bleak for black children. Blacks who are upwardly mobile, whether into the middle or working classes, like most first-generation arrivés, have a low birthrate. Conversely, unmarried young black females from economically deprived origins bear the majority of black children born today. The African-American leadership, as well as many liberal academic scholars, now recognize that Moynihan was right (although they may not give him credit) and acknowledge the need to deal with family dysfunctions.[8]

As Lenin put it, "What is to be done?" In 1965, Moynihan made some policy proposals: that the government provide jobs for those who cannot find them, that the military be more open to blacks, that the very poor be given family allowances to supplement earned income. These analyses and recommendations formed the core of Lyndon Johnson's now famous address at Howard University on 4 June 1965. The president stressed the need for white America to accept the task of providing equality of opportunity for American blacks. He agreed, with Moynihan (who wrote most of the speech), that the civil rights guarantees of the right to vote and the outlawing of segregation cannot automatically provide blacks with equal economic opportunity. He emphasized the continuing growth of the economic gap between blacks and whites. Following Moynihan's lead, Johnson pointed to the causal role of family instability and called for a war on poverty.

The family, as we have seen, has always been at the core of Moynihan's analyses of American social problems. He was, therefore, glad to have his emphasis validated by the largest single social-science project ever undertaken, James Coleman's evaluation of the efforts to bring about equality of educational opportunity.[9] Coleman had conducted a comprehensive study of the effects of integration, school quality, and academic achievement, which involved gathering data on tens of thousands of pupils in hundreds of schools. At the time, most people believed that integrating schools would improve the education and social environment of black students and thus help to reduce or, one hoped, eliminate the racial differences in attainments. In a careful multivariate (regression) analysis, Coleman found that whether schools are integrated or not has little effect on educational achievement. The most important differentiating variable by far is family characteristics. Holding other things—including school characteristics, race, and class—constant, those from stable, better-educated families are more likely to be school achievers.

On reading the report, Moynihan concluded that Coleman had produced the most important finding in social science, that the report's conclusions must be widely disseminated to the policy and academic worlds. To contribute to these objectives, he, together with leading statistician Frederick Mosteller, organized a seminar at Harvard to evaluate the Coleman results.[10] Bolstering Moynihan's longtime assumptions, the research has had a continuing influence on his policy concerns. The way to deal with the problem of family instability is economic improvement. Families can be stabilized by jobs and, if that is not possible, may be made more viable by money. Here I would note that he has been unimpressed by the many books and articles stressing the effects of welfare dependency. He insists that up to the present there is no reliable research demonstrating that government assistance, welfare, undermines work motivation.

Much to Pat's dismay, Richard Nixon was elected president of the United States in November 1968. But then to Moynihan's and others' surprise, he was appointed as the incoming president's domestic policy adviser, later counsellor to the president. Due in part to his role as adviser, but even more important due to Nixon's psychological insecurity and perhaps also to Nixon's somewhat depressed family background, the new administration turned out to be, in economic terms, one of the most liberal the United States has ever had. Moynihan was able to gain the support of the president on a number of policy matters, including the continuation of many aspects of the Johnson poverty program, which Republicans had opposed, particularly the Office of Economic Opportunity. Mostly Moynihan pressed, as he was to do for much of the next three decades, for family-oriented welfare reform. Nixon supported his efforts.

Moynihan's plan, first known as the Family Security System, later as the Family Assistance Program (FAP), provided for a minimum payment of $1,600 a year, part of which would be paid to the working poor, families headed by an employed male, with an earned income of less than $3,920. It called for a "family togetherness incentive," to replace the existing Aid to Families with Dependent Children (AFDC) program, which made a family better off financially if the father left home. It is not surprising that Moynihan's proposals met with criticisms from most Republicans and, for that matter, from conservative Democrats as well. Although the president strongly endorsed these policies, publicly and privately, they were rejected in Congress following a year-and-a-half-long battle. Although the main legislative efforts largely failed, they resulted in passage of Supplemental Security Income (SSI), which, as Moynihan proudly notes, produced "a guaranteed income for the aged, the blind and the disabled."[11] The FAP had been designed to do the same for children and families with children. In the end, they were left out.

Moynihan would later indicate that he always harbored doubts about the FAP's viability.[12] What is amazing about the outcomes of the debate on the FAP is not that it lost, but that it came so close to passing, winning by almost two-to-one in the House and then failing in the Senate in the very last days of the Ninety-first Congress. The plan, in many ways, was one of the most radical measures ever submitted, since it called for income by right. Two political scientists, Bill Cavala and Aaron Wildavsky, attempted, before the congressional debate started, to predict the outcome by gathering information on all of the players involved, the president, the Congress, and the public.[13] They concluded, after interviewing fifty members of Congress and studying the polls, that the measure could not pass. Perceived as a guaranteed-income plan, it went against the grain of deep-rooted American sentiments calling for work and self-reliance. As Cavala and Wildavsky noted, also working against it was its projected high cost. It would have probably required a substantial tax increase. The groups that normally should have been expected to support such a proposal, organized labor and civil rights organizations, did not, for as Moynihan pointed out, "labor unions fear that a guaranteed income would render them superfluous. Militant black leaders take the same position for a similar reason." And, in agreement with Cavala and Wildavsky, he noted that "policies that provide unearned income run counter to widely held and deeply felt American values, such as achievement, work, and equality of opportunity." In fact, as he pointed out, the proposal was not for a guaranteed annual income but rather was an effort "to supplement the income of persons already working, and it sincerely looked to the prospect of finding work for others who were not working."[14]

Basically, the Family Assistance Plan would have provided for a minimum income to everyone, regardless of whether he or she was working at the moment. What is ironic, from the vantage point of the severe ideological cleavages on related issues in the 1990s, is the extent to which the FAP did not seriously divide the liberals and the conservatives. There was a desire in both camps to do something about the condition of the impoverished, to stabilize their families.

The defeat led to a decline in Moynihan's influence within the administration. He lost control of the Urban Affairs Council. Perhaps most disheartening was the revival of bitter attacks on Moynihan from within the African-American and liberal communities. These stemmed from the publication of a confidential document that he had written to Nixon dealing with the black family and its lack of progress. Reacting to the defeat of the FAP, he proposed a policy of "benign neglect," a term his enemies treated as racist. Moynihan felt that the growing use of extreme language and of ideological tension, stemming from the conflicts of the 1960s, made further legislative action difficult. Hence, he proposed a breathing period. The phrase, however, suggested to some a lack of concern for the blacks.

The publication of the "benign neglect" memorandum in the *New York Times* ended Moynihan's usefulness to the Nixon administration.[15] He returned to Harvard, which, like Washington, was no longer a happy place for him. Liberal academics and students saw his racial policies as conservative and disdained his involvement with an administration that pressed on with the Vietnam War, though Moynihan had earlier asked to resign because of the Cambodian incursion.

Following a period most marked by Moynihan's diplomatic activities in India and at the UN, a new role opened in 1977, as a member of the U.S. Senate. The Senate position has been a happy one for him. It gives him a bully pulpit from which to reach out and influence policy. Being from New York makes it even better because the Empire State and Washington are the major centers for news diffusion. Senators also receive considerable staff resources. They are, however, most influential and powerful when they are part of the chamber's majority party and play a leadership role in it. Hence, it was not until he assumed chairmanship of the Finance Committee in 1993 that Moynihan could come fully into his own. But, as we know, that lasted for only two years.

As an advocate in these senatorial years, Moynihan has been able to play an extremely important role for the American political and academic communities. As the senator from academe, he has become a middle man, bringing scholarly-based ideas to his colleagues. He is an opinionated politician, although he has been the model of a centrist. He is too smart and sophisticated to follow a party line, whether left or right. He realizes that the liberal emphasis on throwing money at problems and assuming that all of them can be solved by more funds, schools, social workers, et cetera, just does not hold up. As someone who himself experienced poverty, he cannot accept the libertarian conservative assumption that in a genuinely competitive market economy (which has never existed), almost all the underprivileged will be motivated and able to make it on their own. He also resents the disdain of many on the right for the chronically poor and the implicit, if not explicit, stance of many conservatives of "blaming the victim."

Although a social scientist, Moynihan does not believe that his erstwhile campus colleagues are able to produce the answers policymakers are looking for. As he puts it in *Counting Our Blessings*:

> The explanatory power of the various disciplines is limited. . . . [T]here are not many things social science has to say. . . . [I]ts characteristic product is the null hypothesis. . . . Indeed, if anything, while social scientists tend to be liberal, the tendency of social science findings must be judged conservative, in that they rarely point to the possibility of much more incremental change.[16]

Social scientists can evaluate the outcomes of policy, as the Coleman Report had done. They can, of course, also give advice based on research findings, although these are often conflicting and usually suspect when subject to a methodological critique. As noted, social science at its best teaches its practitioners to think multivariately—that is, to recognize that all behavior is a consequence of many variables, some reinforcing each other, some acting at cross-purposes. It is necessary, therefore, to try to evaluate relationships by using regression analysis or by performing its equivalent by logic, holding qualitative factors constant. Moynihan is a master of this art.

He returns again and again to his insistence that stabilizing and improving the family is the sine qua non, even though he cannot prove it. This has been the principal message of his senatorial years. Moynihan's most important accomplishments during the Reagan-Bush presidencies involved cooperation with Bob Dole and other Senate leaders. The cross-bench alliance was responsible for the Social Security and welfare reforms of 1983 and 1988.

The changes in Social Security adopted in 1983 basically carried out the recommendations of a bipartisan National Commission on Social Security Reform. The reform addressed ensuring the funding of the program at least through 2033. Moynihan pressed for creating incentives for welfare recipients that would encourage them to get off of welfare. The 1988 Family Welfare Reform reflected Moynihan's concerns. It sought to add to the emphasis on income maintenance more spending for education and job training and incentives to encourage those on welfare to find jobs. As the *Congressional Quarterly Almanac* summed up the act, it

> strengthened child-support enforcement procedures, required states to implement work, education and training programs for welfare mothers, required states to pay welfare benefits to poor two-parent families, and offered extended child-care and medical benefits to families in which parents left the welfare rolls for a job.[17]

The election of Bill Clinton in 1992 was seen as a blessing by Moynihan. Clinton had campaigned from the same ideological corner of Democratic moderation or centrism that Moynihan occupied. Clinton was a founding member and a past chairperson of the centrist Democratic Leadership Council (DLC). But more important for Moynihan, the Democrats now had a majority in the Senate and he became chairperson of the Finance Committee. This committee has jurisdiction over everything that needs funding, which means almost everything. Not surprising, the number-one item on his list, which he thought also had high priority on the new president's agenda, was welfare reform. He was in error. The most important administration issue for the 1993 Congress turned out to be health policy. The president and his wife were determined to enact a major health-care reform bill that would ensure medical treatment to every person in the United States, an objective with which Moynihan sympathized.

The procedures followed by the new administration to draw up the legislation unfortunately repeated mistakes of the last previous Democratic president, Jimmy Carter. President Carter had faced a major problem: ensuring energy supplies, largely oil. To find a solution, he created an energy task force headed by James Schlesinger. The task force was under instructions from the president to operate in secret, and not to negotiate or deal with the various interest groups concerned with energy. Schlesinger's team came up with a complex plan, but had failed to mobilize grassroots and interest-group support. The proposals naturally failed.

The Clinton task force, headed by Hillary Rodham Clinton, went much the same route and was equally unsuccessful. That failure was anticipated by many political scientists and journalists, but particularly by two sophisticated policy-concerned academics, Sven Steinmo, who had been a student of Wildavsky's, and Jon Watts. Steinmo had been trained by his mentor to carefully examine political context, as well as the players in the game. They noted that American political institutions prevent major changes except in the context of a severe crisis, and as they documented, there was no crisis in health care in the nineties.[18] And if there was a crisis with respect to the uninsured, the situation was neither experienced nor understood as such by most of the public or the experts. Bill Kristol was to admonish the GOP congressional leadership, which initially had shown willingness to compromise, that there was no need to do so, since there was no perception in the general population of a health care crisis.[19] They followed Kristol's advice in the decisive later months of the debate.

Moynihan, as chair of the Finance Committee, was one of the key actors, since his committee had to authorize most of the eventual bill. But as the Hillary Clinton task force came up with an increasingly complex proposal, which totaled over 13,000 pages and contained extremely detailed regulations, the image of a Rube Goldberg apparatus took hold among the public. Moynihan became increasingly pessimistic, about both the content of the bill and its chances of enactment. The Democrats controlled his committee by only eleven to nine; one defection would prevent approval, and a number of his party colleagues were at least as unhappy as he about aspects of the bill and could not be counted on.

Moynihan's relations with the Clinton administration were strained, and had been so from the start, because he had not supported Clinton for the presidential nomination. Senator Kerrey of Nebraska had been his choice. Within a few months after the new administration had taken office, *Newsweek* noted that Moynihan had not been invited to or visited the White House to talk to the president. When a senior staffer was asked about this, the reply was, "Why should we, what has he done for us?" This behavior was not designed to foster cooperation between the Finance Committee and the White House. The president, naturally disturbed by the comment, announced that if he discovered who said it, the person would be fired immediately. No one was. Comparable anti-Moynihan staff statements were to appear in the press later, and were responded to in kind. Regardless of relations with the White House, the senator was determined to do what he could for the enactment of needed health reforms. He and others, however, strongly recommended to Hillary Clinton and her task force that they accept compromises proposed by some moderate Democrats and Republicans. At one point, enough Republicans had signed on to allow passage of a health bill that would have incorporated most, though far from all, of the Clinton proposals. But compromise was opposed by the White House.

As a senator from New York, Moynihan was especially concerned with the impact of the bill on the complex of teaching and research hospitals located in New York City. Reading and gathering expertise about health matters, he was especially impressed with the significant progress made by medical research. Assuming a continuing rate of progress, he anticipated an escalation of such developments, with the further elimination of some major killers. And he saw in the proposed bill threats to medical research. He assigned himself the task of serving as its protector, particularly in university-affiliated hospitals.

Steinmo and Watts proved to be right. The bill failed. Like Carter's energy plan, its proponents were unable to find sufficient support for a program drawn up behind closed doors. The public, which had initially been in favor of expansion of health care coverage, grew increasingly negative as it was made aware by well-financed health industry opponents of the bureaucratic complexities inherent in the plan. But the debate and its focus on the need to reduce the cost factors in health care helped foster a subsequent rapid expansion of the role of private health maintenance organizations (HMOs). The Clinton proposal had been favorable to HMOs, although Hillary Clinton and other exponents of the plan would repeatedly say erroneously that their proposals would ensure free choice of doctors.

The expansion of HMOs brought about many of the problems that organized medicine had earlier argued were inherent in "socialized medicine." HMOs deny patients open access to physicians. Patients can deal only with health providers who are part of the plan they are enrolled in, and are permitted to see a specialist or get a second opinion only if their primary care provider authorizes the service. Hospital stays require plan approval and are usually rationed carefully. To reduce costs, physicians are under pressure by many HMOs to cut back on tests and use of specialists. For the most part, doctors are no longer free agents if they are part of an HMO, and increasingly, most have to be. They are becoming more like employees who must obey their superiors than independent professionals.

Even access to drugs prescribed by physicians can be limited by pharmacists under instructions from HMOs.

As I have noted, the Clinton administration's focus on its health plan took welfare reform off the agenda of the 105th Congress. Then the following Congress, elected in 1994 with a Republican majority, claimed a mandate to roll back the welfare state. The loss of Democratic control of Congress meant the end of Moynihan's position as chairperson of the Finance Committee.

Moynihan, of course, has continued to play an important role. He has been much involved in debates over welfare, Social Security, and the budget. Although the Clintons perceived his lack of enthusiasm for their health plan as a reflection of Moynihan's more centrist politics, his opposition to the welfare bill, which the president signed, seemed to locate him among the liberal critics. Both positions attest to his pragmatic politics, to his concern with objectives not ideology. The new Welfare Act, while emphasizing workfare, an objective that he had fostered earlier, uses force, as well as incentives, specifying some groups to be denied welfare and specifying time limits for others, regardless of family or personal conditions. Cutting expenditures took priority with the Republican majority and the president; both were concerned with balancing the budget. But Moynihan would not approve the consequent cruelty.

Some technical questions concerning national productivity and estimates of GNP growth have affected his positions on welfare and social security. Long before the Boskin Commission, Moynihan noted that government statistics underestimate productivity by 1 to 3 percent.[20] And if Boskin and Moynihan are right, estimates of recent federal deficits, and of future funding problems for Social Security and Medicare, are exaggerated. The senior senator from New York has also questioned some of the assumptions about the existence of a widespread culture of dependency among those on welfare. He argues that there is no conclusive evidence to this effect. In any case, he believes, as noted earlier, that policy positions on these issues are not research-driven but reflect values and value choices.

What are Moynihan's values? In his early days in political life, he would have been classified as a New Deal liberal, seeking to bring about a more productive and egalitarian society. Like Harry Truman, John Kennedy, Henry Jackson, and Hubert Humphrey, he has been a strong anti-Communist, with respect to both the Cold War with the Soviet Union and the local hot wars with American Communists. He early understood that the latter were agents of and controlled by the former. This background led him, as it did with others, to distrust those who were "soft" on the Soviets and their domestic flunkies, many of whom were active in the Democratic Party. And as the ideological intraparty battle escalated in the late 1960s and early 1970s, Moynihan stood with the hard-liners. Increasingly critical of the Vietnam War, he served as a co-chair of the Committee for Political Settlement in Vietnam, which pressed the United States to negotiate and get out, but on terms that could negate a Communist takeover. His foreign policy positions led to opposition to George McGovern as a presidential candidate in 1972, and to his involvement in the centrist Coalition of a Democratic Majority (CDM), in which he and Henry Jackson played leading roles.

Many of the anti-Communist intellectuals in CDM became the core of those known in the early seventies as "neoconservatives." Almost all of them were Democrats, some like Daniel Bell and Norman Podhoretz were social democrats. Moynihan and the "neocons" also differed somewhat from the liberals on domestic policy. These concerns were made manifest in *The Public Interest*, which they founded in 1965, with Daniel Bell and Irving Kristol as coeditors.[21] Moynihan was a member of the original editorial board; he remains on it.

What has characterized *The Public Interest* has been a respect for facts, no matter what ideology they challenge, and a concern for the "unanticipated consequences of purposive social action," to quote the title of Robert Merton's 1936 essay on the topic.[22] But as Moynihan had learned from the debates over the 1965 Moynihan Report, when research findings conflict with ideology the latter frequently wins. This should not be surprising. One of the founding fathers of sociology, Max Weber, noted that all scholars have a "party line" (his term, which included not only politics but academic theories, past conclusions, et cetera). They are predisposed to report data that coincide with the line and to ignore those that do not or to subject them to severe methodological critiques. Weber, therefore, recommended that when research produces results that are agreeable to your "line," do not publish them but ask others to redo the study, to check it out. He felt it is safe to publish only findings that challenge one's prejudices.[23] Few, if any, follow this dictum.

The Moynihan approach to policy research seeks to de-ideologize it. And, as we have seen, in line with Weber's dictum, this has involved him over the years in serious controversy, particularly with liberal academics, intellectuals, and activist students. Such confrontations had a profound effect on those liberals who took the goal of objectivity seriously. They found a welcome on their right and some joined the ranks of identified conservatives. This has not happened with Moynihan, although his participation in Republican administrations must have encouraged him to do so. Many of his *Public Interest* neoconfreres who have grown more conservative than he has have been unhappy with his failure to move as far as they in the same direction.

Why has Moynihan not gone along with most of the cofounders of the *Public Interest?* In *The Moynihan Report and the Politics of Controversy*, Lee Rainwater and William Yancey suggest that Moynihan's continuing "views on social welfare were strongly influenced by Catholic welfare philosophy, which has emphasized the idea that family interests are the central objective of social welfare and social policy in general."[24] He remains a believing and practicing Catholic. But many good Catholics, like the Buckleys, Mike Novak, or George Weigel, well-versed in Catholic philosophy, have sharply different views.

More relevant to understanding Moynihan, I think, is his family background. He is the product of a broken family. His father left home when he was ten years old; his mother remarried, but that marriage broke up when he was fourteen. As he notes in *Coping*, "I was raised in chancy circumstances in an already sufficiently threatening world."[25] In discussing African-Americans, Pat, as Rainwater and Yancey report, specifically recalls his relations with black shoe-shine boys with whom he worked side by side, and being impressed that "their world . . . [and his] seemed to be much the same worlds." He could see "parallels between the 'wild Irish slums' of the late nineteenth century and the Negro ghettos of today."[26]

When Pat talks about the need for family stability, he is speaking from experience. Since it takes one to know one, I can also testify about the effects of poverty and of unemployment on the family and on the morale and psyche of young people. Unemployment and poverty are not statistics for us, or events which, though regrettable, are necessary consequences of economic adjustments. They result in unbearable human misery. As Pat put it in a discussion of African-Americans in 1964, "problems of unemployment . . . [are] absolutely devastating, and they are not Negro problems, they are American problems generally."

But whatever the sources of Pat's views and politics, the fact remains that he is neither a liberal nor a conservative. And his reading as a social scientist has led him to draw on the best scholarship, from Emile Durkheim's analysis of *anomie* to Robert Merton's discussion of "unanticipated consequences." The latter gives him insights in the need to be cautious, to try to trace through potential consequences. But as Moynihan notes, Merton also shows how social science predictions can change the course of events.

Why is Moynihan so prescient? I would say because he has known from the start that there is no first cause, not in politics, not in social science. No, I am wrong, as I told Pat over thirty years ago, when he was forty, "Coleman finds, it's all the family."

Pat knew about the family all along. And those who do not know about it, whether they are liberals or conservatives, whether they think genes determine where people wind up or do not believes genes have much effect on intelligence or learning, are wrong. What Pat teaches is that not only are there no utopias, there are no solutions, not in the state or in the completely uncontrolled market. There are only approximations, only the continuing struggle for decency, for morality, for equality of opportunity and respect.

NOTES

1. Seymour Martin Lipset and Gyorgy Bence, "Anticipations of the Failure of Communism," *Theory and Society* 23 (April 1994): 201–2.

2. Douglas Schoen, *PAT: A Biography of Daniel Patrick Moynihan* (New York: Harper & Row, 1979), 231.

3. Ibid., 243.

4. President's Task Force on Manpower Conservation, *One-Third of a Nation: A Report on Young Men Found Unqualified for Military Service* (Washington, D.C.: GPO, 1964).

5. Daniel P. Moynihan, *Miles to Go: A Personal History of Social Policy* (Cambridge: Harvard University Press, 1996).

6. See Daniel P. Moynihan, *Maximum Feasible Misunderstanding: Community Action in the War on Poverty* (New York: Free Press, 1969), esp. 169–201.

7. See "The Moynihan Report—The Negro Family: The Case for National Action," reprinted in Lee Rainwater and William L. Yancey, *The Moynihan Report and the Politics of Controversy* (Cambridge: MIT Press, 1967), 39–124.

8. Lyndon Johnson, "To Fulfill These Rights," speech drafted by Richard N. Goodwin and Daniel P. Moynihan. See ibid., 125–32.

9. James S. Coleman, *Equality of Educational Opportunity* (Washington, D.C.: U.S. Office of Education, 1966).

10. Frederick Mosteller and Daniel P. Moynihan, eds., *On Equality of Opportunity* (New York: Random House, 1972).

11. See Daniel P. Moynihan, *The Politics of a Guaranteed Income: The Nixon Administration and the Family Assistance Plan* (New York: Random House, 1973).

12. Daniel P. Moynihan, *Coping: Essays on the Practice of Government* (New York: Random House, 1973), 166.

13. Bill Cavala and Aaron Wildavsky, "The Political Feasibility of Income by Right," *Public Policy* (spring 1970): 321–54.

14. Moynihan, *The Politics,* 8, 11.

15. "Text of Moynihan Memorandum on the Status of Negroes: Memorandum for the President," *New York Times,* 1 March 1970, 69.

16. Daniel P. Moynihan, *Counting Our Blessings: Reflections on the Future of America* (Boston: Little, Brown & Co., 1980), 147–48.

17. "After Years of Debate, Welfare Reform Clears," *Congressional Quarterly Almanac* 44 (100th Cong., 2d sess., 1988): 349.

18. Sven Steinmo and Jon Watts, "It's the Institutions, Stupid! Why Comprehensive National Health Insurance Always Fails in America," *Journal of Health Politics, Policy, and Law* 20 (summer 1995): 325–72. This article was written much earlier and presented at the 1994 annual meeting of the American Political Science Association.

19. See a series of memos written by William Kristol and distributed by fax to Republican leaders and the press by the Project for the Republican Future, from December 1993 to September 1994.

20. For a detailed presentation by Michael Boskin, see an interview with him in Kathleen O'Toole, "The Trillion-Dollar Man," *Stanford* (May/June 1997), 53–55.

21. For a discussion of the much-misunderstood politics of the "neoconservatives," see Seymour Martin Lipset, *American Exceptionalism: A Double-Edged Sword* (New York: W. W. Norton, 1996), 193–202.

22. Robert K. Merton, "The Unanticipated Consequences of Purposive Social Action," *American Sociological Review* 1 (December 1936): 894–904.

23. See Max Weber, *The Methodology of the Social Sciences* (Glencoe, Ill.: Free Press, 1949), 55, 84.

24. Rainwater and Yancey, *The Moynihan Report,* 20.

25. Moynihan, *Coping,* 5.

26. Rainwater and Yancey, *The Moynihan Report,* 22.

CHAPTER FOUR

DANIEL PATRICK MOYNIHAN, EPIDEMIOLOGIST

NICHOLAS N. EBERSTADT

Anyone even vaguely familiar with his work will already know that Daniel Patrick Moynihan is a polymath. Indeed, this sometime political adviser, sub-cabinet member, special assistant to the president, Harvard professor, diplomat, and senator has occupied himself as an established expert—if not a preeminent authority—in an unnerving multiplicity of intellectual disciplines and academic fields: American history, architectural criticism, arms control, educational policy, ethnology, income policy, international law, public finance, public policy research and evaluation, the sociology of the family, and urban planning. It should come as no surprise that the intellectual ambit of this evidently incorrigible trespasser among fields of specialized learning has taken him into many other areas not enumerated above. What may nonetheless surprise even some of his friends and admirers is that Daniel Patrick Moynihan's writings show him to be a formidable student of epidemiology.

Epidemiology, in the careful but inelegant definition of a recent dictionary devoted to the topic, is the "study of the distribution and determinants of health-related states or events in specified populations, and the application of this study to control of health problems."[1] In Dr. Ian Rockett's somewhat more lucid explanation, epidemiologists investigate "why disease and injury afflict some people more than others, and why they occur more frequently in some locations and times than at others—

knowledge necessary for finding the most effective ways to treat and prevent health problems."[2] In the epidemiological approach to public health problems, "the primary units of concern are *groups* of persons, not separate individuals,"[3] and the method, in the classic formulation of Dr. W. H. Frost, "includes the orderly arrangement of [established facts] into chains of inference which extend more or less beyond the bounds of direct observation."[4] From these specifics, it will be apparent that Daniel Patrick Moynihan has demonstrated an epidemiological inclination, and displayed an epidemiological virtuosity, in his nearly forty years of study of three contemporary American social issues: traffic safety, crime, and drugs.

Violent crime, illicit drug use, and traffic hazards are, of course, more than just public health questions. But public health questions they most assuredly are. And when considered as health problems, there is a characteristic similarity among them. Indeed, the International Classification of Diseases (ICD), the standard taxonomy against which doctors issue diagnoses and coroners fill out death certificates, groups the adverse consequences of these three ills together under a single broader heading: "Injury and Poisoning." And although relatively few nonepidemiologists might recognize this to be the case, "Injury and Poisoning" have posed a major, and by some indices a mounting, threat to the nation's health over the postwar period—that is, during an era in which the United States not only has enjoyed an unsurpassed and still growing affluence but also has suffered only negligible losses and injuries due to military conflict.[5] Indeed, even as the U.S. life span has steadily lengthened, deaths due to "external causes" (unintentional injuries, including motor vehicle crashes, suicide, and what is termed "homicide and legal intervention") have assumed a troubling prominence in the modern American mortality structure.

In 1960, according the National Center for Health Statistics (NCHS), deaths from "external causes" accounted for 8.6 percent of all deaths in the American population; in 1993, the proportion had risen to 10.4 percent.[6] (These figures are age-standardized and thus unaffected by intervening shifts in the nation's demographic composition; no less telling, the ominous upward trend is evident for every major subpopulation, from black males to white females.) Trends are even more dramatic when cast in terms of "years of potential life lost" (YPLL), a measure of premature mortality among those under age 65. In 1970, deaths due to "external causes" were calculated to compose 24.7 percent of total YPLL; by 1993, they composed 28.9 percent—a higher proportion for the general American population than had been characteristic for black males just twenty-three years earlier.[7] In 1993, the toll in YPLL from "unintentional injuries" (principally, motor vehicle crashes) was greater than from all types of cancer ("neoplasms") combined; by the same measure, "homicide and legal intervention" that year resulted in more premature loss of life than did heart attacks ("ischemic heart disease"). Despite continuing and dramatic improvements in emergency room and paramedic intervention capabilities, moreover, the age-standardized death rate in America due to "homicide and legal intervention"—injuries that were crimes in themselves or were caused by crime—more than doubled between 1960 and 1993.[8] Of all the deadly risks in postwar American daily life, perhaps only the AIDS epidemic has proven more stubbornly resistant to the diverse public and private therapies that have been applied in the attempt to subdue it.

The phenomenon of violent injury in modern American life is in some sense similar to a number of other public policy challenges with which Moynihan's name has become associated: It is a problem (or set of interrelated problems) with major consequences for the nation's well-being, surprisingly poorly understood even by specialists, and seemingly unsubmissive in the face of sustained policy intervention. Moynihan the epidemiologist did not discover cures to the afflictions he analyzed. In epidemiology, there usually are no "cures." A good epidemiologist, instead, can help to reduce the burden on a population from given health risks by devising strategies based on an informed assessment of the "etiology" (what social scientists might call "dynamics") of the hazard in question. American policymakers today understand the "etiology" of traffic injury, crime, and drugs more clearly thanks to Daniel Patrick Moynihan's insights.

TRAFFIC SAFETY

Moynihan has been a student of automobile safety since the late 1950s, when he worked on highway safety policy (among other things) for New York Governor Averell Harriman. An early expression of this interest can be found in his piece "Epidemic on the Highways," published in *The Reporter* in 1959.[9] His most important analytical contribution to the study of vehicular injury was his essay "Traffic Safety and the Body Politic," which originally appeared in *The Public Interest* in the spring of 1966.[10] This is, quite simply, an extraordinary piece of work. Even thirty years after publication, the reader cannot help but be impressed by the originality and the intellectual power of its exposition. In less than ten thousand words,

Moynihan revolutionized the American approach to auto safety, transforming the then deadly-dull topic of "road safety" into an intriguing (and researchable) area of policy inquiry, and outlining the directions by which private and collective action could progressively reduce the human toll exacted by the driving machine. This remarkable article is less famous than it should be, so it deserves some special attention here.

The central insight in "Traffic Safety and the Body Politic" is derived directly from basic epidemiological teaching: namely, that there was nothing accidental about traffic "accidents." In any given episode, a car crash or a collision with a pedestrian might seem a random and inexplicable tragedy. But when viewed in the aggregate (remember that the epidemiological method examines "groups of persons, not separate individuals"), quite predictable overall patterns of risk could be discerned; there was a regular structure to, or an "etiology" of, motor vehicle injury. Yet, neither policymakers nor the public seemed to be aware of this. "Just as classical forms of disease were in general treated by magic until perhaps two centuries ago," wrote Moynihan, "accidents have until this moment been thought of as somehow 'wild' occurrences which do not conform to the sequential chain of causal events that define the way things in general take place."[11]

Because interventions at the individual, corporate, or governmental level could alter the various risk schedules associated with driving, Moynihan reasoned, it should correspondingly be possible to contain and diminish the human cost of motorized travel. "There is a considerable body of empirical evidence," he argued, "that automobile accidents can be reduced without substantially compromising the essential transportation system by which they are generated."[12]

In Moynihan's diagnosis, the central impediment to a more effective traffic policy was that government authorities had embraced an approach to enhancing public safety completely inadequate to the task. For peculiar historical reasons, America was applying the wrong "paradigm" to auto injury prevention. As he explained,

> The entire pattern of State Police management of the automobile complex is derived directly from the model of the prevention, detection, and punishment of—crime. . . . This involves intense concentration on the guilt of individuals, as measured by conformance to statutes, and belief in the efficacy of punishment, either threatened or carried out, as a means of social regulation. There is not much evidence that this works. . . .

> [T]here is no evidence [, for example,] that drivers who are arrested for speeding, or similar offenses, are in fact any different from other drivers, or that they act differently thereafter. . . . [W]e must live for the moment with the probability that most "convicted speeders" are little more than innocent victims of the Poisson distribution.[13]

By contrast with the existing juridical framework for auto injury control, an epidemiological approach to the dangers of motor travel (what Moynihan called "federal concern with automobile transportation, properly conceived") not only would offer the possibility of substantially reducing vehicular casualties but also would

> as much as possible put an end to the present idiocies of armed police arresting and often imprisoning hordes of citizens who are then haled [*sic*] before courts incompetent to judge a problem that in any event is almost impossible to define in legal terms.[14]

"Traffic Safety and the Body Politic" identified three key syndromes that were, in Moynihan's estimate, exposing the public to unnecessarily high risk of auto injury: "the venality of the automobile industry," "the psychological role of the automobile" in daily life, and "the failure of government."[15]

American automakers in those days, as he explained in painful and convincing detail, were defiantly indifferent to issues of design safety in their product. ("I have come to the conclusion," commented an exasperated Moynihan, "that for brute greed and moral imbecility the American automobile industry has no peer.")[16]

The public, for its part, was "ambivalent on the question of traffic safety," for the automobile constituted "a prime agent of risk-taking in a society that still values risk-taking, but does not provide many outlets."[17] (As Moynihan tartly observed, "The largest reason we have not done anything to tame the automobile is that we have not much wanted to.")[18]

Then there was the government. Not only had federal, state, and local authorities opted for the wrong tools for the job, they did not even collect the sorts of information that would permit an evaluation of performance:

> Directly related to the absence of facts about safety design is the absence of facts about the whole subject. . . . [T]here are in fact no standard national statistics about traffic safety. The United States government does not collect

> them. The only moderately reliable statistic that exists is the number of persons killed . . . a dependable but meaningless number, in the sense that it provides no guide to action of any sort. . . . It is hardly a complicated matter to conceive what basic national data ought to be collected. . . . Most of the data could be gathered by standard sampling techniques.[19]

Legislation then just introduced—the Highway Safety Act of 1966—had "the potential," Moynihan noted, for redirecting auto safety policy toward more promising strategies. "The issue now," he mused, "is whether the forthcoming legislation will evoke the sustained and responsible concern of those who have so neglected the subject in the past."[20] It did, and in the following decades, the dangers of road travel were dramatically reduced.

Mortality statistics convey some impression of the transformation in risk schedules. Between 1950 and 1970, America's age-standardized death rate from motor vehicle crashes had risen by almost a fifth; between 1970 and 1991–93, on the other hand, it declined by over two-fifths.[21] All the while, however, Americans were driving more and spending more time in the car and on the road; thus mortality rates per se understate the gains against the deadly risks of driving as an activity. In 1965, the U.S. traffic death rate per 100 million vehicle miles was 5.1; in 1993, this figure had fallen by two-thirds, to 1.7 (Figure 4.1).

In 1966, Daniel Patrick Moynihan was not persuaded that such statistics conveyed meaningful information about underlying public health risks: Trends derived from them, he warned, could be biased or even dominated by the secular advance of modern medicine, which steadily increased the survival chances for crash victims. Yet other data can now corroborate the general trends indicated by motor mortality figures. National data on auto injuries, for example, are available from 1975 onwards; between 1975 and 1992, nonfatal injuries per 100 million passenger miles dropped by almost 30 percent (Figure 4.2). "In 1960," Moynihan wrote, "I made some tentative calculations that something like a third of the automobiles manufactured in Detroit ended up with blood on them."[22] For the early 1990s, a comparably tentative computation would suggest that the odds for domestically purchased cars and light trucks had dropped to about one in 4.5 or less.[23]

How, exactly, are these improvements to be explained? In quantitative terms, it is not possible to allocate the change among the various contributing factors. Nevertheless, it is clear that the overall trend was influenced by generally auspicious responses by each of the three sets of

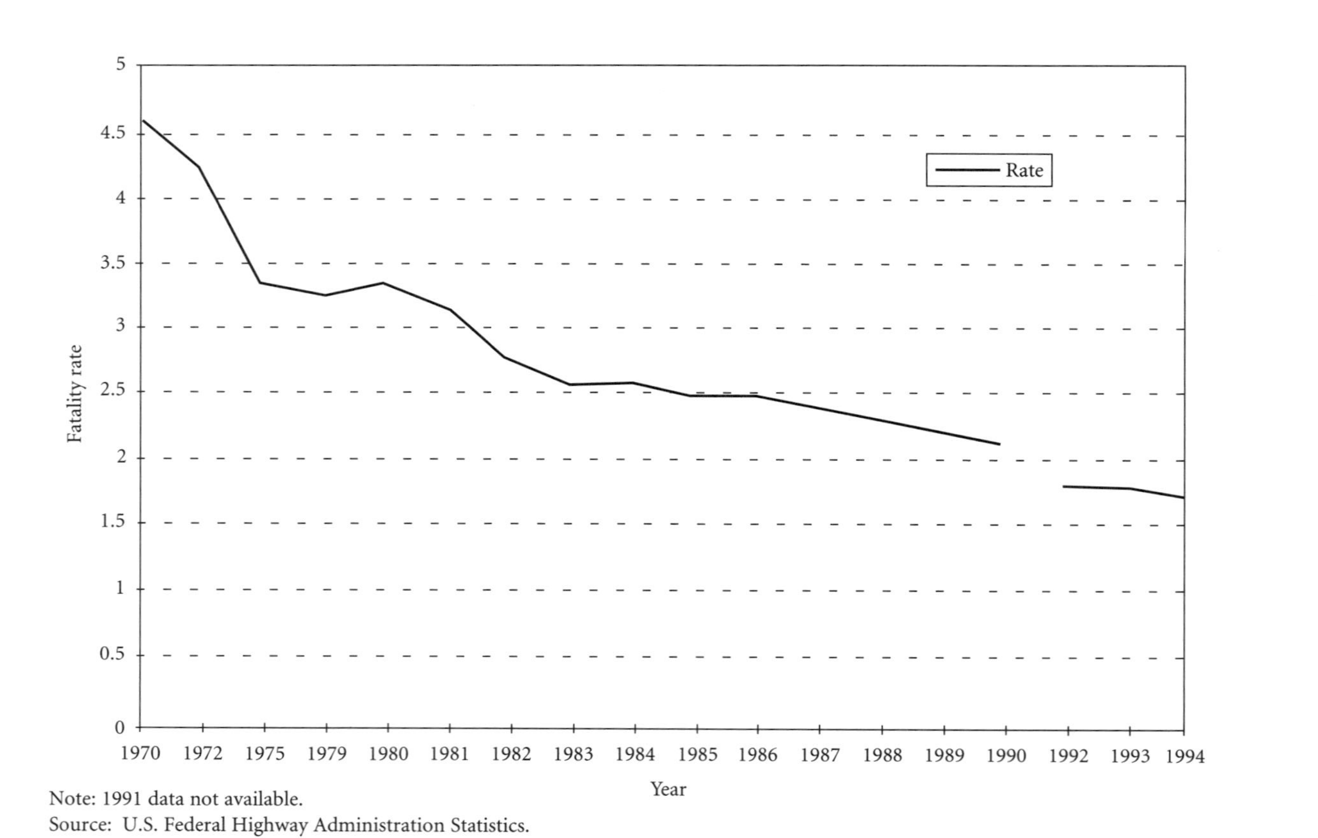

Note: 1991 data not available.
Source: U.S. Federal Highway Administration Statistics.

Figure 4.1 Rate of fatalities per 100 million miles of vehicle travel (1970–1994)

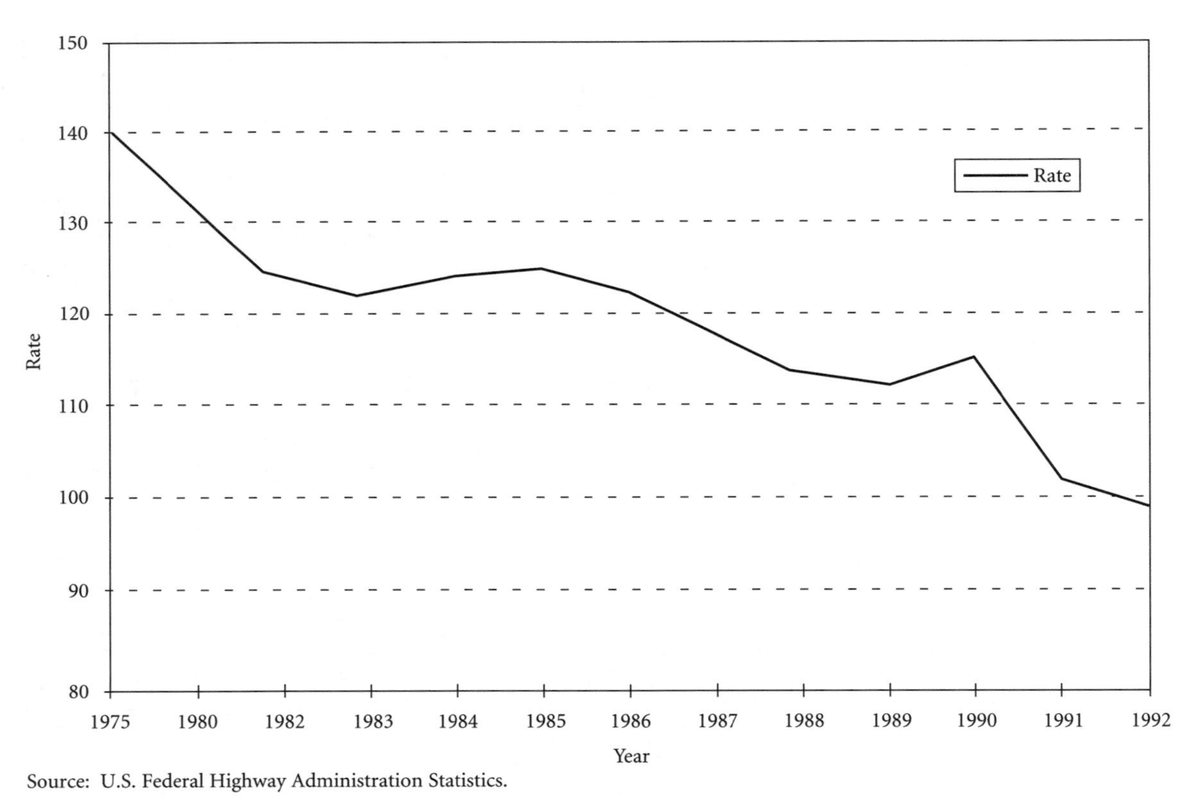

Source: U.S. Federal Highway Administration Statistics.

Figure 4.2 Rate of nonfatal accidents per 100 million vehicle miles traveled, 1975–1992

independent actors Moynihan had identified: the auto industry, the motorist, and the government.

In the early 1960s, it is fair to say that Detroit did not take auto safety terribly seriously; in the 1990s, on the other hand, the entire auto industry had completely internalized the concept of design safety into its corporate cultures, assigning it a high and enthusiastic priority. This was a more mature attitude for a more mature industry; it could be explained almost in terms of "life passages." At a point between the early 1960s and the early 1990s, the American auto industry had faced its own version of a "near-death experience." Suddenly confronted by increasingly restrictive regulation, expensive tort litigation, disenchanted consumers, and adept foreign competitors, the survival of the three major American auto manufacturers was no longer taken for granted. For some time, in fact, it seemed to be seriously in doubt. The now international auto industry that has developed in the wake of that corporate trauma is firmly committed to "selling safety." Demographics has probably played a role here. At one end of the business, the auto industry's *ancien regime* has been replaced by a younger generation of decisionmakers to whom safety issues were profit issues; for another, the "feminization" of the auto market—the growing importance of mothers and other women in the selection and purchase process—has rewarded the orientation toward design safety, reinforcing its new standing within corporate strategy.

Demographics alone, however, do not explain the shift in American driving habits. If safety-consciousness is a feminine trait, all American motorists have become more "feminized"—men and women alike. Americans may be no more likely today than in the past to observe the strict letter of the law when it comes to speed limits, but they are much more likely to buckle up, and considerably less likely to drive drunk. Significant changes in behavior have occurred over relatively short periods of time. The National Highway Traffic Safety Administration (NHTSA), for example, estimates that between 1982 and 1991, seat belt use increased from about 11 percent of all American auto passengers to about 50 percent[24] (Figure 4.3). At much the same time, the proportion of fatal crashes in which the driver's blood alcohol concentration measured 0.10 or above dropped sharply: from an average of approximately 25 percent in 1982 to less than 20 percent in 1994 (Figure 4.4). This drop in blood alcohol concentrations, incidentally, was totally pervasive: among men and women; the young the old; drivers of trucks, cars, and motorcycles alike; and irrespective of the time of day (or night) of the crash.

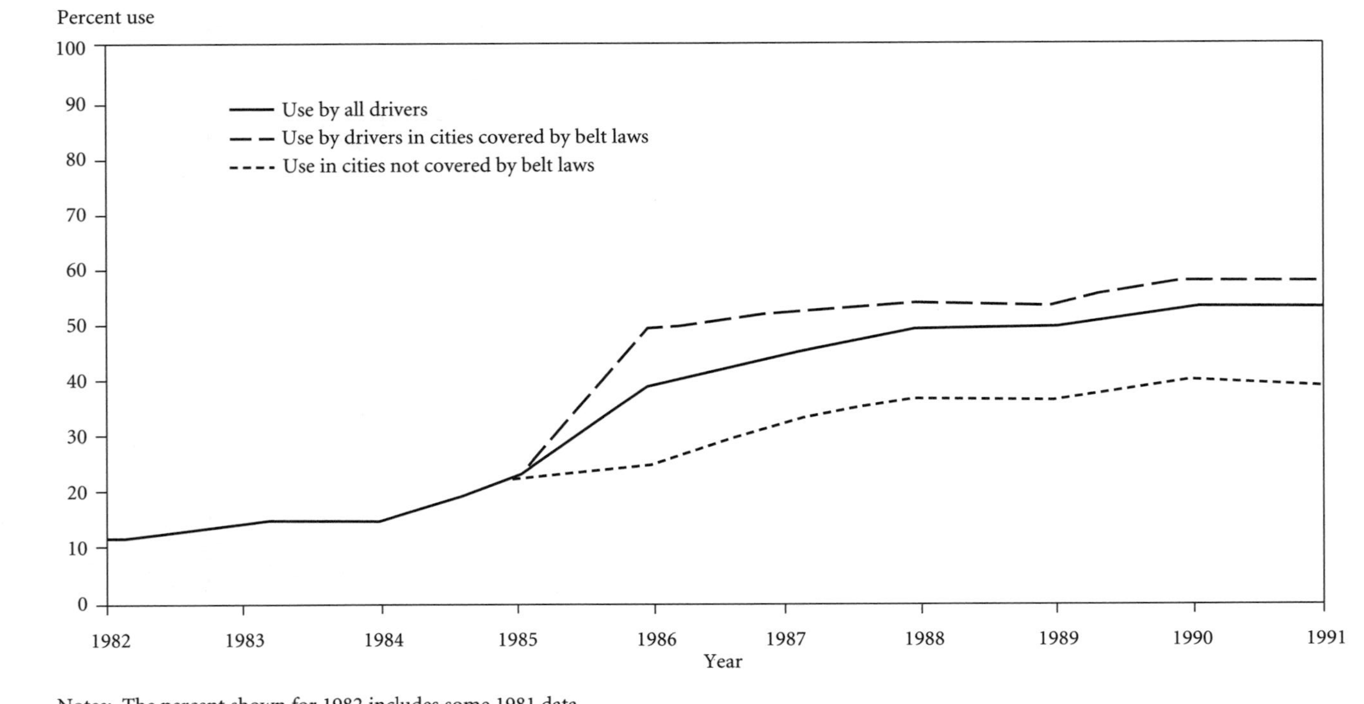

Notes: The percent shown for 1982 includes some 1981 data.
Data for 1989 and later were computed somewhat differently than were earlier data.
Source: National Highway Traffic Safety Administration.

Figure 4.3 Trends in drivers' use of safety belts

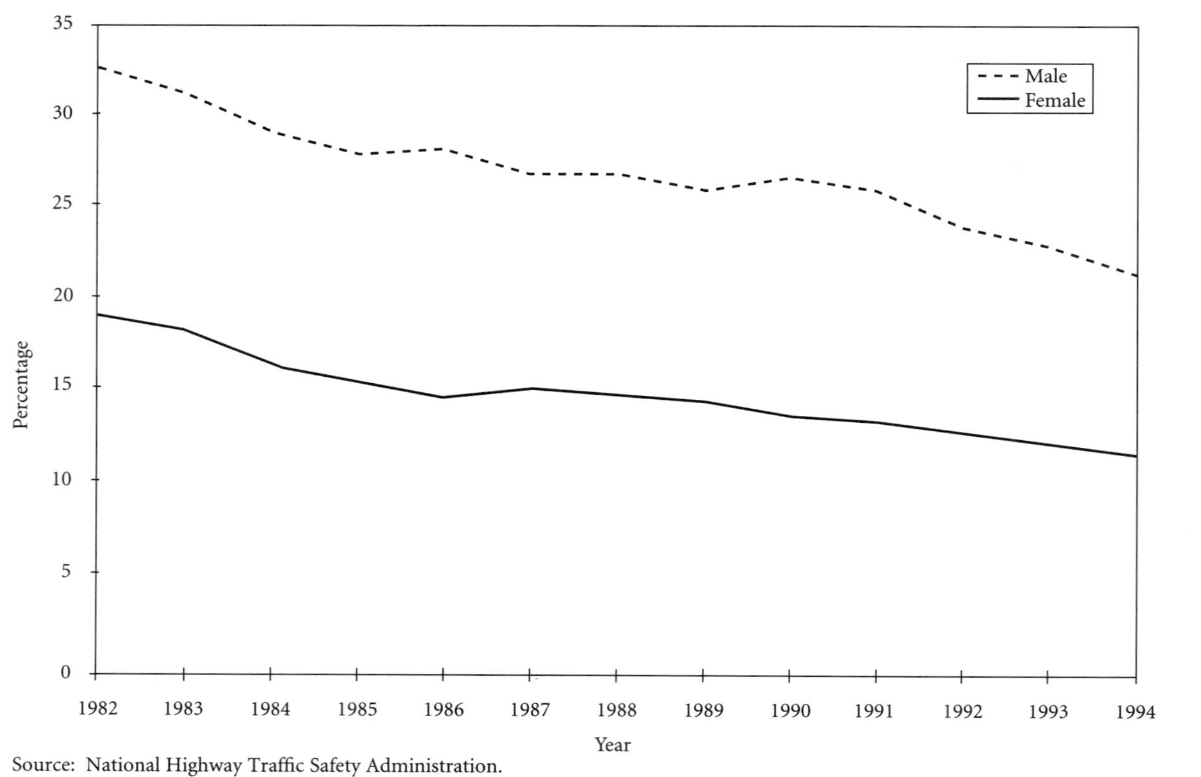

Source: National Highway Traffic Safety Administration.

Figure 4.4 Percentage of drivers in fatal crashes with blood alcohol concentration 0.10 or higher

Legislation and enforcement may have played some part in these shifts, but much more can probably be credited to "public education"—broadly construed. In an increasingly affluent and healthy nation, the general public tends to place a progressively higher value on its time, and on its life; information that reliably augments or preserves these quantities tends to result in behavior modification. To be sure, a tolerance for risk—even a taste for it—is reflected in some driving behavior, as Moynihan pointed out in 1966. In response to safety improvements, some drivers may choose to take greater risks than before.[25] But such instances appear to be anomalous. On the whole, recent American driving habits suggest that tolerance for these sorts of risks has been far from immutable, much less perverse. In this particular respect, Moynihan may have underestimated the scope for traffic safety enhancement.

The impact of government interventions on actual achieved traffic safety has hardly been unidirectional. Micromanagerial stipulations on the "corporate average fuel economy" (CAFE) of the manufactured "fleets," for example, have been pure epidemiological idiocy; the enforced heterogeneity in highway vehicle size dictated by this "environmental" ukase has predictably consigned hundreds, perhaps thousands, of Americans to violent death each year since *ceteris paribus*, people in the smaller car are more likely to be hurt in a collision.[26] New safety regulations, moreover, cannot automatically take credit for saving lives: As Sam Peltzman's econometrics persuasively attested over twenty years ago, the same demand for and use of life-saving seat belts would likely have been accomplished by American auto buyers of their own free will as was legislated into new autos after the Highway Safety Act.[27] Yet, when all is said and done, government attention to traffic safety post-Moynihan incontestably saved vastly more lives than it cost (although its financial cost-effectiveness may be another story). Government concern with auto safety and control of construction purse strings resulted in better and less hazardous highways and roads. The government's hectoring of the U.S. auto industry about design safety almost certainly accelerated life-saving innovations—at least in the early phase of that regulated relationship. And introduction of the data-gathering and evaluation systems that Moynihan had advised provided far-reaching guidance for corrections and new directions in auto safety for the public, the individual driver, and the corporate sector.

The complaint has been lodged at times that auto safety policies have made no difference whatever to the well-being of the American driver: that reductions in fatalities per 100 million miles driven, for example, follow an almost smooth trajectory, unaffected over time by changing policy interventions or regimens. This is true, at least as far as past mortality trajectories are concerned. But from the standpoint of the safety policymaker, this is rather beside the point; safety innovation does not occur spontaneously, any more than new highways design and build themselves.

In a rational and risk-averse population, increases in income, education, and information will be expected to drive down the incidence and cost of transportation-related injuries. But how this happens at different junctures, and by how much, are not preordained. The spread and gradual inculcation of epidemiological reasoning over the past generation and a half was partly responsible for the specific auto safety improvements that were actually achieved over that period, and Daniel Patrick Moynihan was a prominent vector in the process.

VIOLENT CRIME

Although the orders of magnitude for injuries and deaths from driving and crime happen to be similar in America today, the etiologies obviously are not. Driving is not axiomatically a social pathology; criminal activity, on the other hand, is. Unlike criminal assault, physical or emotional injury of other people is not a necessary consequence of every trip in a car. And while the risks of both road hazard and crime derive in large measure from concentrated subpopulations, crime—unlike reckless driving—can be and often is a way of life for its practitioners: a profession, a pastime, simply an attractive challenge.

Given the characteristic differences between the agents of auto injury and the agents of criminal injuries, it should be no surprise that public policy has been markedly more successful in controlling the former than the latter. Indeed, the virtual explosion of crime, and the spread of criminality, within the American population over the past three and a half decades arguably demarcate one of the greatest social—and policy—failures in modern American history. Epidemiologists can claim no special credit for helping to quell this still-raging epidemic. Nevertheless, Daniel Patrick Moynihan has offered us valuable observations and intriguing hypotheses about the epidemiology of contemporary American crime.

Demography is a regular tool for the epidemiologist. In his study of domestic criminal violence, Moynihan the epidemiologist collaborated closely with Moynihan the demographer. One product of this partnership was an essay titled "Peace," first published in his collection *Coping*, in 1973. Addressing the question of "peace at home," Moynihan ventured that

> most of the events that tore American society almost apart, or so it seemed in the 1960s, arose from conditions unique to the decade in which they occurred. They had not existed before. They will not exist again. They involve the interaction of demographic and political-cultural changes. . . . [T]he 1960s saw a profound demographic change occur in American society which was a one-time change, a growth in population vaster than any that had ever occurred before or any that will ever occur again, with respect to a particular population subgroup, namely those persons fourteen to twenty-four years of age.[28]

Moynihan went on to explain that the "people who cause most of the trouble in society, as you probably know, are people fourteen to twenty-four. . . . Societies, no matter where they are, are mostly organized around the problem of how to get people from fourteen to twenty-four."[29] Because the baby boom of the 1950s resulted in an unprecedented increase in the absolute number of infants, there was an unprecedented increase in the absolute number of adolescents and very young adults a decade and a half later; and because America was already heading toward subreplacement fertility by the late 1960s, there were no repeat performances on the horizon. Thus, in the coming decades, Moynihan predicted, "we shall have peace, but it will in some respects be a peace of exhaustion."[30]

"Peace," it should be emphasized, addressed the prospects for domestic social disturbance in general, rather than crime in particular. The demographic reasoning undergirding the analysis, moreover, was eminently sound. Even so, we now know that events subsequently unfolded in a manner that Moynihan's audience in 1973 would have been poorly prepared to anticipate. In the late 1970s, the absolute number of Americans age 15–24 finally peaked and commenced a steady decline—but the number of Americans "getting into trouble" continued to rise seemingly inexorably. From the late 1970s to the mid-1990s, the trends for total youth population in America and total arrests in America were heading in opposite directions (Figure 4.5). Like the famous "scissors" in the 1965 Moynihan Report, which depicted Aid to Families with Dependent Children caseloads rising even as nonwhite male unemployment rates were falling,[31] this was an ominous and unexpected divergence.

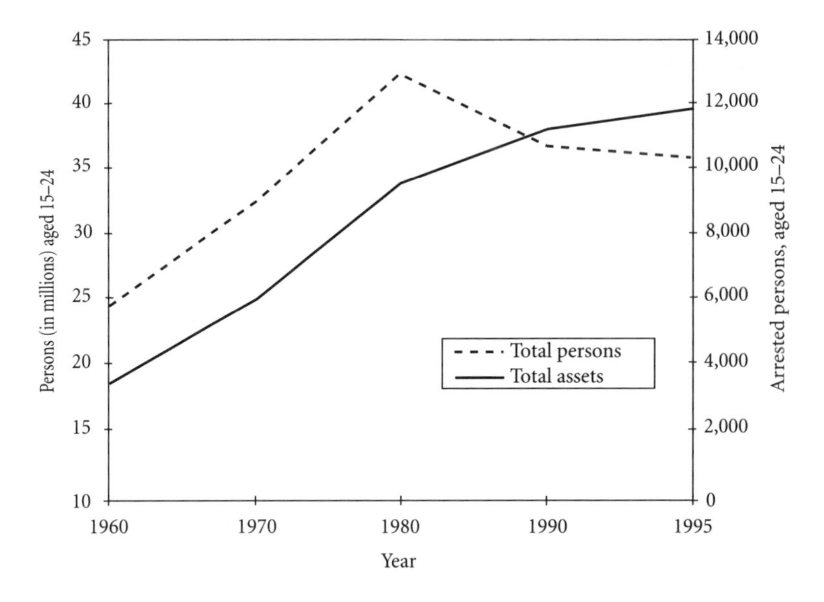

Source: U.S. Bureau of the Census, *Statistical Abstracts of the United States.*

Figure 4.5 Persons aged 15–24 arrested, per annum, vs. total persons aged 15–24, 1960–95

In retrospect, it may be that the 15-to-24-year-old population is a less suitable "risk group" to track for violent crime than for other social disturbances. Despite all the attention to the young offender in social work and criminology, after all, the fact is that most delinquents in America today are not chronologically juvenile. To judge by homicide mortality rates, for example, the prime risk cohort in America between 1950 and 1989 was the 25-to-34-year-old male[32] (Figure 4.6). Men in this age group also record higher arrest rates, and higher proportions of alcohol-related driver fatalities, than younger cohorts. The actual existing crime problem in contemporary America, it would seem, can largely be defined in terms of adult predators and "problem-case" grown-ups at large in a graying, child-scarce society.

The crime problems of tomorrow are surely affected not only by the absolute size of today's rising cohorts but also by their composition. Daniel Patrick Moynihan pointed this out over thirty years ago, and has been reminding us of this central fact ever since. In his 1965 essay "The Case for a Family Policy,"[33] Moynihan warned that

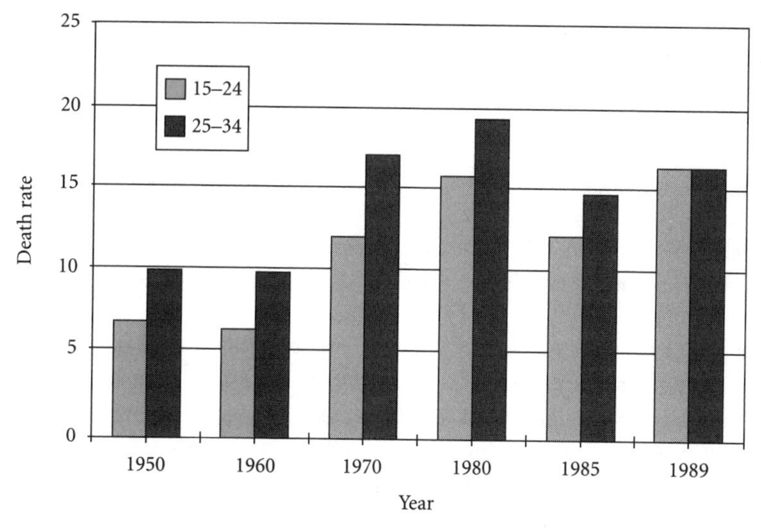

Source: *Health, United States,* 149.

Figure 4.6 Death rates for homicide and legal intervention, 1950–1989 (per 100,000 resident population)

> there is one unmistakable lesson in American history: a community that allows a large number of young men to grow up in broken families, dominated by women, never acquiring any stable relationship to male authority, never acquiring any set of rational expectations about the future—that community asks for and gets chaos. Crime, violence, unrest, unrestrained lashing out at the whole social structure—that is not only to be expected; it is very near to inevitable.[34]

Not even Moynihan, though, could have guessed in 1965 how characteristic the broken home and the fatherless family would become for America over the next thirty years. By the early 1990s, the fraction of white families that were fatherless, and the ratio of white illegitimate births, were about the same as they had been for nonwhites in the early 1960s[35]—conditions Moynihan had then judged sufficiently alarming to warrant his 1965 report *The Negro Family* and his essay "The Case for a Family Policy."

The trend of young males raised in fatherless homes has proven to be a fearsomely good predictor of overall trends for violent crime over the past generation. By this indicator, pressures for future crime epidemics continue to mount. How are we to cope with this coming onslaught?

In early 1993, in *The American Scholar*, Moynihan described how we were coping: by "Defining Deviancy Down."[36] "I offer the thesis," writes Moynihan,

> that over the past generation . . . the amount of deviant behavior in American society has increased beyond the levels the community can "afford to recognize" and that accordingly we have been redefining deviancy so as to exempt much conduct previously stigmatized, and also quietly raising the "normal" level in categories where behavior is abnormal by any earlier standard.[37]

The public reaction to steadily rising incidences of crime, Moynihan continued, "is curiously passive. . . . James Q. Wilson comments that Los Angeles has a St. Valentine's Day Massacre every weekend. Even the most ghastly reenactments produce only moderate responses."[38] Having described the new "denial" mechanisms in discomfiting detail, Moynihan admonished that

> we are getting used to a lot of behavior that is not good for us. . . . If our analysis wins general acceptance—if, for example, more of us came to share Judge Torres' genuine alarm at "the trivialization of the lunatic crime rate" in his city (and mine)—we might surprise ourselves how well we respond to the manifest decline of the American civic order. Might.[39]

"Defining Deviancy Down" is a masterful essay—in social psychology, not epidemiology. Although Moynihan invokes the need for epidemiological reasoning in addressing the crime problem in this study,[40] he refrains from broadly describing the shape such an approach would take. He does propose a particular intervention—federal regulation of the domestic supply of handgun bullets—that might well affect current homicide rates if enacted. But surely bullet rationing would only be a small component of an overall epidemiologically grounded anticrime strategy.

Generally speaking, epidemiology addresses public health problems from two directions: prevention or control. If the supply of violent criminals in the nation is closely related to the supply of fatherless younger men, prevention is problematic; we have not yet been able to devise a workable way to purposely halt, much less reverse, this rising tide of fatherlessness. On the other hand, we may understand more about control than is always apparent. (As recent experience in New York City suggests, moreover, we are learning—or relearning—things about crime control from time to time.)[41]

One sure fact about crime control is that jailed criminals do not prey on the public. Over the past thirty years, an explosion of incarceration has accompanied the explosion in crime. By 1994, nearly 1.5 million Americans were jailed or imprisoned on any given day: nearly every hundredth white adult male and every fifteenth black adult male.[42] This is, incontestably, a disturbing development and a sorry commentary on America today. But what is its epidemiological significance?

Studying the crime epidemic unleashed since the 1960s, an epidemiologist might well conclude that we are currently underprisoned, that incarceration rates in America are presently too low, and that public policy is devoting too few resources to punishment: that we are not, in other words, adequately availing ourselves of the one sure avenue of crime control we know to work. Daniel Patrick Moynihan's epidemiological writings, however, have not directly indicated his own view on this troubling question.

DRUGS

Though there is considerable overlap today between the public health problems posed by crime and illicit drugs, the etiologies of the two syndromes can be distinguished from one another. In 1993, Moynihan published a probing assessment of America's drug problem in *The American Scholar* under the title "Iatrogenic Government."[43] "Iatrogenic," one may dimly recall, is a medical term referring to illnesses caused or exacerbated by the physician's own interventions. As one may surmise from that title, Moynihan's estimate of government efforts to mitigate the drug problem was less than sanguine.

In the expanded version of the essay, published as chapter 3 of his 1996 volume, *Miles to Go*, Moynihan put his thesis and his critique bluntly:

> There are discernible rhythms in drug epidemiology. They appear to burn themselves out as the initial enthusiasts succumb to the effects of the drug, or to lateral afflictions (HIV/AIDS, in the case of the 1960s heroin cohort), or disappear into prison. Their behavior has become aversive; fewer recruits are attracted, and the episode subsides. No thanks, or little thanks, to the federal government, and here is the point. . . . The problem of drug abuse in the United States today—which is to say, the use of illicit drugs—is the direct, unambiguous consequence of federal law prohibiting their licit use.[44]

Heroin, cocaine, and now crack, Moynihan reminds us, are only the latest in a long series of powerful new intoxicants made possible by technological advance. In eighteenth-century England and early-nineteenth-century America, the advent of high-proof distilled spirits resulted in enormous social and public health problems; for a time, gin may even have exerted something like a Malthusian check on the growth of the population of the city of London.[45]

In the United States, as in England before it, a (religiously based) temperance movement helped to reduce alcohol consumption dramatically. But Americans then attempted to eliminate alcohol use through a national legislative prohibition—the Eighteenth Amendment, enacted in 1919 and repealed in 1933. As Moynihan recounts, "Alcohol prohibition was a convulsive event that, among other things, led to the creation of a criminal underworld of exceptional influence and durability."[46] Extending the analogy, Moynihan wryly comments that

> in dealing with drugs [today] we are required to choose between a crime problem and a public health problem. In choosing to prohibit drugs, we choose to have a more or less localized—but ultimately devastating—crime problem rather than a general health problem. . . . It is essential that we understand that by choosing to prohibit drugs we are choosing to have an intense crime problem concentrated among minorities.[47]

Moynihan's criticism of government policy is stinging:

> Clearly the federal drug policy is responsible for a degree of social regression for which there does not appear to be any equivalent in our history. The number of inmates imprisoned for drug offenses now exceeds those in prison for property crimes.[48]

But he also has harsh words for the American medical profession, which, he asserts, "finds drug research aversive behavior."[49] In the final analysis, he concludes, "only the development of a blocking or neutralizing agent will have any real effect, given the setting in which our drug problem now occurs"; "interdiction and 'drug busts' are probably necessary symbolic acts, but nothing more."[50]

Though "Iatrogenic Government" stands as a foray into epidemiology, one would not describe it as an essay of clinical detachment. There is a tone of resignation—some would say pessimism—out of keeping with a usual

Moynihan study. Reading his analysis, one suspects that Moynihan, in his heart of hearts, expects that the current drug problem in America is beyond positive strategies for solution—or rather, is amenable to solution only by long-term demographic trends, as the high-risk subgroups destroy or inoculate themselves and are replaced.

Such a grim prognosis may ultimately prove accurate; Moynihan's predictive record, as we all know, has been amazingly good over the years. Yet, other readings of the epidemiological evidence at hand can also be suggested. The possibilities for prevention, for example, may be greater than, and somewhat different from, those Moynihan outlines.

The great distilled alcohol epidemic in the English-speaking world, after all, was tamed by religious temperance movements. These were not constructs of government—they arose from civil society itself—but they seemed to prove considerably more effective in their time than today's government-sponsored programs for drug "treatment on request." Successful anti-intoxicant movements, moreover, continue to spring up from society itself, unsummoned by the state: think of Alcoholics Anonymous and Mothers Against Drunk Driving.

Flawed as they arguably may be, existing control policies, for their part, may also have their virtues. Current drug laws, after all, are used for more than just drug control; like the income tax statutes that eventually snared Al Capone, they are now routinely used against violent criminals by law enforcement officials lacking evidentiary basis for prosecution on other offenses. The prisons have indeed swelled with felons convicted of drug offenses; between 1980 and 1994, those ranks increased by over 180,000.[51] But the number of prisoners convicted of violent offenses rose even more dramatically over those same years—by over a quarter-million—and some fraction of the "drug" offenders in reality were something even less attractive. Given this state of affairs—"set and setting," so to speak—an epidemiologist might entertain the possibility that a relaxation of current controls on illicit drugs could lead, for some period of time, to a worsening of both the crime problem and the public health problem.

CONCLUDING OBSERVATIONS

It is sometimes supposed that rigorous policy research requires the analyst to be value-neutral. But as Daniel Patrick Moynihan has proven by long and honorable personal example, this is not the case. Indeed, there is a distinct hazard when policy research becomes unmoored from ethical norms or inured to moral distinctions. As Moynihan recently noted, the same holds for epidemiology:

> Epidemiologists have powerful insights that can contribute to lessening the medical trauma, but they must be wary of normalizing the social pathology that leads to such trauma.[52]

Within epidemiology, that risk is greatest with respect to injuries and deaths due to "external causes." The great figures of epidemiology have long recognized this to be so. As Dr. H. O. Lancaster has written,

> the one unifying feature of many of these deaths, which include suicides, homicides, accidental poisonings, and external violence, is a lowered appreciation of the sanctity of human life. Therefore, ultimately the prevention of a proportion of these deaths is a moral problem.[53]

In his writings on auto safety, crime, and drugs—to mention only the three topics discussed above—the moral element of the epidemiological problem has always been obvious and inescapable to Moynihan. America's foremost political epidemiologist has never been one to shrink from the hard questions, or to neglect their moral dimension. That is a legacy to be ignored only at considerable risk to the health of the nation and its people.

NOTES

1. John M. Last, ed., *A Dictionary of Epidemiology* (New York: Oxford University Press, 1988), 42.
2. Ian R. H. Rockett, "Population and Health: An Introduction to Epidemiology," *Population Bulletin* 49, no. 3 (1994): 2.
3. Gary D. Friedman, *Primer of Epidemiology* (New York: McGraw-Hill Book Company, 1974), 1.
4. W. H. Frost, *Snow on Cholera* (New York: Commonwealth Fund, 1936), ix.
5. Demographically negligible, that is. Between 1947 and 1997, over ninety million deaths were recorded in the United States. Of these, fewer than 90,000 were battle deaths. Derived from U.S. Bureau of the Census, *Statistical Abstract of the United States,* 1996 edition, 74, 360.
6. Derived from U.S. National Center for Health Statistics (hereafter, NCHS), *Health, USA: 1995,* 1996, 110–11.

7. Ibid., 112–13.

8. Ibid., 110. For some subgroups in some periods, the impact of trends in "external cause" mortality has been not only adverse, but dominant. For black males during the years 1984–89, for example, the losses in life expectancy at birth due to homicide and unintentional injury were of sufficient magnitude to cancel out all the longevity improvements that would otherwise have accrued from progress against heart disease (Kenneth D. Kochanek, Jeffrey D. Maurer, and Harry M. Rosenberg, "Causes of Death Contributing to Changes in Life Expectancy: United States, 1984–1989," *Vital and Health Statistics*, ser. 20, no. 23 [1994]:11).

9. See Daniel P. Moynihan, "Epidemic on the Highways," *The Reporter* 20, no. 9 (30 April 1959): 16–23. Moynihan has credited the late Dr. William Haddon Jr., an epidemiologist who served with the New York State Health Department and, later, was the first head of the National Highway Traffic Safety Administration, as having originally piqued his interest in auto safety policy.

10. Initially titled "The War against the Automobile," *The Public Interest*, no. 3 (spring 1966): 10–26, retitled "Traffic Safety and the Body Politic," in Daniel P. Moynihan, *Coping: Essays on the Practice of Government* (New York: Random House, 1973), 79–99.

11. Moynihan, *Coping*, 98.

12. Ibid., 81.

13. Ibid., 93–94.

14. Ibid., 99.

15. Ibid., 82, 88, 89.

16. Ibid., 83.

17. Ibid., 89, 88.

18. Ibid., 88.

19. Ibid., 91–92.

20. Ibid., 99.

21. NCHS, *Health, United States, 1995* (Hyattsville, Md.: NCHS, 1996), 146.

22. Moynihan, *Coping*, 91, 83.

23. Derived from U.S. Bureau of the Census, *Statistical Abstract of the United States*, 1981 edition, 622, 1995 edition, 632, 638. This crude computation recalibrates Moynihan's original estimate according to the proportional change in reported traffic injuries and in registered vehicles between 1960 and 1993. Note that this method likely understates intervening improvements, insofar as injuries were more likely to be underreported in 1960 than in 1993 and injuries sustained in 1993 were less likely to draw blood than in 1960.

24. U.S. General Accounting Office (GAO), *Highway Safety: Safety Belts Save Lives and Reduce Costs to Society*, Report GAO/RCED-92-106, July 1992, 8–9.

25. For two of the studies that appear to document this effect, see Christopher Garbacz, "Do Front-Seat Belt Laws Put Rear-Seat Passengers at Risk?" *Population Research and Policy Review* 11, no. 2 (1992): 157–68, and Alf Erling Risa, "Adverse

Incentives from Improved Technology: Traffic Safety Regulation in Norway," *Southern Economic Journal* 60, no. 4 (1994): 844–57.

26. One careful econometric study, for example, predicted that CAFE regulations would be responsible for 2,200 to 3,900 additional fatalities in America over a ten-year period from 1989-model-year autos alone! Robert W. Crandall and John W. Graham, "The Effects of Fuel Economy Standards on Automobile Safety," *Journal of Law and Economics* 32, no. 1 (1989): 97–118.

27. Sam Peltzman, "The Effects of Automobile Safety Regulation," *Journal of Political Economy* 83, no. 4 (1975): 677–725.

28. Moynihan, *Coping*, 422–23.

29. Ibid., 423.

30. Ibid., 428.

31. U.S. Department of Labor, *The Negro Family: The Case for National Action* (Washington, D.C.: Department of Labor, Office of Policy Planning and Research, March 1965), 12.

32. This pattern, however, appears to be changing in the 1990s. For 1991–93, according to the NCHS, mortality rates for homicide and legal intervention were higher for the 15–24 age group than the 25–34 age group, irrespective of race or sex (NCHS 1996, 149–51).

33. Originally titled "A Family Policy for the Nation," *America* 113, no. 12 (18 September 1965): 280–83.

34. Published in Moynihan, *Coping*, 76.

35. Derived from U.S. Bureau of the Census, *Statistical Abstract of the United States*, 1996 edition, 63, 78; U.S. Department of Labor, 1965, 59, 61.

36. Daniel P. Moynihan, "Defining Deviancy Down," *The American Scholar* (winter 1993): 17–30. An expanded and updated version of that essay stands as chapter 3 in Daniel Patrick Moynihan, *Miles to Go: A Personal History of Social Policy* (Cambridge, Mass.: Harvard University Press, 1996).

37. Moynihan, *Miles to Go*, 144.

38. Ibid., 153.

39. Ibid., 157.

40. Ibid., 155–56.

41. For details and preliminary analysis, see John J. DiIulio Jr., "Arresting Ideas: Tougher Law Enforcement Is Driving Down Urban Crime," *Policy Review* (fall 1995), 12–16; Clifford Krauss, "Bratton Hailed as Pioneer of New Style of Policing," *New York Times*, 27 March 1996, B5.

42. Derived from Jodi M. Brown et al., *Correctional Populations in the United States, 1994* (Washington, D.C.: U.S. Department of Justice, Bureau of Justice Statistics, 1996), 7.

43. Daniel P. Moynihan, "Iatrogenic Government," *The American Scholar* (summer 1993): 351–62.

44. Moynihan, *Miles to Go*, 193.

45. Ibid., 197–98.

46. Ibid., 199.

47. Ibid., 200, 206.

48. Ibid., 207.

49. Ibid., 202.

50. Ibid., 208.

51. Brown et al., *Correctional Populations,* 10.

52. Quoted in ibid., 156.

53. H. O. Lancaster, *Expectations of Life: A Study in the Demography, Statistics, and History of World Mortality* (New York: Springer-Verlag, 1990), 341.

CHAPTER FIVE

DANIEL PATRICK MOYNIHAN AND THE FALL AND RISE OF PUBLIC WORKS

ROBERT A. PECK

What did Pat Moynihan know and when did he know it? When it comes to public works and the city, as in so many other public policy fields, he has known more than everyone else—and earlier, too. In public works, he has transformed the debate. Public architecture he has single-handedly disinterred from a public policy grave and restored to the political agenda. If you would see his monuments in this field, look about you—literally.

On public buildings, urban design, highways, transit, waterways, and water supply he has brought to bear his trademark qualities: an eclectic historical memory, a rapier tongue and typewriter, a nose for demography and geography, a sixth sense for data, and an immunity to ideological blinkering. In this field in particular, Moynihan the political vote-counter and Moynihan the passionate New Yorker rival Moynihan the political scientist. Moynihan's achievements are worthy of the great public builders, from Hadrian to Georges Haussmann to Robert Moses, only Moynihan's are humane.

HISTORY AND GEOGRAPHY

In 1977, the U.S. Senate reorganized, and the Committee on Public Works, dating to 1837, was renamed the Committee on Environment and Public Works. Soon after the name change, the committee receptionists began answering the phones "Environment Committee" and so confirmed the displacement of public works by the more contemporary issue, as it was thought, of the environment. Certainly the environment was the principal focus of the committee members and staff, lobbyists and journalists.

It was Pat Moynihan's first year in the Senate, and he was a member of the committee. Although he had begun compiling a creditable environmental record that would soon include support for strengthened clean-water and clean-air legislation and the cleanup of New York's Love Canal and West Valley nuclear dump, he bemoaned the committee's casual abandonment of its public works origins.

Moynihan had chosen Public Works and Finance as his two major committee assignments. His choices surprised many who had assumed the former ambassador would head straight for Foreign Relations. With New York City in fiscal extremis, Moynihan lobbied for the seat on Finance, declaring that there he could best help out and noting that it had been decades since a New Yorker had served on Finance. As became clear, he thought Public Works could help New York, too.

In 1986, the Environment and Public Works Committee reorganized following the Democratic recapture of the Senate. Moynihan, with considerable seniority, passed over the chairmanship of the five or so subcommittees pegged to environmental issues and sought instead the establishment and chairmanship of a new consolidated Subcommittee on Water Resources, Transportation, and Infrastructure. No one objected; they were not much interested in public works.

Only months later did complaints begin to arise when it became clear that, by scooping up all of public works, Moynihan had gained control of some 80 percent of the federal funds authorized by the committee. He also held sway over authorization of public works projects, which, since the beginning of the Republic, have mattered to members of Congress, especially around election time.

Moynihan was mindful that this subcommittee chairmanship would extend his influence. Just as important, he believed that public works matter and have mattered for the longest time. Public works systems are the foundations of the economic activity and urban development that characterize human society. Moynihan would write that public works in the last century were "understood to be the foundation for economic growth. . . . The intense competition for public works projects among cities, among regions, and among entrepreneurs, was a competition over the distribution of future wealth."[1]

In his view, attention should be paid today, too. We had long understood the importance of public works but had seemingly now forgotten. His first hearing in 1991 on what would become the Intermodal Surface Transportation Efficiency Act (P.L. 102-240, known as ISTEA, pronounced by cognoscente as "ice tea") was led off by a panel of economists who had done research on the relationship between the rate of public works investment and productivity in the economy, here and abroad.[2]

From his early days on the committee, he would lecture about the debates over federal support for "internal improvements" that had consumed the Congress throughout the first decades of the nineteenth century.[3] Colleagues and hearing witnesses would appear bemused or bored, most apparently learning all this for the first time and caring not in the least.

But for Moynihan, history lives and instructs; geography and economics determine. Inattentive to his lessons and intent, in the Washington fashion, on the latest news curio, the capital's wonkaholics left the public works field wide open to Moynihan. He used the opening to fashion innovative public policy and to benefit New York.

Here is the lesson that opened the Environment and Public Works Committee's introductory statement—authored by Moynihan—on the surface transportation legislation that, with minor modifications, was enacted as ISTEA and revolutionized the federal highway and transit programs:

> The first federal highway program was signed into law by Thomas Jefferson on March 29, 1806 (2 Stat. 357). It was part of the arrangements whereby Ohio was admitted to the Union. The National Road, as it came to be known (more recently, U.S. 40), was to connect the new state with the Eastern seaboard. As has been the case ever since, the legislation both divided the states and united the nation.[4]

Moynihan went on to recall the South's opposition to the road (it could drain off population toward the West, and besides, it skirted Richmond) and Pennsylvania's (ditto for Philadelphia). "Even so," Moynihan noted, "no state failed to give the measure at least one supporting vote. The age of internal improvements had begun, as had the debate concerning them."[5] Moynihan was signaling that he knew a thing or two about sectional fighting.

In a way rare for our times, the ISTEA debate raised fundamental policy questions about federal support for public works. But the debate was dominated, in time-honored tradition, by fighting over funding allocations among the states. Some progressive transportation advocates (that is, anyone not in the highway lobby) held that the planning and cost-sharing reforms in Moynihan's bill carried only because the entrenched interests were so engrossed in the "formula fight" over the states' shares of highway funding that they failed to see the bill's longer-range threats to their dominion. Moynihan can be assumed to have known this would occur, because it has always occurred. Not coincidentally, while fashioning progressive national policy, he also significantly improved New York's position in the state-by-state highway funding formulas.

Moynihan has never failed to put the stamp of his historic-geographic sensibility on his public works innovations. He won on ISTEA. Twelve years earlier, he had been less successful in an attempt to reform water resources policy. Wielding much less seniority than he would on ISTEA, he had been just as forthright about the sectional underpinnings of the effort, his first at comprehensive public works legislation.

With the cosponsorship of Senator Pete Domenici (Republican of New Mexico), in May 1979, he introduced a bill that would have reallocated some of the billions of federal dollars spent on dams, canals, and water supply networks. In lieu of project-by-project congressional approvals—the time-honored, pork barrel, logrolling tradition—there would be a formula based on states' land areas and populations. The states would get to decide how to spend the funds.

"Blasphemy: Senate Heretics Poke Fun at Sacred Dams" is how the *Washington Post* headlined its story about the defeat of the measure in subcommittee.[6] The newspaper piece reported the two heretics, Moynihan and Domenici, joined by Senator Alan Simpson (Republican of Wyoming), went down to defeat "as expected" but not before "bad projects were actually called 'turkeys'" and "public works projects were described as 'capers' and 'pork.'" Moynihan noted that the prevailing system had resulted in New York getting "not one penny" of the more than one billion dollars authorized under a 1958 water supply act.

Moynihan also opposed but could not stop the federal grant of $4 billion for a water-distribution system to make the implausibly sited desert city of Phoenix amenable to rampant growth. Supporters of the Central Arizona Project clung to the clumsiest of ruses that the project's purpose was to support irrigation in the exurban Phoenix desert. They had to. Federal funds have been available for decades for irrigation where water isn't and for flood control where water runs in torrents, no matter the improbability of development in either kind of location. Federal funds just haven't been available, overtly at least, for the single purpose of helping to build and maintain basic urban water-supply systems. Water supply could be funded only if combined with some other purpose such as navigation, irrigation, or flood control.

The irrigation and flood-control fictions were not available even as a ruse to get federal assistance for construction of the Third City Water Tunnel for New York City, a project necessary to avert catastrophe in the nation's largest city should either of the two other ancient and dangerously leaky main underground aqueducts ever fail. Moynihan would thunder: "You can live without oil. You can even live without love. But you can't live without water."[7] He would bemoan the fact that New York State and other eastern states had been, in essence, born too soon, sharing the misfortune to have been settled and to have built their infrastructure solely with their own resources in the centuries before federal subsidies were available.

After the Domenici-Moynihan bill went down to narrow defeat in subcommittee, Moynihan mused that he "just might decide that New York needs some of the same kinds of absurd things that the rest of the country has been getting . . . I want ocean liners in the Erie Canal. I want a billion-dollar Poughkeepsie dam. I want a brand-spanking-new canal from Lake Erie to Rochester."[8] Moynihan did work relentlessly, with eventual success, to get federal aid to restore the Erie Canal (and the larger New York State Barge Canal, of which it is now a part). In each Senate reelection campaign, he would go "navigatin'" on the canal, whistle-stop style. He saw the restoration as a boost to tourism, a fitting historical monument to American public works and engineering, and a geography lesson to New Yorkers about the days when the grain crops of New York and the Midwest, transported on the canal, had helped make New York a commercial power.

Even the New York State Thruway, a model for the interstate system, was built too soon. It took Moynihan a decade and a half in the Senate to secure a federal payback for the thruway, which had been incorporated into the interstate system in name only.

SEEDS OF DISINVESTMENT

In 1983, Moynihan spoke to the American Planning Association. It was a time when alarms over the "crumbling infrastructure crisis" briefly put public works on the front pages. Moynihan had been speaking about the problem in hearings since at least 1980, before the media discovered it.[9]

Moynihan reported that public works spending by all levels of government had declined nearly 30 percent during the previous decade, but "no one seemed to realize this was occurring."[10] He suggested that, although no one had accurate information, the rate of investment had probably declined by half in twenty years and that there was probably a net disinvestment in infrastructure.[11] Seeking an explanation, Moynihan, of course, went back to history and geography first. He rehashed the "internal improvements" debate:

- the Senate's 1807 request, at President Jefferson's urging, for a Treasury report on the opportunity and constitutionality of federal assistance to road, waterway, and canal projects;
- Secretary Gallatin's ten-year plan for a federally supported system; western support for the projects and reluctance from "Eastern traders whose customs duties would have to pay for them";
- President Madison's veto in 1817 on grounds the Commerce Clause would not allow such federal assistance;
- the Supreme Court's decision in *Gibbons v. Ogden* (22 US 1 [1824]), affirming federal supremacy in governing the inland waterways; and
- the 1824 congressional order to the Army Corps of Engineers to prepare a plan for a national transportation system and the plan's defeat by regional rivalries and President Jackson's states' rights opposition.[12]

Of course, as Moynihan noted, the federal government subsidized and channeled development anyway, usually indirectly by establishing forts, lighthouses, courthouses, and customhouses and by providing land grants and railroad land surveys.[13] (For several decades beginning in 1838, there was a Corps of Topographical Engineers in the army.) Some individual projects received direct subsidies, such as the Cumberland Road and some river and harbor navigation works.

Moynihan suggested that it was the failure of the government to undertake coordinated planning that "sowed the seeds of disenchantment with public improvements that infests the infrastructure debate today. . . . Public works, which were always bound up in political give and take, and properly so, at some point became synonymous with pork barrel."[14] Moynihan is no political naïf. He knows that to win passage of any federal public works assistance at all, it has always been necessary to spread the wealth around. He simply says that there ought to be some planning before the spending.

He observed, moreover, that once we had our essential water and transportation systems in place, we forgot about them. He mused that it may be more accurate to say that we created highway and water departments so that we could forget about them and so public works ceased to be a "significant, continuing public issue."[15] In the classical tradition, Moynihan takes politics to be a continuing dialogue about how to carry out the polity's common business. Remove an issue from the political agenda, and you can expect it to fade from public consciousness and, thereafter, its funding to wither as well. For Moynihan, there should be public debate—with an engaged public and attentive elected officials—about how to satisfy a region's transportation, water, or waste-management needs. Consigning those decisions to technocratic bodies gives the false impression that their solution is only an engineering exercise: devoid of value choices, complex and mechanistic, crushingly boring in any event.

In public works debates, Moynihan adduced another reason that public works had been stymied: government regulations and an excess of public process. He had in mind a case that struck home. By the early 1980s, the long-running acrimony over construction of the below-grade Westway to replace the elevated West Side Highway was headed for a conclusion disappointing to Moynihan.

To environmentalists' fear that replacing the elevated West Side Highway with the below-grade Westway could diminish air quality, Moynihan had replied to no avail that nearly one-third of the funding would go to create a park, "the equivalent in our century of Central Park in the last."[16] The environmental movement at the time was perilously close to being a no-growth movement when it came to public works. (Among its other achievements, ISTEA outlined a "sustainable" transportation program, and the drafting and implementation of the act inspired environmentalists to think more constructively about public works.)

Moynihan pointed out that Westway had finally come down to a decade-long, litigious dispute over the issuance of a federal permit to dredge and fill in the Hudson River waterfront. The average time to complete a Corps of Engineers navigation project from the time of its first recommendation to Congress was something like twenty-seven years. In contrast, Moynihan loved to remind New Yorkers that

- starting in 1900, the IRT subway was tunneled through Manhattan from City Hall to 145th Street in four and a half years;

- the Empire State Building opened thirteen and a half months after its groundbreaking in 1930; and
- LaGuardia Airport opened just three years after Mayor LaGuardia landed at Newark in late 1936 and declared, "My ticket says New York, and that's where I expect to land." [17]

Moynihan has consistently criticized instances of overexuberant, politically dysfunctional forms of citizen participation.[18] He believes deeply in electoral representative government, and he mistrusts attempts to get around it, especially when the attempts are claimed to be in the better interests of the "people." *Maximum Feasible Misunderstanding* was Moynihan's tale of the federal antipoverty program that foundered when its bureaucrats tried to create centers of power in the inner city that would literally fight City Hall, which is to say, the elected local government.[19]

Moynihan thinks that elected officials are the power of the people. If citizen participation means a heated campaign aimed at influencing elected officials, Moynihan is for it. He opposes drawn-out citizen-participation processes that seem designed to frustrate the decisions elected officials have already made.

Similarly, Moynihan has trust in the constitutional compromise that gave us our geographically based Congress. That is what drives Moynihan, who has tried to stop some of the most egregious pork barrel, to dedicate himself above all to ensuring that public works funds are equitably distributed. He is not a project-by-project utilitarian, insisting on some bloodless cost-benefit formula. Rather, he seems to be a follower of John Rawls's theory of fairness: Moynihan thinks if everyone is sure that, over time, they will get a fair share, public works spending will be supported.

Moynihan argued that for all these reasons—amnesia toward infrastructure's historic role in the nation's development, the pork barrel image, relegation to technocratic bodies, and prolonged process—it should come as no surprise that American governments, and the federal government in particular, were disinvesting in infrastructure. Moynihan titled his American Planning Association address, "If We Can Build Saudi Arabia, Can We Not Rebuild America?" Moynihan had discovered that the Army Corps of Engineers was engaged in more construction in Saudi Arabia than in the United States. Though he could not have known the corps was establishing the Gulf War's infrastructure, Moynihan said: "If they want some practice building airfields in deserts, that is fine by me. . . . But they shouldn't leave home altogether! And the United States government should not be putting their services up for hire, when we won't do at home what needs doing."[20] (He later discovered that, among other things, the corps had built forty-six mosques. Moynihan wryly commented that this was "excellent as a *limited* exercise, but even mosque building can be carried to excess.")[21]

Finally, Moynihan speculated that the decline in public works investment also was "a consequence of haphazard and diffuse decision-making. We have failed to organize budgetary information on long-term capital spending projects in any meaningful and useful form."[22]

Here, Moynihan was adverting to an insight that he has had, and a weapon he has wielded, in other policy fields as well: we tend to solve problems in America only once we begin measuring them. For Moynihan, it became important to get the numbers right and continually to call attention to them. After all, the disinvestment in infrastructure that was so suddenly discovered in the early 1980s had been going on for at least a decade and a half and no one had noticed.

Moynihan's Public Works Improvement Act of 1984 was aimed at developing reliable public works data and correcting the federal budget's systematic accounting bias against capital investment. As the bill's title implies, Moynihan was also on a campaign to excise the word "infrastructure," which he termed "ponderous."

The first version of the bill, introduced in 1982, tried to go all the way. It would have put the federal government on the road to creating a capital budget separate from the operating budget.[23] Most states have one. Certainly those states with balanced budget requirements have one (because only the operating budget must be balanced). If a federal balanced budget amendment were ever to pass, one can be relatively certain that the federal government would have one, too. In fact, the threat of passage of a balanced budget amendment in early 1997 prompted President Clinton to appoint a Capital Budget Commission.

The idea makes sense, of course. Public works are assets with long useful lives. Annual funding effectively prohibits amortization and ignores depreciation, discourages maintenance, and conversely, encourages disproportionate spending on new capacity. In the end, with the unstinting opposition of OMB—which opposes capital budgeting through good times and bad, Democratic and Republican administrations alike—Moynihan settled for an attempt at a consolidated accounting of the federal government's infrastructure investment.

More successful was Moynihan's attempt at a new Gallatin plan. The 1984 Public Works Improvement Act (P.L. 98-501) established a National Council on Public Works Improvement. The council's 1988 report, *Fragile Foundations*, provided much of the analytical and policy framework for ISTEA. The council debunked the idea that large portions of American infrastructure were in peril. But it reported that improved economic productivity and competitiveness could require an increase in annual investment of up to 100 percent. It also recommended clarifying respective federal, state, and local roles in infrastructure and management; improving the performance and efficiency of existing facilities; a capital budgeting process "at all levels of government"; incentives to ensure adequate maintenance; and more use of techniques for reducing the load on infrastructure, such as demand management, land-use planning, and waste reduction.[24] The council helped set the tone of public works debate, such as it has been, for the past decade.

The debate has been muted. Congress and the media declared the infrastructure crisis over with passage of the 1982 gas tax increase, trumpeted as an infrastructure fix. The vast proportion of the increase went to new highway construction, which *Fragile Foundations* and subsequent studies would show to be largely unneeded. The gas tax program was nothing but an antirecession jobs stimulus that, like all its predecessors since the Depression, began delivering its "stimulus" too late, in this case into a recovered economy in time for the 1984 Reagan reelection. (Ironically, the Senate Democratic leadership originally proposed an antirecession bill in 1982 that nearly ignored traditional public works altogether; it would have targeted funds more toward job training and other social programs, perhaps on the assumption that unemployment was severest among social workers.)

INTERSTATES TO INTERMODALS

The development of ISTEA has to be viewed as Moynihan's most comprehensive demonstration of his command of public works data, his concomitant resistance to conventional opinion, his understanding of economics and politics, and his belief that public works fundamentally determine development patterns and the quality of life. Transportation experts were stunned at how he deployed this knowledge to overturn the highway interests' hegemony, which had lasted nearly fifty years. Everyone thought that this would be another routine highway bill reauthorization.

Late in 1990, the Bush administration unveiled a proposal that could be considered moderately progressive, compared with earlier highway bills. Moynihan trumped it, and the Bush Department of Transportation never was of much consequence in the ensuing debate.

Progressive transportation advocates and environmentalists were even more stunned when, early in 1991, they discovered an article by Moynihan that had appeared in *The Reporter* magazine in 1960 entitled "New Roads and Urban Chaos."[25] Written just four years after the interstate highway program was enacted, and just as construction was beginning to go full tilt, the article exposed the questionable assumptions underlying the program, explained the politics that motivated it, and accurately predicted its drastic impact on the city and American life. Activists in 1991, many of them veterans of some two decades of "stop the freeway" battles, and perhaps having mistakenly chalked up Moynihan's support of Westway to conventional politics, could not believe that thirty years before, he—or anyone—could have seen so clearly through the highway lobby's smog.

"New Roads" has to be read. Moynihan astutely started:

> The *Wall Street Journal* does not commonly describe any undertaking of the Eisenhower administration as "A vast program thrown together, imperfectly conceived and grossly mismanaged, and in due course becoming a veritable playground for extravagance, waste and corruption."[26]

He went on to trace the program's origins, from the calls for transcontinental highways in World War I, to its revival as a New Deal public works project projected to require 14,000 miles. A 1939 Bureau of Public Roads study "revealed that there was surprisingly little cross-country traffic and suggested that the concept be changed to a 25,700-mile intercity system."[27] In 1944, Congress authorized an interstate system of 40,000 miles. The Clay Committee appointed by President Eisenhower found that only 8,500 miles could expect enough traffic to pay for themselves as toll roads and, of those, 5,000 miles had already been completed or were being built. Moynihan remarked: "Thus, from the outset, there has been more mileage authorized for the system than anyone knew exactly what to do with."[28]

In 1956, Geoffrey Crowther of the *Economist* had given a speech in New York following a cross-country trip. He said he found himself "puzzled by the statements—that are taken for granted in this country now—that your highways are obsolete. . . . Your highway system is magnificent. It is overburdened in the immediate vicinity of the largest cities; but get away from the large cities and your highways are empty. . . . I wonder if the matter [the interstate program] has been investigated as thoroughly as it should be."[29] Moynihan commented: "It had been. Any number of congressmen had wondered if it could not be made bigger. It was."[30]

Moynihan said that city streets were, indeed, "chockablock with cars" and that half the cost (though a fraction of the mileage) of the interstate program would be spent on urban roads. But he endorsed the "Malthusian specter" that had been raised by a New York city official: "the number of automobiles increases to fill all the space provided." (In 1991, Moynihan said of congestion: "This is the oldest of urban problems. Rome struggled with it until the day the Goths arrived.")[31]

Here, Moynihan was countering in advance almost every delusional notion that has shaped the conventional wisdom in highway debates since. Transportation advocates in 1991 were still trying to counter that convention's hold on the public mind. They could report that, by 1990, the vast proportion of the congestion on the interstate system occurred on urban mileage representing less than 10 percent of the system; that experience proved that building new highway capacity only generated more traffic that ultimately overwhelmed any temporary relief from the new construction; and that building highways in urban areas was becoming prohibitively expensive.[32]

"New Roads" tried to explain how the interstate program got going despite the lack of need. There was the automobile industry for one; there were conservatives who thought roads good for business and liberals who (back then) thought of roads "as part of the litany of public investment they so love to chant: Better Schools, Better Hospitals, Better Roads." There were southern and western Democrats in Congress who knew that the mileage would tilt toward their more rural regions.[33] The Interstate and Defense Highways Act of 1956 was sponsored by Senator Albert Gore Sr., of Tennessee. Superhighways run in the family: His son, as we know, would later champion the information superhighway.

Finally, Moynihan noted that "the urge to have the highways was not matched by an urge to pay for them."[34] The 1944 interstate authorization had been moot. By 1952, even with the federal share of funding increased to 60 percent, and the states in a general postwar road-building frenzy, less than 1 percent of the interstate system had been built. But in 1956, the combination of 90 percent federal funding and the establishment of a trust fund to direct federal gas tax receipts solely to highway building did the trick. Moynihan pointed out that with a 90–10 split (under some circumstances 95–5), states could not afford not to come up with the small match required.[35]

In 1991, Moynihan returned to this point about subsidies, a theme of his in public works. What data there were indicated growth in transportation productivity to be near zero. To Moynihan, this was to be expected. Echoing economists, he said, "Public goods tend to be perceived as free goods, and consumed as if they had no cost. . . . Just as there is no such thing as a free good, there is no such thing as a freeway."[36]

Fortuitously, by 1991, the interstate system was all but completed—finally—having cost more than $125 billion and taken thirty-five years, rather than the $27.5 billion and ten years predicted in 1956. Moynihan made much of the completion, because it laid the groundwork for realigning federal transportation assistance.

One of ISTEA's foundation-shaking realignments was to require, before federal assistance flows, local and state plans that take into account all forms of transportation, not just highways. Even more astounding was ISTEA's insistence that the plans be limited to foreseeably available funding; what had previously passed for highway planning had been the compilation of local wish lists that far outstripped potential funds.

In addition to requiring serious planning, Moynihan addressed the public good problem by altering the federal-state sharing formulas. Over the years, new construction on federally designated highways other than the interstate had been funded at an 80–20 ratio; mass transit, subsidized for the first time in 1964 (but out of hard-to-get general tax revenues, not the gas tax trust fund), was at a ratio of 60–40 or lower for construction and 50–50 for operating assistance. Federal highway and bridge repairs were sometimes funded to the states at a lower rate than new construction.

Criticizing this bias toward new highways, particularly with evidence that repair needs were underfunded and that older sections of the interstate were beginning to need total rehabilitation, Moynihan declared in 1991: "We've poured enough concrete." This was not the sort of statement ever heard previously from a congressional overseer of the highway program. Moynihan's bill leveled the field. He proposed a 75–25 federal-state ratio for highway construction, highway maintenance, and public transit capital projects.

In the early 1980s, Moynihan had taken a similar approach to reforming federal subsidies for waterway improvements. Unable to prevail on their more comprehensive overhaul of the program, he and Senator Domenici did succeed in reducing the federal share of costs for harbor dredging. Suddenly, a number of cities with dreams of becoming deep-water ports decided that their shallow draft harbors worked just fine. Moynihan and Domenici spoke persuasively about the disparity in transportation efficiency brought about by the waterways having a subsidy while the railroads had none. (One has to assume the railroads' federally provided route surveys and land grants to have been long since fully depreciated.)

Moynihan's ISTEA bill characteristically included provisions expressing an optimism that applied research could also improve public works productivity. ISTEA authorized experiments in "congestion pricing" that would impose fees to ration highway access, discouraging use at peak hours. States were required in their planning to consider using their federal highway funds for intermodal improvements to rail and air terminals, the bottlenecks around which had been shown to be among the most serious impediments to improving the nation's freight-hauling efficiency. Federal research would be conducted on the feasibility of high-speed magnetic levitation transportation, a technology already under development in Europe and Japan.

Finally, Moynihan promoted the use of a small percentage of highway funds (but still amounting to billions of dollars over the six-year authorization of ISTEA) for transportation "enhancements," basically environmental and aesthetic improvements, including the conversion of abandoned rail lines to bike trails, the rehabilitation of historic transportation structures, and the creation of new wetlands. This aspect of Moynihan's bill surprised no one in 1991 who knew anything of his reputation and record in urban planning.

It surprised even less those who had read "New Roads and Urban Chaos." As the title suggests, a significant part of the article was devoted to an eerily prescient evaluation of the interstate's effect on the nation's cities. Moynihan wrote:

> It is not true, as is sometimes alleged, that the sponsors of the interstate program ignored the consequences it would have in the cities. . . . They exulted in them. Thanks to highways, declared the Clay Report, "We have been able to disperse our factories, our stores, our people; in short, to create a revolution in living habits. Our cities have spread into suburbs, dependent on the automobile for their existence.". . . In general the program is doing about what was to be expected: throwing up a Chinese wall across Wilmington, driving educational institutions out of downtown Louisville, plowing through the center of Reno. When the interstate runs into a place like Newburgh, New York, the wreckage is something to see.[37]

In 1991, Moynihan would cite the economist William J. Baumol for an update on the urban effects of the interstates: "By encouraging the substitution of truck transport of freight for railroads it eliminated one of the major advantages of the city as a manufacturing location. This, and other forces, drove manufacturing jobs elsewhere, and left the cities with excessive populations relative to the employment possibilities they offered."[38] In other words, the highway wreckage in Newburghs the nation over was not just physical; it was social, too.

A MAN, A PLAN, AN AVENUE

No one was surprised in the ISTEA debates that Moynihan cared so much about the cities. Moynihan's first act of note on the national stage was as city planner.

As everyone knows, in 1962 it was Moynihan, then an assistant to Labor Secretary Arthur Goldberg, who wrote up a recommendation to have the federal government redevelop Pennsylvania Avenue. History has it that President Kennedy noted the dilapidation of the private structures on the north side of the avenue on his inaugural ride to the White House. History does not explain how John Kennedy had failed to notice this condition during all the years he commuted as senator from the Capitol to his residence in Georgetown. In light of the fact that the Pennsylvania Avenue proposal appeared amid the banal-sounding "Report of the Ad Hoc Committee on Federal Office Space," as did the unsolicited Moynihan contribution of a set of "Guiding Principles for Federal Architecture," some think that the whole thing, including the Kennedy apocrypha, was a Moynihan invention.

The story of Moynihan's siring and half a lifetime of squiring the Pennsylvania Avenue plan through successive presidencies is well-known. (He had help from some others, most notably Jacqueline Kennedy. She requested of Lyndon Johnson only two things as legacies of President Kennedy: rename the Cape Canaveral space center and continue the Pennsylvania Avenue effort.)[39] Along with Moynihan's accomplishments in other fields, Pennsylvania Avenue and ISTEA are the only public works achievements that seem to make the standard accounts of his career. Those accounts generally miss the broader themes in Moynihan's public works career.

For example, the long Pennsylvania Avenue planning period, and the longer period still before development took shape, confirmed Moynihan's view that public works are not for the short-winded. Not until 1974 was the Pennsylvania Avenue Development Corporation chartered. PADC was the financial engine, armed with condemnation powers and fueled by Treasury borrowing, that got the job done. By the time PADC got under way, the plan was in its third or so incarnation. (Each successive plan was a bit less monolithic, a bit more, well, urban. Delay is not always bad.) Not until 1990 or so was there a high-rise residential flat that Moynihan could purchase.

Moynihan himself illuminated the time frame this way:

> I like to think President Kennedy would approve the results: I know he would understand the time it has taken. He was fond of telling the story of some grizzled French imperialist, Marshal Lyautey, if memory serves, who observed his Algerian gardener dawdling at his work one afternoon and ordered the poor wretch to get to digging. The hapless gardener explained he was planting a cactus that had just bloomed and it would not do so again for a hundred years. "Then plant it immediately," bellowed the Marshal. "For the more time things take, the more is the reason to get going."[40]

The extended time span required for public works may help explain its lack of appeal in contemporary government, with its daily-headline-to-daily-headline focus. The long time it takes for deferred maintenance to become manifest, compared with shorter elective terms, definitely accounts for the short shrift given to public works upkeep.

Moynihan's vision for Pennsylvania Avenue was unusually urban for a city plan of the time. He thought the avenue should not only impress but also enliven the city. The 1962 recommendation said, "care should be taken not to line the north side with a solid block of public and private office buildings which close down completely at night and on weekends. . . . Pennsylvania Avenue should be lively, friendly and inviting, as well as dignified and impressive."[41] In view of the fact that the recommendation was hitching a ride on a report to alleviate a shortage in federal offices, there must have been many who assumed that the report would endorse, not criticize, cloning the impressive but lifeless Federal Triangle across the avenue. Instead, from the very first plan, the northern side was to be reserved for mixed development, including housing.

Moynihan's prescription of a "lively, friendly and inviting" downtown would be commonplace today but was not so then. Moynihan articulated his Pennsylvania Avenue goals contemporaneously with the publication of

Jane Jacobs's *The Death and Life of Great American Cities.*[42] It would take several years for this book to make its mark. Since the 1920s, the adoption of Le Corbusier's vision of the city by the planning elite and the development of zoning codes had made popular the idea—indeed had made it the law in most places—that cities and their suburbs should be carved into single-use zones: housing here, retail there, workplaces somewhere a distance away, all connected by autos (or by autogiros in some Corbusian renderings, but definitely not by foot). Jane Jacobs simply noted that cities, on the other hand, thrive on what we would now call diversity. They need homes, shops, factories, and offices juxtaposed to achieve the dynamism we celebrate in successful cities. Moynihan instinctively understood that.

Hardly anyone knows, because tragedy intervened, that Moynihan advocated deploying a concert hall, theater, and opera house at points along the avenue to help bring it to life. Beginning in the 1950s, there had been talk of creating a National Cultural Center in Washington, talk owed less to some freak Eisenhower-era love of high culture than to Cold War belief that there was a Kulturkampf going on, too. At President Kennedy's behest, Moynihan and colleagues were to have presented their Pennsylvania Avenue plan, including this idea, to congressional leaders following Kennedy's trip to Dallas on November 22, 1963. The National Cultural Center became the memorial to Kennedy and was shanghaied to its riverfront site, more convenient to suburban drivers and severed from downtown by a mishmash of freeways. Only now is there talk again of a downtown opera house, this time a proposal to house the Washington Opera in the once-flagship building of the defunct Woodward & Lothrop department store chain and not too far from Pennsylvania Avenue.

Moynihan and friends had the city dweller's appreciation of earthier culture, too. At an early planning meeting, William Walton and Moynihan speculated that a "bawdy house" might just add the right spice to the redevelopment stew. Walton produced a sketch of a bawdy house lady, captioned by Moynihan "Miss Pennsylvania Avenue of 1965, or How to Revive the Grand Parade Route."[43] Moynihan still has the sketch. Ironically, construction of the Federal Triangle had displaced Washington's red-light district (and Chinatown and the central farmers' market) in the 1930s.

In fact, those bawdy ladies of yesteryear worked on the site of the new Ronald Reagan Building, which is the last link in the Triangle and the avenue and will soon house the Woodrow Wilson Center. Moynihan sponsored the 1987 legislation to build it. And he made sure that the building would be architecturally worthy of its site. (In 1983, arriving for a Blair

House meeting of the commission on social security, Moynihan assailed the members with a blast about the ugly brown brick facade of the J.W. Marriott Hotel, then newly constructed across from what is now the Ronald Reagan Building. Moynihan joked that it must be "a cheap Republican trick." David Stockman, President Reagan's budget director replied, "Pat, that's a redundant statement.")[44]

Moynihan believes in planning: Of public works in general, recall, he said that planning ought to precede spending, and he made this happen in ISTEA. But he is skeptical of the planning profession's ideology, which seems to have become self-hypnotic. Of city planners, Moynihan expressed both frustration and hope in 1969: "It has been said of urban planners that they have been traumatized by the realization that everything relates to everything. But this is so, and the perception of it can provide a powerful analytic tool."[45]

Hailed following his victory on ISTEA for its planning requirements, Moynihan told a band of celebrants that he hoped the planners would adequately perform, because "there hasn't been any real planning since Daniel Burnham died." [46] He is surely right; once city planning was divorced from physical planning, it became an obscured and diminished discipline and cultivated a shallow generalism. Moynihan has noted that, in contrast to architecture, an individualistic art which has flourished in our age of individualism, city planning "tends to be done by committees of the . . . cultured," and that leads to "lots of entropy." [47] More charitably, he has said that we have difficulty making large plans and seeing them through over the inevitably long haul because of the "general erosion of the power of political parties and social elites." [48]

The singular success of the Pennsylvania Avenue plan was due in large measure to the redevelopment commission and the corporation put in place by Moynihan and his cohorts. They made physical plans, juggled many interrelated factors, and invented open but not endless procedures. Public-private "committees of the cultured," they were able to effectuate a large plan over a very long haul.

ARCHITECTURE TELLS

Moynihan holds a special brief for public architecture. Perhaps in no other area of public works has he so completely dominated the field. Perhaps in no other had so few others cared at all for so long until he came along.

His reinvention of a noble, humanist public architecture can be dated, too, to the "Report of the Ad Hoc Committee on Federal Office Space." Moynihan penned for the report (there is no question but that this was entirely his idea) a one-page statement of "Guiding Principles for Federal Architecture." A virtual ballad of the New Frontier, the "Guiding Principles" called for "an architectural style and form which is distinguished and which will reflect the dignity, enterprise, vigor and stability of the American National Government . . . designs [which] embody the finest contemporary American architectural thought . . . development of an official style must be avoided." [49] In less official prose, Moynihan has put it: "build whatever the Whiskey Trust is building and over the years you'll get the good with the bad." [50]

That the government should not have an "official" style today seems self-evident. It was not so when Moynihan wrote. In 1901, the annual report of the supervising architect of the treasury, the office which then designed and built federal buildings, announced that the "classic style of architecture" was the appropriate style for the government and would, indeed, be the official style.[51] And so it was throughout the 1920s and 1930s, despite the "Modern" or "International style" holding sway with the avant-garde here and abroad. Even after World War II, when one would have thought the Nazis' propagandistic use of neoclassical architecture might have at least temporarily discredited the classical style, if not the idea of an official style altogether, the federal government held to a "stripped down" classicism.

You have to be careful here. Neoclassicism does not equal totalitarianism, of course. Nearly every government in the 1920s and 1930s was building classical public buildings. The Federal Reserve Board headquarters of 1937 by Paul Cret in Washington bears an eerie resemblance to Hitler's chancellery by Albert Speer in Berlin. Conversely, until Stalin conducted an architectural purge, the Soviets commissioned Constructivist masterpieces that appeared free-spirited even if the regime was not; Mussolini flirted with the Modern, at least until his alliance with Hitler; Goering's Luftwaffe headquarters of the mid-1930s had a definite tinge of the Bauhaus. Any style can be authoritarian if anointed and overblown: Under the patronage of Governor Nelson Rockefeller, Albany's International-style Empire State Mall of the late 1950s presented what the critic Robert Hughes aptly described as an "architecture of coercion."[52]

In any event, Moynihan's statement has held. It is the peculiarly American, anti-official declaration about official architecture. It has held on, Moynihan has often said, not least because it is also so unbureaucratically brief.[53]

As Moynihan predicted, the "Whiskey Trust" mandate of the "Guiding Principles" has not guaranteed a distinguished federal architecture. But his statement did have the immediate effect of causing the General Services Administration and other government agencies to begin hiring the best American architects, something the government had not done much of since 1901. (One hastens to add that the federal buildings of the 1930s, designed predominantly by civil service architects, were quite good.) That the results have been mixed through the years says more about the state of American architecture than about the government's attitude in commissioning it.

Moynihan's influence in architecture extends beyond rhetoric and policy-making. His intervention in specific projects may be of even greater import in reestablishing government interest in public architecture of lasting quality.

Buffalo: Prudential Building and Connecticut Street Armory

In 1977, Moynihan's first year in the Senate, he was walking around Buffalo, New York, when he turned a corner and spied the dilapidated Prudential Building, one of the best-known early American skyscrapers by the architect Louis Sullivan. Moynihan told Buffalo's mayor that if the city could see to it that the building was rehabilitated, people the world over would come to Buffalo to see it. (The mayor is reported to have replied with an eight-letter bovine reference.) On the spot, Moynihan said he would secure federal assistance and move his Buffalo office in when renovations were complete. He did both. Some years later, when a nineteenth-century neogothic National Guard armory in Buffalo burned and the Pentagon offered only enough funding for a utilitarian drill hall, Moynihan forced the Pentagon to capitulate. The armory was restored.

New York City Federal Buildings: Custom House, Social Security in Queens, Foley Square

Moynihan used his position on the Public Works Committee (and engaged in some horse trading with the House Public Works Committee) to ensure restoration of the Custom House at Bowling Green in lower Manhattan, c. 1907, a Beaux Arts landmark by Cass Gilbert, and to build a new Social Security payment center that helped anchor revitalization in Jamaica, Queens. He was the force behind the innovative financing and construction of the landmark-quality new Foley Square federal courthouse and federal office building. (Of the earlier, 1960s Foley Square federal building, *New York Times* architecture critic Paul Goldberger said it showed that "maybe the federal government does have it in for New York after all.")[54] Moynihan weathered some withering criticism on the costs and then took the occasion of the courthouse dedication to remind the mayor that the city had still to make good on a promise to build a park between the federal and municipal buildings facing the square.

New York City: Pennsylvania Station

He is even now trying to rectify one of New York's worst architectural crimes: the 1964 demolition of the Roman-inspired Penn Station and its replacement by a subterranean hovel. Architectural historian Vincent Scully said of this: "Through it [Penn Station] one entered the city like a god. One scuttles in now like a rat." [55] Moynihan has breathed life into a plan to convert the neoclassical James Farley Post Office Building a block away into a more worthy successor. Does Moynihan take these things as seriously as what others take to be his weightier issues? In a New York speech in late 1993, President Clinton said he had not yet had a conversation with Senator Moynihan that had not included a plea for the Penn Station project.[56]

Washington: Old Post Office Building, Pension Building/ National Building Museum, Union Station, Thurgood Marshall Judiciary Building, Capitol West Front and Grounds

As a member of the Pennsylvania Avenue Commission, Moynihan helped save from demolition the neo-Romanesque Old Post Office Building on Pennsylvania Avenue; as a Senate member, he got it rehabilitated. He wrote the legislation that turned the run-down Pension Building into the National Building Museum. When no one else in public life would lift a finger to save Union Station, because of an earlier ill-conceived and wasteful congressional scheme to turn it into a visitor center, Moynihan spoke up so forcefully that his bill creating a public-private, train station–commercial redevelopment effort passed without dissent. A few years later, he saw through the construction of the Thurgood Marshall Judiciary Building that finally completed, eighty years later, the building grouping that was originally contemplated by Union Station's architect.

Moynihan is the architectural conscience of the Congress. When he threw in with the opposition to extending the Capitol's West Front, the plan collapsed. He faced down architect Philip Johnson at a hearing and took the Senate floor to denounce Johnson's proposed fifty-two-story skyscraper on the Potomac that would have diminished Washington's monumental views. Helped finally by a fear of terrorism, he got parking off the East Plaza of the Capitol and is trying to push the car-free salient even farther out beyond the Capitol.

Moynihan's architectural speaking and writing show a solid grounding in architectural history, though he never had formal training. Moynihan says his interest in architecture grew up with him as a youth in Hell's Kitchen, when he could not fail to walk by Raymond Hood's art deco McGraw-Hill Building. However derived, his critical faculty in architecture is acute, creative, and fearless:

- Speaking at the ceremony to name the 1960s federal building in Foley Square for Jacob Javits, Moynihan looked up from his text, craned his neck to look at the building, and declared that Javits deserved better than to have his name on this surpassingly ugly building.[57]
- In the spring of 1981, construction was nearing completion on the banal Hart Senate Office Building. All winter, the scaffolding had been sheathed in heavy plastic against the weather to allow the exterior marble to be installed. One day, the plastic came off. Moynihan promptly introduced a resolution: "Whereas the plastic cover has now been removed revealing, as feared, a building whose banality is exceeded only by its expense; and Whereas even in a democracy there are things it is as well the people do not know about their government: Now, therefore, be it *Resolved*, That it is the sense of the Senate that the plastic cover be put back."[58]
- Urged at a Public Works Committee hearing to fund roof repairs for the Kennedy Center, Moynihan noted that the center's architect, Edward Durrell Stone, had designed the U.S. Embassy in New Delhi, which bore a strong family resemblance to the Kennedy Center, as did all of Stone's noted buildings. Moynihan had personal knowledge that the embassy's roof also leaked. Moynihan said that Stone reminded him of the character in the Disraeli novel described as someone "distinguished for ignorance" as he had but one idea and it was wrong.[59]
- In 1970, commenting on visions of technology and the city, Moynihan considered the then-new and highly acclaimed Ford Foundation

> Building in New York. Noticing, as most critics did, its "quiet, unassertive" exterior and its signature atrium dominated by a lush public garden, Moynihan noticed something else: "[T]he building has been built as a factory. . . . The huge, heavy lateral beams . . . the saw-tooth roof, the plant managers' eyrie hung from the ceiling . . . the perfectly standardized, interchangeable fixtures in each office . . . triumphantly evoke the style and spirit of the primeval capitalist factory. Corten [steel beams, designed to rust]. Red. Rouge. River rouge. Of course! And why not for $16 million of Henry Ford's money?" [60]

Just as Moynihan loves architecture, but critically, he respects its profession, but guardedly. In this, too, Moynihan is not blinded by his enthusiasm and cannot be captured by ideology. Architects so often are; so, too, are city planners and historic preservationists. Moynihan has not hesitated to criticize them.

Keynote speaker for the national convention of the American Institute of Architects in 1969, Moynihan was anything but coddling: "The plain fact is that architects are, with respect to the quality of public building, much in the position of stock brokers. Whether the market rises or falls, you still get your commissions. And the present American city is the result." [61]

In 1979, he introduced a bill to overhaul the GSA's public buildings program.[62] It would have reduced costs by increasing government ownership and reducing long-term leasing, and it would have mitigated the worst excesses of pork barrel by reforming the congressional authorization process.

The bill also proposed instituting design competitions to overturn the closeted, "old boy network" nature of the GSA architect-selection process. The American Institute of Architects opposed this. Another provision would have established a chief GSA "architect" to ensure that good architects were selected and good designs commissioned and built. This the AIA endorsed, but on the condition that only a registered architect be allowed to hold the office. Moynihan told the AIA witness his testimony "smacked of professional stuffiness." [63]

Nevertheless, only a few years later, the AIA made Moynihan an honorary member and then, in 1992, named him the first "lay" recipient of a new Thomas Jefferson Award for Public Architecture. Given as a memento a replica of Jefferson's silver drinking goblet, Moynihan promptly poured his wine from a plastic cup into the goblet and offered an impromptu toast.

Speaking to preservationists, Moynihan has cautioned against the parochialism, almost a kind of atavism, that seems to overcome them at times. He supports preservation out of a sense that there are certain things that we just do not do anymore, but he warns against the "stultifying timidity" that comes from "the fear of not doing as well as others have done; the sense of having been outthought and outperformed by earlier generations." [64]

What is it that makes Moynihan care so much about architecture and public works? He believes that architecture, in particular, is a visible decoder of inchoate public values, or as he put it, criticizing the UN bureaucracy in *A Dangerous Place:* "As with most matters concerning government, architecture told most." [65]

Moynihan spun out an architectural parable on the triumph of the international apparatchiks. The International Labor Organization had a building up by 1920, he wrote, that was "sensible . . . both a monument of sorts to the international labor movement *and* a place where work got done." The League of Nations building, c. 1937, "was verily a palace," but still principally for delegates. However, in Turtle Bay, the postwar UN headquarters

> had quite a different symbolism . . . the Secretariat was apotheosized, its shimmering glass stele towering forty stories over assembly hall and meeting rooms alike, reducing delegates and delegators to the insignificance of tiny markings on the plaza far below. In the 1960s in Geneva there had been a great building boom by the specialized agencies. Here delegates were dispensed with altogether. . . . The new International Labor Office, high up on the slope now, was luxurious to the point of sensuality. The restaurant was of an *haute cuisine* decor such that there cannot have been a workman in the world who would have felt free to enter there, save to fix something.[66]

Moynihan takes this conviction two steps farther. First, he argues that "architecture is the one inescapably public art . . . that government can have as little involvement with the arts generally as it chooses, save that it cannot avoid architecture. . . . [A]rchitecture is inescapably a political art, and it reports faithfully for ages to come what the political values of a particular era were." [67] Another time, he called architecture "as fundamental a sign of the competence of government as will be found." [68] He believes that in the long run, history will judge our governance more by the quality of our public buildings than by the daily trivia in the press or even by the outcome of momentous social and foreign policy debates. Our own opinion of the ancient Egyptians, of Greece and Rome and the Middle

Ages, based so much on architectural remains, would seem to confirm his opinion.

Second, Moynihan believes that public architecture does not just reveal, it actually inculcates public values. He declared to the AIA: "the American polity—the experience as well as the sense of community and shared convictions—has . . . atrophied in our time because of the retreat from architecture and public buildings as a conscious element of public policy and a purposeful instrument for the expression of public purposes. . . . If we are to save our cities and restore to American public life the sense of shared experience, trust and common purpose that seems to be draining out of it, the quality of public design has got to be made a public issue because it is a political fact." [69]

"Shared experience, trust and common purpose" are for Moynihan the backing of the American patchwork. Again and again in his essays in *Toward a National Urban Policy*, the volume he edited when the "crisis of the cities" was at its height, Moynihan returned to the theme that the American city—and in turn America, which has become an urban society—will succeed or fail in the same measure that they succeed or fail in promoting that credo. Only that, he argues, will engender faith in and adherence to public laws and public order.

Good architecture and urban design have a role to play in public order, but America seemed gripped by "uglification" which "may first have developed in Europe, but as with much else, the technological breakthroughs have taken place in the United States. . . . Social peace is the primary objective of social policy. To the extent that this derives from a shared sense of the value and significance of the public places and aesthetic value of the city, the federal government has a direct interest in encouraging such qualities." [70]

A similar theme pervades all of Moynihan's writing and achievement in public works. He holds that public works, as of old, are still the indispensable underpinning of economic productivity. Yet, there is a spiritual element to his enthusiasm, too, and it begins in his belief that public works knit communities together in "shared experience, trust and common purpose." As have others, he counts as one of the achievements of the Brooklyn Bridge the fact that, fifteen years after it opened, the separate cities of Brooklyn and New York merged. But he also wrote this about the bridge:

> It was a typically 19th Century American public works project. To be sure, it shared with public works projects of our century financial problems, safety

disputes, and allegations of political chicanery. But it was thought of also as an object of pride, of awe; as a dramatic new means of imposing the idea of America on the geographical mass of the continent. It was conceived as a conquest of nature, a demonstration of American boldness and ingenuity, and a knitting together of civic cultures. . . . [I]t soared and inspired.[71]

This is a declaration of faith, not of political science. Clearly, there is more at issue here than Moynihan's observations that there is a nexus between public works spending and productivity, between public works and functional communities. There is emotional and, in the case of architecture, aesthetic attraction, too.

Moynihan used to advert to Evelyn Waugh's phrase, "the retreat from magnificence," in decrying the decline of public works, urban planning, and public architecture.[72] It is only a vision of the far horizon of history, a belief in public magnificence, that could have given Moynihan the confidence to stand up for spending on more beautiful highways, triumphal train stations, and ennobling public buildings. In fact, Moynihan once cited approvingly the oath of ancient Athens:

We will ever strive for the ideals and sacred things of the city, both alone and with many;

We will unceasingly seek to quicken the sense of public duty;

We will revere and obey the city's laws;

We will transmit this city not only not less, but greater, better and more beautiful than it was transmitted to us.[73]

The New York City of Moynihan's youth was the New York of Central Park, City College, the Public Library, and old Penn Station, a city that invested its public wealth, in other words, in places of high aspiration and learning, places accessible to all citizens where public magnificence inculcated shared experience, trust, and common purpose.

In contrast, in many cities and suburbs today, the public wealth is so often spent on convention centers and sports arenas. Even if some approach a degree of magnificence, they are not public works in the traditional sense; indeed, it is only in this generation that sports arenas have come to be on the public dole. They are not universally accessible. The convention center and attendant hotels are gathering places for visitors, not the city's residents. And even if the basketball franchise is the city's most universally shared passion, the price of a season ticket to the arena is steep and the "common purpose" is narrow and banal. As Moynihan put it, "we get convention centers and hotels. But we don't get any extra *city*."[74]

Amid the turmoil of the 1960s, Moynihan called for architectural "magnificence" but not necessarily "monumentality," for "a public architecture of intimacy, one that brings people together in an experience of confidence and trust."[75] In a passage that revealed, as well as any, both his urban dream and nightmare, he called attention to "the essential fact in the age of the automobile: namely, that cities, which had been places for coming together, have increasingly become machines for moving apart."[76]

What will happen if the information superhighway triumphs? Like earlier highway advocates, its promoters exult in the dispersion that it will allow. It is open to question whether "virtual" shared experience can provide a satisfying substitute for actual gathering places woven into the urban fabric, whether cyber villagers will feel shared experience and trust or will just feel lost in cyberspace. This is a subject for a Pat Moynihan: virtual roads and social chaos.

NOTES

1. Daniel P. Moynihan, "If We Can Build Saudi Arabia, Can We Not Rebuild America?" (Robert C. Weinberg Fund Lecture, American Planning Association, New York University Club, New York, 18 June 1983), 4.

2. U.S. Senate Committee on Environment and Public Works, *Demographic Trends and Transportation Demand: Hearing before the Subcommittee on Water Resources, Transportation and Infrastructure,* 102d Cong., 1st sess., 7 February 1991.

3. Personal observations of the author, a committee staff member beginning in mid-1979.

4. Senate, *The Surface Transportation Efficiency Act of 1991,* 4 June 1991, Senate Report 102-71, 102d Cong., 1st sess. (hereinafter ISTEA Introduction), 1.

5. Ibid., 2.

6. Ward Sinclair, "Blasphemy: Senate Heretics Poke Fun at Sacred Dams," *Washington Post,* 29 November 1979, A2.

7. The author witnessed many speeches and interviews in which the phrase was used.

8. Harrison Rainie, "Moynihan Mixes Water-Project Reform with Wry," *New York Daily News,* 3 December 1979, 28.

9. Personal observations of the author.

10. Moynihan, "If We Can Build," 5.

11. Ibid.

12. Ibid., 3–4.

13. Ibid., 4.

14. Ibid.

15. Ibid., 5.

16. Daniel P. Moynihan, quoted in "The Battle by the River Drags On," *New York Times*, 31 July 1995, B3. The author heard this quotation countless times during the actual Westway debate more than a decade earlier.

17. Moynihan, "If We Can Build," 7.

18. See, e.g., Daniel P. Moynihan, "Toward a National Urban Policy," in Daniel P. Moynihan, ed., *Toward a National Urban Policy* (New York: Basic Books, 1970), 13.

19. Daniel P. Moynihan, *Maximum Feasible Misunderstanding: Community Action in the War on Poverty* (New York: Free Press, 1969).

20. Moynihan, "If We Can Build," 6.

21. ISTEA Introduction, 5.

22. Moynihan, "If We Can Build," 6.

23. *Rebuilding of America Act*, S. 2926, 97th Cong., 2d sess.

24. National Council on Public Works Improvement, *Fragile Foundations: A Report on America's Public Works; Final Report to the President and the Congress*, February 1988, 2–3.

25. Daniel P. Moynihan, "New Roads and Urban Chaos," *The Reporter* (14 April 1960), 13 et seq.

26. Ibid., 13.

27. Ibid.

28. Ibid.

29. Quoted in ibid., 15.

30. Ibid.

31. ISTEA Introduction, 4.

32. Ibid., 4–5 (describing testimony about construction not alleviating congestion).

33. Moynihan, "New Roads," 14.

34. Ibid., 15.

35. Ibid., 17.

36. ISTEA Introduction, 8.

37. Moynihan, "New Roads," 19–20.

38. ISTEA Introduction, 10.

39. Interview, Mrs. Kennedy in New York City, 11 January 1974, with Professor Joe B. Franz of the University of Texas at Austin, cited by Senator Moynihan in *Congressional Record*, 14 July 1994, 140, pt. 91: S8940.

40. Moynihan, "If We Can Build," 1–2.

41. "Report of the Ad Hoc Committee on Federal Office Space," 23 May 1962 (presented to the president on 1 June 1962).

42. Jane Jacobs, *The Death and Life of Great American Cities* (New York: Vintage Books, 1961).

43. Daniel P. Moynihan, "William Walton Revealed, or The Secret 1962 Plan to Revive the Grand Parade Route" (unpublished remarks at a National Archives author lecture, 19 January 1989, on the occasion of the publication of Carol M. Highsmith and Ted Landphair, *Pennsylvania Avenue: America's Main Street* [Washington, D.C.: American Institute of Architects Press, 1989]).

44. Moynihan, in contemporaneous conversation with the author.

45. Moynihan, "Toward a National Urban Policy," 6.

46. Moynihan, in conversation with the author, 1991.

47. Daniel P. Moynihan, foreword to Highsmith and Landphair, *Pennsylvania Avenue,* 8.

48. Ibid., 11.

49. "Report of the Ad Hoc Committee on Federal Office Space."

50. Daniel P. Moynihan, "The Politics of Conservancy" (lecture to the New York Landmarks Conservancy at the Metropolitan Museum of Art, New York City, 7 November 1984).

51. Cited in Lois Craig, *The Federal Presence: Architecture, Politics, and Symbols in United States Government Building* (Cambridge: MIT Press, 1978), 236.

52. Robert Hughes, *The Shock of the New* (New York: Knopf, 1981).

53. Comments to the author, among others.

54. Paul Goldberger, *The City Observed, New York: A Guide to the Architecture of Manhattan* (New York: Random House, 1979), 35.

55. Vincent Scully, *American Architecture and Urbanism,* new rev. ed. (New York: Henry Holt and Company, 1988), 143.

56. The author was in attendance, New York City, 13 December 1993.

57. Reported to the author contemporaneously by several attendees.

58. S.R. 140, 97th Cong., 1st sess. (19 May 1981).

59. The author was present. For the same point about Stone's architecture, see Moynihan, "The Politics of Conservancy," 8–9.

60. Daniel P. Moynihan, "The City in Chassis," in Moynihan, *Toward a National Urban Policy,* 332.

61. Daniel P. Moynihan, "Architecture in a Time of Trouble," *AIA Journal,* September 1969, 67.

62. S.R. 2080, 96th Cong., 1st sess. (1979).

63. The author was in attendance.

64. Moynihan, "The Politics of Conservancy," 6.

65. Daniel P. Moynihan (with Suzanne Weaver), *A Dangerous Place* (Boston: Little, Brown, and Company, 1978), 86.

66. Ibid., 87.

67. Moynihan, "The Politics of Conservancy," 5.

68. Moynihan, "Architecture in a Time of Trouble," 66.

69. Ibid., 68.

70. Moynihan, "Toward a National Urban Policy," 23.
71. Moynihan, "If We Can Build," 2.
72. Moynihan, "Architecture in a Time of Trouble," 68.
73. Moynihan, "Toward a National Urban Policy," 25.
74. Moynihan, foreword to Highsmith and Landphair, *Pennsylvania Avenue,* 11.
75. Moynihan, "Architecture in a Time of Trouble," 68.
76. Moynihan, "The City in Chassis," 327.

CHAPTER SIX

DANIEL PATRICK MOYNIHAN ON SECRECY

ROBERT A. KATZMANN

The day of 4 March 1997 might very well have been remembered—but for the Twentieth Amendment, which moved Inauguration Day to January 20[1]—as the historical moment when the president once again took the oath of office. It may come to be known as the day when government began to change its mindset about secrecy. For that is when the Commission on Protecting and Reducing Government Secrecy issued its report.[2]

Most commissions receive scant attention. Rare is the commission report that has a life beyond its issuance; most are consigned to the microfiche collection in the basement of some federal depository library. But this report on secrecy would be different because of its chair, Senator Daniel Patrick Moynihan. If the typical commission is concerned with moving organizational units from one place to another, this would seek to change the way we think about a problem so as to better address it. It is vintage Moynihan—using an instrument of government, in this case a commission—to shape the very definition of policy and its debate. By a unanimous vote, across the political spectrum, the commission determined: "It is time for a new way of thinking about secrecy. . . . The best way to ensure that secrecy is respected, and that the most important secrets *remain* secret, is for secrecy to be returned to its limited but necessary role. Secrets can be protected more effectively if secrecy is reduced overall."[3] By the commission's count, there are over 1.5 billion pages of government records in government vaults, more than twenty-five years old, that are still classified. "Some of these are still highly sensitive and should remain secret, but others are at the end of their life cycle and should be moved out of the classification system." [4]

The commission report is framed by Senator Moynihan's "Chairman's Foreword" and by his *Secrecy: A Brief Account of the American Experience.*[5] I would hope that these important contributions, together with Senator Moynihan's Bernstein Lecture at Georgetown University, "Secrecy as Regulation," would be separately published as a book, and thus made accessible to a larger audience.[6]

SECRECY AS REGULATION

The central theoretical insight of the commission report is Senator Moynihan's concept that "secrecy is a mode of regulation."[7] As he put it: "In truth, it is the ultimate mode, for the citizen does not even know that he or she is being regulated. Normal regulation concerns how citizens must behave, and so regulations are widely promulgated. Secrecy, by contrast, concerns what citizens may know; and the citizen is not told what may not be known." [8]

Senator Moynihan's concern with organizational behavior and regulation is long-standing; his writings on secrecy are sprinkled with references to Weber, Wilson, Downs, Shils, Light, and Hess.[9] In a lecture delivered at Lehman College, drawing on Wilson and the nineteenth-century German sociologist Simmel, Moynihan set forth "The Iron Law of Emulation"—organizations in conflict become like one another. His interest, then, was in the means by which the branches of government compete with one another. In the area of secrecy, his concern is with the techniques used by agencies within one branch, the executive.

It was in 1995, while writing an introduction to the paperback edition of Edward A. Shils's *The Torment of Secrecy: The Background and Consequences of American Security Policy* (first published in 1956), that Senator Moynihan first conceived of the "secrecy as regulation" concept.[10] And thus he began with Max Weber in his chapter "Bureaucracy" in *Wirtschaft und Gesellschaft*:

> Every bureaucracy seeks to increase the superiority of the professionally informed by keeping their knowledge and intentions secret. Bureaucratic

> administration always tends to be an administration of "secret sessions": in so far as it can, it hides its knowledge and action from criticism. . . . The pure interest of the bureaucracy in power, however, is efficacious far beyond those areas where purely functional interests make for secrecy. The concept of the "official secret" is the specific invention of bureaucracy, and nothing is so fanatically defended by the bureaucracy as this attitude, which cannot be substantially justified beyond these specifically qualified areas. In facing a parliament, the bureaucracy, out of a sure power instinct, fights every attempt of the parliament to gain knowledge by means of its own experts or from interest groups. The so-called right of parliamentary investigation is one of the means by which parliament seeks such knowledge. Bureaucracy naturally welcomes a poorly informed and hence a powerless parliament—at least in so far as ignorance somehow agrees with the bureaucracy's interests.[11]

"Secrecy," Moynihan writes, "can confer a form of power without responsibility, about which democratic societies must be vigilant."[12] At the same time, he recognizes at the outset the "unavoidable tension between the right of the public to know and the need for government, in certain circumstances, to withhold knowledge."[13] It may be in the interest of the citizenry that "some information not be generally available."[14] Mature democracy must make the distinction between necessary and unnecessary secrets and ensure that the secrecy system be kept under review.

If we are to understand what is to be done, then we must appreciate what contributed to the system as we know it. Senator Moynihan sets forth three central propositions. The first is that a "vast" secretive security system emerged in part as reaction against immigrants, thought to retain strong attachments to their native countries—countries that were thought hostile to the United States. Hence, "secrets came about largely *because* there was a perceived threat. . . . Loyalty would be the arbiter of security."[15] Moynihan's second proposition is that the statutory foundation for secrecy has been so elusive that "violations of secrecy occur with relative impunity."[16] A final proposition is that "secrecy, unless carefully attended to, is a source of considerable sorrow in government."[17]

For Senator Moynihan, the costs of secrecy are many; secrecy "can be a source of dangerous ignorance."[18] In his view, it "hugely interfered with the free flow of information" upon which sound analysis depends. "As information becomes less free, markets become ever more imperfect, decisions less informed and, accordingly, less efficient." Thus, the American government overestimated the capacity of the Soviet economy with consequent effects for our foreign policy. The culture of secrecy prevented the nation from learning the degree of Communist subversion in the 1930s and 1940s. It also, in Moynihan's judgment, "abetted a form of threat analysis which led to all manner of misadventure"—the most costly being the Vietnam War.[19]

Senator Moynihan's concept of "secrecy as regulation" proved a powerful organizing concept around which to form a consensus. In a time when conservatives and liberals alike attack overregulation, Moynihan proposed deregulation. Declassification also had the potential of releasing information of interest to those who believed that it would confirm their view of the extent of Communist subversion. Senator Moynihan's argument raised the tantalizing question: Would things have been different in matters of policy, domestic and foreign, had the nation (including its political leadership) been aware of what had been stamped "secret"? For still others, dismantling of secrecy promised to improve decision making and analysis, and to restore the public's right to know.

TWO REGULATORY REGIMES: ONE PUBLIC, ONE SECRET

In the Marver H. Bernstein Lecture at Georgetown University, Senator Moynihan placed the secrecy apparatus in the context of the administrative state of the twentieth century. He insightfully observed that we have created not one but two regulatory regimes. The first, "public regulation," provides for all kinds of disclosure, discovery, and due process. That regime, Senator Moynihan writes, is under constant scrutiny. The second regulatory regime—the secrecy regime—is, he writes, "concealed within a vast bureaucratic complex. There is some Congressional oversight: some Presidential control. Do not overestimate either. Note that the public is excluded altogether, save as bureaucracies or bureaucrats think it to their advantage to make some things public."[20]

The course to which Moynihan refers, the almost simultaneous development of two regulatory regimes, is worth pondering. In the 1930s, opponents of the New Deal feared unfettered executive discretion.[21] In 1938, Roscoe Pound, chairman of the American Bar Association Special Committee on Administrative Law, attacked "those who would turn the administration of justice over to administrative absolutism . . . a Marxian idea."[22] The president-elect of the ABA called on his colleagues to join the "titanic struggle" against those " 'progressives,' 'liberals,' or 'radicals' who desire to invest the national Government with totalitarian powers in the teeth of Constitutional democracy."[23]

If opponents of the New Deal led the charge against what they perceived to be administrative absolutism, others called for openness in government as a means of ensuring fairness. In 1934, Erwin Griswold of the Harvard Law School wrote "Government in Ignorance of the Law—A Plea for Better Publication of Executive Legislation."[24] Arguing that administrative regulations "equivalent to law"[25] had become important elements in the ordering of everyday life, Griswold decried the fact that such rules and regulations were not available to the public. To emphasize the point, he began with a quote from Jeremy Bentham: "We hear of tyrants, and those cruel ones: but, whatever we may have felt, we have never heard of any tyrant in such sort cruel, as to punish men for disobedience to laws or order which he had kept them from the knowledge of."[26] Griswold called for the publication of such rules and regulations, hitherto effectively hidden from the public. In 1935, Congress enacted the Federal Register Act,[27] from which the Federal Register comes.

Still, such remedial measures fell short in the view of New Deal critics. Against this background, at the suggestion of Attorney General Homer Cummings, President Franklin D. Roosevelt asked the attorney general in 1939 to appoint a distinguished committee to study existing administrative procedures and to formulate recommendations. In his letter to the president urging the creation of such a body, Cummings emphasized the value of "proper safeguards for the protection of substantive rights and adequate, but not extravagant, judicial review."[28] But in establishing the committee, President Roosevelt underscored the benefits of administrative reform to the Justice Department "in endeavoring to uphold actions of the administrative agencies of the Government, when the validity of their decisions is challenged in the courts."[29] Thus, as John Rohr observed, "the correspondence initiating the AGR [Attorney General's Report] presaged its two dominant themes—protection of rights and effective administration."[30] If the tension between these two objectives was not wholly resolved, the final version of the report was weighted on the side of rights.

The Attorney General's Committee on Administrative Procedure, chaired by Dean Acheson, produced a series of monographs on agency functions, and submitted its "Final Report" to the president and the Congress in 1941. "It is also plain that persons dealing with the Government have an interest—

one might say a right—to prompt knowledge of the official understanding of the law, of the way in which it will be enforced, of the path by which it is intended to achieve the congressional purpose." These materials, together with extensive hearings of the Senate Judiciary Committee, were central elements in the passage of the Administrative Procedure Act (APA) of 1946.[31]

The Administrative Procedure Act, which has assumed quasi-constitutional status, is premised on the idea that agencies should be required to keep the public currently informed of their organization, procedures, and rules; the public should be able to participate in the rule-making process; uniform standards for the conduct of formal rule making and adjudicatory proceedings should be prescribed; and as appropriate, judicial review should be available. The APA seeks to make government proceedings more accessible and open to the public. As administrative law scholar Kenneth Culp Davis, himself a staff member of the attorney general's committee, observed, there is to be no "secret law."[32] The Administrative Procedure Act has, in time, been supplemented by the Freedom of Information Act (enacted as an amendment to the Administrative Procedure Act).

The Administrative Procedure Act recognized few exceptions, one of them being in section 3, namely: "Any function of the United States requiring secrecy in the public interest." According to Attorney General Tom Clark's interpretation:

> This would include the confidential operations of any agency, such as the confidential operations of the Federal Bureau of Investigation and the Secret Service and, in general, those aspects of any agency's law enforcement procedures the disclosure of which would reduce the utility of such procedures. . . . It should be noted that the exception is made only "to the extent" that the function requires secrecy in the public interest. Such a determination must be made by the agency concerned. To the extent that the function does not require such secrecy, the publication requirements apply. Thus, the War Department obviously is not required to publish confidential matters of military organization and operation, but it would be required to publish the organization and procedure applicable to the ordinary civil functions of the Corps of Engineers.[33]

If the thrust in 1946 of the Administrative Procedure Act, fueled by the work of Dean Acheson's committee, was toward openness, the National Security Act of 1947, at least as implemented, embedded a contradictory impulse. Both acts envision regulation: the APA, regulation in the service of openness; the National Security Act, as implemented, regulation (indeed, the ultimate regulation) in the service of secrecy. It is a puzzle worth pondering.

By way of a coda, I note that thirty-seven years after writing his piece in the *Harvard Law Review* supporting openness in government, Erwin Griswold, then solicitor general of the United States, represented the United States in its opposition to publication of the Pentagon Papers (*New York Times v. United States* and *United States v. Washington Post*). In 1989, eighteen years after the fact, Griswold reflected that the position of the U.S. government had been in error:

> It quickly became apparent to any person who has considerable experience with classified material that there is massive overclassification and that the principal concern of the classifiers is not with national security, but rather with governmental embarrassment of one sort or another. There may be some basis for short-term classification while plans are being made, or negotiations are going on, but apart from weapons systems, there is very rarely any real risk to current national security from the publication of facts relating to transactions in the past, even the fairly recent past. This is the lesson of the Pentagon Papers experience, and it may be relevant now.[34]

SECRECY AND THE DELEGATION OF POWER

Article I, section 1, of the Constitution declares that "[a]ll legislative powers shall be vested in a Congress of the United States." By these words, the framers both vested power in the legislative branch and constrained its use. Over the last two centuries, cases abound about whether vague and broad delegations are unconstitutional delegations of legislative power to administrative agencies. It was in 1813, in *Brig Aurora*, that the Supreme Court first considered the nondelegation clause in the context of a statute that authorized the president to remove trade embargoes against France and England when they "ceased to violate the neutral commerce of the United States."[35] The Court sanctioned the statute because the executive's discretion was limited to taking the specific action authorized by Congress when the "named contingency" took place. In the years since, the "named contingency" test has been replaced by other tests. For a period in our history, during the early part of the New Deal, the Court struck down delegations of power to the executive branch, with *A.L.A. Schecter Poultry Corp. v. United States* being the classic case.[36] But since the New Deal, the Supreme Court has sustained all of the legislation reviewed under the nondelegation clause. In all these cases, the Court has determined that the executive branch has acted pursuant to some knowable standard. That has been so in regard to what Moynihan refers to as "public regulation." With regard to the secrecy regime, however, the actions taken tend not to be known and, hence, not reviewable. By Senator Moynihan's account, in 1995 there were 21,871 "original" Top Secret designations and 374,244 "derivative" designations.[37] Absent some manner of accountability, it becomes difficult to know what actions conform to legislative authority, however broadly defined.

SENATOR MOYNIHAN CREATES A COMMISSION

Concerned about the culture of secrecy, Senator Moynihan crafted legislation creating a commission to conduct "an investigation into all matters in any way related to any legislation, executive order, regulation, practice, or procedure relating to classified information or granting security clearances" and to issue a final report making pertinent recommendations.[38] The commission's inquiry was the first authorized by statute to examine government secrecy in four decades, only the second in history.[39] Aided by an able staff, the twelve-member commission included a wide diversity of individuals: vice chair Representative Larry Combest (Republican of Texas); director of Central Intelligence John Deutch; former assistant secretary of the air force Martin Faga; Alison Fortier of Lockheed Martin Corporation; Ambassador Richard K. Fox Jr.; Senator Jesse Helms (Republican of North Carolina); journalist Ellen Hume; Professor Samuel Huntington; Maurice Sonnenberg, a member of the president's Foreign Intelligence Advisory Board; and John Podesta, at various times assistant to the president, staff secretary, Georgetown University law professor, White House deputy chief of staff, and widely acknowledged as the White House's expert on issues of secrecy and declassification. The commission stated in its report:

> In undertaking our mission . . . we have observed when the system works well, and when it does not. We have looked at the consequences of the lack of adequate protection. We have sought to diagnose the current system, and to identify what works and the ways the system can work better. Above all, we have sought to understand how best to achieve both better protection and greater openness. . . . The system will perpetuate itself outside intervention,

> and in doing so maintain not only its many positive features, but also those elements that are detrimental to both our democracy and our security.[40]

Accordingly, the commission urged enactment of a statute that sets forth principles for what may be declared secret, much in the way that the Administrative Procedure Act created a law to guide behavior. Senator Moynihan acknowledged that a "statute defining and limiting secrecy will not put an end to overclassification and needless classification, but it will help."[41] Such a law would enable classifiers to know when they are acting properly. The proposed statute, which would create a general classification system and a national declassification center, would have the following elements: "Sec. 1: Information shall be classified only if there is a demonstrable need to protect the information in the interests of national security, with the goal of ensuring that classification is kept to an absolute minimum consistent with these interests. Sec. 2: The president shall, as needed, establish procedures and structures for classification . . . [and] a parallel program to declassification . . . ; Sec. 3: In determining whether information should be or remain classified, such standards and categories shall include consideration of the benefit from public disclosure of the information," weighed "against the need for initial or continued protection under the classification system. If there is significant doubt whether information requires protection, it shall not be classified."[42] In addition, under the terms of the proposed legislation:

> Information shall remain classified for no longer than ten years, unless the agency specifically recertifies that the particular information requires continued protection based on current risk assessments. All information shall be declassified after 30 years, unless it is shown that demonstrable harm to an individual or to ongoing government activities will result from release. Systematic declassification schedules shall be established. Agencies shall submit annual reports on their classification and declassification programs to the Congress.[43]

CHANGING THE TERMS OF THE DEBATE

Even before the release of its report, the commission's influence was already felt. Largely because of Senator Moynihan's prodding, the Central Intelligence Agency released the first group of the National Security Administration's "Venona" translations—Soviet intelligence messages decoded in the

1940s, which recount purported espionage activities in the United States.[44] Those documents will no doubt be a treasure trove for historians.

Press reaction has been supportive, too, suggesting that the Secrecy Commission will continue to have an impact. The *Washington Post, New York Times*, and *Christian Science Monitor* published highly favorable editorials, and the *Los Angeles Times* devoted a page-one, column-one feature to the subject of secrecy.[45]

As to the long-term objectives of the commission, Senator Moynihan recognizes that changing organizational culture will be difficult. James Q. Wilson has written: "Every organization has a culture, that is, a persistent, patterned way of thinking about the central tasks of and human relationships within an organization."[46] "Culture," he continued, "is to an organization what personality is to an individual. Like human culture generally, it is passed on from one generation to the next. It changes slowly, if at all."[47] An organization need not have just one culture. Therein lies Moynihan's hope. It is that a "competing culture of openness might develop which could assert and demonstrate greater efficiency."[48] But that culture of openness, Moynihan asserts, will not develop unless the present culture of secrecy is "restrained by statute."[49] As he put it in the Bernstein Lecture:

> This second regime [the secrecy regime] is in need of radical change. We have sensed this for some time. But I now submit that change will only come if we recognize it as a *bureaucratic regime* with recognizable and predictable patterns of self-perpetuation which will never respond to mere episodic indignation.[50]

In this new environment, painstaking decisions will still have to be made, weighing the costs and benefits of secrecy, and assessing such other factors as the vulnerability of the information, the estimated harm from its disclosure, the risk of its loss, its value to adversaries, and the cost of protecting it. Secrets, of necessity and in the national interest, will still have to be kept. But for Senator Moynihan, the frame of reference will have changed—"a climate which assumes that secrecy is not the starting place."[51] And that will be a major shift indeed.

NOTES

1. Amend. 20, sec. 1: "The terms of the President and the Vice President shall end at noon on the twentieth day of January, and the terms of Senators and Repre-

sentatives at noon on the third day of January, of the years in which such terms would have ended if this article had not been ratified; and the terms of their successors shall then begin." The Twentieth Amendment was ratified in 1933.

2. Report of the Commission on Protecting and Reducing Government Secrecy, *Secrecy*, S. Doc. 105-2 (Washington, D.C.: GPO, 1997) (hereinafter Secrecy Report).

3. Ibid, xxi.

4. Ibid., xxiv–xxv.

5. Ibid., xxxi–xlvi, A-1–A-86.

6. Senator Moynihan's Georgetown lecture—the Marver H. Bernstein Lecture—can be found in Daniel Patrick Moynihan, "Secrecy as Government Regulation," *PS: Political Science & Politics* 30, no. 2 (June 1997): 160 (hereinafter Bernstein Lecture).

7. Secrecy Report, xxxvi.

8. Ibid.

9. See, for example, Bernstein Lecture, 160–61.

10. Edward A. Shils, *The Torment of Secrecy*, with an introduction by Daniel P. Moynihan (1956; reprint, Chicago: Ivan R. Dee, 1996), vi–xxiii.

11. From *Max Weber: Essays in Sociology*, trans. and ed. H. H. Gerth and C. Wright Mills (New York: Oxford University Press, 1946), 233–34; *Wirtschaft und Gesellschaft* (Economy and Society), 1922.

12. Secrecy Report, A-6.

13. Ibid.

14. Ibid.

15. Ibid., A-1.

16. Ibid., A-2.

17. Ibid., A-5.

18. Ibid., xxxix.

19. Bernstein Lecture, 164.

20. Ibid., 165.

21. Walter Gellhorn, "The Administrative Procedure Act: The Beginnings," *Virginia Law Review* 72 (1986): 219–33; John A. Rohr, *To Run a Constitution* (Lawrence: University Press of Kansas, 1986), 154–70; Paul C. Light, *Tides of Reform: Making Government Work* (New Haven: Yale University Press, 1997), 76.

22. Roscoe Pound, *ABA Report* 63 (1938): 331, 339–40, quoted in Gellhorn, "Administrative Procedure Act," 221 n. 21.

23. Jacob M. Lashly, "Administrative Law and the Bar," *Virginia Law Review* 25 (1939): 641, 658.

24. Erwin Griswold, "Government in Ignorance of the Law—A Plea for Better Publication of Executive Legislation," *Harvard Law Review* 48 (1934): 198–213.

25. The phrase is taken from *Hampton & Co. v. United States*, 276 US 394, 409 (1928).

26. Griswold, "Government in Ignorance," 198.

27. United States Statutes at Large 49 (1935): 500, 501.

28. Report of the Committee on Administrative Procedure, Appointed by the Attorney General, at the Request of the President, to Investigate the Need for Procedural Reform in Various Administrative Tribunals and to Suggest Improvements Therein, *Administrative Procedure in Government Agencies*, 77th Cong., 1st sess., 1941, S. Doc. 8, appendix A, 251–52.

29. Ibid., 253.

30. Rohr, *To Run a Constitution*, 154.

31. Public Law 404, 79th Cong., 2d sess. (11 June 1946), ch. 324, sections 1–12.

32. As Rohr points out, the phrase is Kenneth Culp Davis's. Rohr, *To Run a Constitution*, 254 n. 6. Davis was a staff member of the attorney general's committee.

33. U.S. Department of Justice, *Attorney General's Manual on the Administrative Procedure Act* (Washington, D.C.: GPO, 1947), 17–18.

34. Erwin N. Griswold, "Secrets Not Worth Keeping," *Washington Post*, 15 February 1989, A25.

35. *Brig Aurora*, 11 U.S. (7 Cranch) 382 (1813).

36. *A.L.A. Schecter Poultry Corp. v. United States* 295 US 495 (1935).

37. Secrecy Report, xxxix.

38. Public Law 103-236, 103d Cong., 2d sess. (30 April 1994), section 905.

39. The first was the Commission on Government Security, created in 1955 by the 84th Congress.

40. *Secrecy Report*, xxii.

41. Ibid., xxxvii.

42. Ibid., xxiii.

43. Ibid.

44. Robert Louis Benson and Michael Warner, eds., *Venona: Soviet Espionage and the American Response, 1939–1957* (Washington, D.C.: National Security Agency, Central Intelligence Agency, 1996).

45. "400,000 New Top Secrets a Year," *Washington Post*, 17 May 1997, A24; "Bipartisan Sunshine," *New York Times*, 22 May 1997, A32; "Democracy Declassified," *Christian Science Monitor*, 19 May 1997, 20; Eleanor Randolph, "Is U.S. Keeping Too Many Secrets?" *Los Angeles Times*, 19 May 1997, 1.

46. James Q. Wilson, *Bureaucracy: What Government Agencies Do and Why They Do It* (New York: Basic Books, 1989), 91.

47. Ibid.

48. *Secrecy Report*, xxxvii.

49. Ibid.

50. Bernstein Lecture, 165.

51. *Secrecy Report*, xxxix.

PART TWO

OFFICE

CHAPTER SEVEN

THE FEDERAL EXECUTIVE

STEPHEN HESS

From time to time a professional intellectual wanders into high elective office in the United States; there also have been politicians who take late-life fliers at intellectual pursuits. Rarely, however, are they intellectuals and politicians at the same time. They seem almost to have an internal on-off switch that allows them to be one or the other. Take the case of the senior Henry Cabot Lodge, a Ph.D. in political science, the first granted by Harvard, editor of one of the most serious journals of his day, author of a prodigious amount of creditable historical writing, who traded scholarship for polemics once he entered the Congress.[1]

The special case we honor, however, manages to be the U.S. senator from New York, seventeenth-most senior in that chamber, while writing a book a year on such subjects as international law or the Establishment Clause of the Constitution.

My assignment in relating the saga of Daniel Patrick Moynihan is his Washington career in the executive branch, first in the Labor Department during the Kennedy and Johnson administrations (1961–65) and then on the White House staff of President Richard Nixon (1969–70).

Being an assistant to a secretary of labor (under Arthur Goldberg) and then the department's first assistant secretary for policy planning (under Willard Wirtz) was not necessarily grim work or heavy lifting. The agency is old enough, as are the tenets of federal labor law, that its essential duties are routinely handled by the permanent employees.[2] This has had two contradictory consequences on the political level. Presidents can use the cabinet slot as a reward for past services without having to worry that the appointee will do too much harm, hence the numerous oil paintings of forgettable leaders that grace the department's walls. Or the position of labor secretary can be a grand opportunity for a creative and ambitious person to roam well beyond the department's mandate. The latter, of course, is the Goldberg variation.

It was political scientist Louis Koenig who noted that the great presidents always interpreted their constitutional powers "with maximum liberality."[3] And it was Pat's habit, learned at the elbow of Arthur Goldberg, to do the same.

Two examples follow from Moynihan's days at Labor.

The first relates to something that in theory only a bureaucrat could love, by title, *Report to the President by the Ad Hoc Committee on Federal Office Space*, "For release Friday A.M., June 1, 1962." The committee consisted of the secretaries of labor and commerce, the budget director, the head of the General Services Administration, and a White House assistant.

As the 1960s commenced, Pat later explained to me, there had been almost no public construction in Washington since the Depression brought work to a stop on the Federal Triangle. Goldberg wanted a new building for his department and would use the Ad Hoc Committee to promote this enterprise. Young Moynihan was assigned to draft the report, which was only sixteen pages. It set forth the problem, proposed priorities, and outlined the role of the GSA. In the final four pages, however, Moynihan interpreted his duties "with maximum liberality." Page thirteen stated "Guiding Principles for Federal Architecture." Remember, the committee's assignment was "office space," not "architectural policy" (a subject of greater interest to Moynihan). With one sweep of the pen, the report declared, "The belief that good design is optional, or in some way separate from the question of the provision of office space itself, does not bear scrutiny." (Given the history of federal buildings, Pat's assumption did not bear scrutiny, but was the perfect segue into what he wanted to propose.) Among the recommendations: There should be no "official style" ("Design must flow from the architectural profession to the Government, and not vice versa"); design must reflect the regional traditions of where buildings are located and should emphasize the work of living American artists. With hardly anyone noticing at the time, Moynihan had written what has been the U.S. government's policy on the architecture of federal buildings for thirty-five years!

Pages fourteen through sixteen of the office space report gave Moynihan another creative opportunity: to propose the redevelopment of Washington's Pennsylvania Avenue, transforming "a vast, unformed, cluttered expanse" into a great thoroughfare linking Article I of the Constitution (The Capitol) and Article II (The White House). President Kennedy liked the idea, and Moynihan put together the "President's Council on Pennsylvania Avenue," a totally informal group without official standing, which drew up the plan. Almost the last thing the president did before leaving for Dallas was to ask whether a meeting was arranged with congressional leaders when he got back to show them the plan. Today the Pennsylvania Avenue redevelopment is just about finished. And when Liz and Pat Moynihan are in Washington, they reside in an eleventh-floor apartment looking down on the splendid avenue whose restoration Pat, more than any other living American, is responsible for.

Example number two of what might be called Moynihan's creative engineering is the Presidential Medal of Freedom, which Kennedy announced on Washington's Birthday, 1963, and which was then described by Tom Wicker in the *New York Times* as "similar to the annual honors list of the British monarch."[4]

This was a project that Goldberg assigned to Pat after a conversation with Kennedy. There had been previous efforts, notably under President Eisenhower, to establish an honors system. Leonard Carmichael, secretary of the Smithsonian Institution, headed a commission that came out with an elaborate proposal for legislation that might have passed had Senator Wayne Morse not decided it smacked of monarchy. Moynihan concluded that such would be the fate of a Kennedy effort as well. Surely there must be some scheme that would not have to go through the nattering legislature.

Moynihan took his cue from British history. According to Pat, Disraeli wanted an award to give to his new Civil Service and hit upon something called the Order of St. Michael and St. George. This medal had been struck on the occasion of the British occupation of the Ionian islands in 1818, handed about to a few admirals, and then forgotten. On being suddenly resurrected by the prime minister, the medal became the symbol of the higher Civil Service.

In the United States there was a "Medal of Freedom," produced after World War II for spies who had not been in uniform. As Pat remembers, "We simply announced to a still very trusting press that the Medal of Freedom, the nation's highest civil honor, would henceforth be known as the Presidential Medal of Freedom and conferred once a year. No one asked when was the last time it had been conferred. I had the wit to provide that the announcement should be on July 4th, but the president could make the actual presentation whenever he found it convenient. He was going to do so when he got back from Dallas."[5] President Lyndon Johnson presided over the first awards ceremony on 6 December 1963. Recipients included Pablo Casals, Edwin Land, George Meany, Ludwig Mies van der Rohe, Thornton Wilder, Ralph Bunche, Felix Frankfurter, and posthumously, John F. Kennedy. The rest is history, or as President Clinton said on 9 September 1996 at the White House, "We're here to award the highest honor our nation can bestow on a citizen, the Presidential Medal of Freedom."

Moynihan's broad-ranging mandate at Labor also gave him an opportunity to explore questions of federal support for the arts,[6] auto safety (an interest that predated Ralph Nader's), and through a new interest in the African American family, a subject that thereafter was to dominate his political life: welfare.

The Negro Family: The Case for National Action was released by the Johnson White House shortly after the Watts riot in 1965. Also known as the Moynihan Report, the author's analysis was based on a strange change in Aid to Families with Dependent Children statistics. From the end of World War II until the early 1960s, whenever black male unemployment rose, so too did new welfare cases. Then, suddenly, unemployment went down and welfare cases went up. Did this reflect a new urban underclass, which if it continued to grow might lead to a whole range of social conflict? Moynihan saw his report as a brief for a national income strategy. But his conclusions were deeply threatening to the black leadership, and the Johnson administration dissociated itself from Moynihan's position.

Most remarkable then was Moynihan's next incarnation as a federal executive. For it was during his tenure as an adviser to Richard Nixon, who had opposed the negative income tax during the 1968 campaign, that a president would become the champion of an income strategy. "If what the poor lacked was money," Moynihan wrote, "giving it to them directly was, on the face of it, a reasonable response: direct, efficient, and immediate."[7] And for a while, at least, he convinced Nixon of the logic.

The tortuous path of the Nixon administration's Family Assistance Plan, from development in the agencies and the White House, through adoption by the president, 'til death at the hands of the Senate Finance Committee, has been brilliantly told by Moynihan in *The Politics of a Guaranteed Income: The Nixon Administration and the Family Assistance Plan.* As an objective case study of how ideas and politics interact in Washington, the book is unsurpassed, in my judgment, all the more remarkable in that the author was one of the key actors in this drama.

Rather than summarize what Moynihan laid out in over five hundred pages, I shall try to recall the specialness of Pat's role at the White House of 1969. I was there as deputy assistant to the president, essentially as Pat's chief of staff.

When Pat was surprisingly (one might say audaciously) asked by President-elect Nixon to be his assistant for urban affairs, he had a temporary home and office waiting in Washington. By night there was the Georgetown house of his old boss, Averell Harriman, complete with staff and wine cellar; by day he settled in at the Pennsylvania Avenue Commission, where he was now vice chairman. The aides he chose for his White House staff appeared to be on average a year or two removed from undergraduate days at Harvard. The youngest, Christopher DeMuth, was twenty-two. This was to be a Moynihan habit (nicely explained in a July 1996 article in the *Washingtonian* on the "savvy mentor").[8] There always would be an eager young person prepared to stay up all night to get "the data" to him. This is an obvious point, perhaps, but one that gave Moynihan an edge over less well-served adversaries. More exceptional is that most of Pat's young assistants proved to be cool and calculating, while well mannered and deferential to their elders. For instance, one of the smaller pieces of Moynihan's White House portfolio was the District of Columbia in those days before Home Rule. He assigned oversight to Richard Blumenthal, who operated with skill and tact. What residents of Washington did not know was that their shadow mayor was twenty-three years old. (Today Blumenthal is attorney general of Connecticut; DeMuth is president of the American Enterprise Institute.)

There is no reason to believe that Nixon as president favored a staff system of creative tension, an operating style most associated with Franklin Roosevelt and Democrats. In 1969, however, it happened that way. Arthur F. Burns, the distinguished Columbia University economist and a close associate of Nixon's during the Eisenhower presidency, was going to be appointed chairman of the Federal Reserve when the position became available in 1970. The president, in the meantime, gave Burns cabinet rank, the title of counselor, and responsibility for domestic policy. If Burns and Moynihan were inadvertently placed on a collision course, the advantages were with Burns, insider-conservative, who had higher status and a broader mandate. That Moynihan, outsider-liberal, ultimately "won" (at least on the issue of greatest importance) speaks in part to his understanding of how presidents (*all* presidents) operate. There is, for example, the law of propinquity, otherwise known as "nearness to the throne." Burns had chosen an elegant suite of offices across West Executive Street from the White House, where his staff could be efficiently consolidated; Moynihan had chosen two small offices (for himself and me) in the west basement of the White House, even though it meant that our staff would be housed somewhere else. This was, as Pat noted, "an intangible but unmistakable advantage." Indeed, at a later point in our story, Moynihan realized that it was crucial for Burns to have a "victory" as well.

Neither Moynihan nor Burns operated as so-called "honest brokers," a staff role dearly loved by a school of public administration. Rather, they were advocates. Each had a philosophy of domestic government. (Strangely, given his long political career, Nixon did not, which is why a struggle for his mind was possible.) Notable was that Burns and Moynihan were scholars (Ivy League professors to boot!), and the resulting argumentation was exceptional by Washington standards. At one point, for instance, their competing memos to the president were about the history of the Speenhamland system, a late-eighteenth-century British scheme of poor relief. (Our side, by the way, had historical advice from Gertrude Himmelfarb and Cambridge University's Jack Plumb.)

It is necessary here to make one quick yet important aside, given the ultimate fate of Richard Nixon's presidency. Nixon kept staff functions in airtight compartments. The policy people discussed policy with the president, period, often on a remarkably elevated level, while, at the same time, Nixon was plotting with his political handlers in language that was subsequently labeled "expletive deleted." (In hundreds of hours of conversation with Nixon, I cannot recall his cursing: I was a policy person.) No members of the Moynihan or Burns staffs, science advisers or economists, were implicated in Watergate.

Burns and Moynihan were attached to different advisory systems, which were reflected in the weight awarded to their respective proposals within the White House. Burns was given a group of task forces, made up of busy people from outside government. In a sense, this amounted to cadging ideas on the cheap. Moynihan, on the other hand, was given a cabinet committee, called the Urban Affairs Council, whose tasks were thrashed out by those who would be most immediately responsible for their success (or failure), and with departmental staff appropriate to the job at hand. Increasingly Burns was put on the defensive, responding to the UAC's initiatives. Moreover, the system assured Moynihan of three cracks at the president per week—setting the UAC meeting agenda, council meeting, and postmeeting debriefing. Just as long as Moynihan could make the meetings interesting, the president would attend, and Moynihan could retain this subtle advantage.

Moynihan raised creating an agenda to an art form. At one meeting he brought before the Urban Affairs Council the question of where to locate a building that was to be constructed in Fresno, California. This is the sort of matter that presidents need not be bothered with. The amount of money is modest by federal budget standards; yet Moynihan saw the issue as an intellectual puzzle that would intrigue Nixon. The building was to be used by the Internal Revenue Service to process tax returns. The IRS wanted it in a "good" neighborhood because during tax-collection time a lot of temporary workers were needed, housewives and students, and (according to the IRS's brief) the agency "can effectively utilize this labor pool only if employees encounter little or no travel problems and find favorable environmental conditions." In short, put the building where it can best help accomplish the agency's mission. But the General Services Administration had other interests and another proposed site. The GSA wanted to put the building in a "bad" neighborhood so that the construction would contribute to Fresno's urban renewal and (according to GSA's brief) help "efforts directed toward the reduction in the number of our citizens who are unemployed or tied to public welfare."[9] Thus it came to pass that in December 1969 the director of the IRS and the director of the GSA debated this issue before the president of the United States in the White House cabinet room. As Moynihan expected, Nixon was delighted with the exchange.

(Who won? I don't think I ever knew, so I recently asked Pat. "The IRS Service Center [today] is on a site in a relatively nice middle-income neighborhood, but is surrounded by poorer neighborhoods that are heavily black, Hispanic, and Asian.")

On another occasion (29 September 1969), Moynihan gathered the president and the domestic cabinet to hear about "the demography of American youth" and "the patterns of youth unrest" from two students who had been summer interns and a young staffer. Instead of the usual anecdotes and speculations that defined most of what was in the popular press during the Vietnam era, the three presenters had meticulously charted the institutional characteristics of major campus protests: 6.2 percent of colleges and universities had experienced at least one incident of "violent" protest during the past academic year; 22.4 percent had experienced "disruptive" protest; protests were twice as likely to occur at private institutions as at public institutions, three to four times more likely in nonsectarian institutions than in church-related schools, least likely to occur at two-year colleges, and so forth.[10] It was an electric performance. The intern presenters were Franklin D. Raines, twenty, Harvard College, and Martin M. Fischbein, twenty, Antioch College; the staffer was Chester E. Finn Jr., twenty-five, a former student of Moynihan's. (For the record: Raines is today the U.S. budget director; Finn is a senior fellow at the Hudson Institute and a former assistant secretary of the U.S. Department of Education; and Fischbein, along with his fiancée, TV personality Jessica Savitch, died tragically in a freak car accident.)

What soon became clear was that Moynihan was charming Nixon with his wit and words.[11] Only a Moynihan, when challenged by an adversary at an Urban Affairs Council meeting with "Let us call a spade a spade," would reply with Oscar Wilde's adage, "Anyone who would call a spade a spade should be compelled to use one."[12] Only a Moynihan could describe the expected "peace dividend," revenues that might come from ending the Vietnam War, as "evanescent like the morning clouds around San Clemente."[13] Memos Pat sent the president were so engaging that Nixon often passed them around the higher reaches of government, causing Pat some embarrassment when they found their way into the press. Even a Nixon needed relief from the grayness of his Haldeman-created staff. As the president said when Pat returned to Harvard, "I disagreed with a lot of what he said—but he certainly did light up the place!"

Finally, on 8 August 1969, the president addressed the nation, and the winners and losers were announced. The welfare system was "a colossal failure," Nixon said, and in its place he was proposing "that the Federal government build a foundation under the income of every American family with dependent children that cannot care for itself. . . . Thus, for the first time, the government would recognize that it had no less an obligation to the working poor than to the nonworking poor."[14] He also announced a proposal for revenue sharing, a transfer of resources from the federal government to states and municipalities, an idea that Burns very much favored.

The Family Assistance Plan was passed by the House of Representatives, but ultimately failed in the Senate Finance Committee. What would be the state of poverty today if it had become law? Pat doesn't want to speculate. As Adam Yarmolinsky has recently written, "For a major political figure, Moynihan is refreshingly aware of how much he—and we—don't know."[15]

The story of Moynihan's influence in the conversion of a Republican president might be explained solely in terms of processes and staff and charm and such, but, in Nixonian parlance, that would be wrong. What really made the difference could be called "The Disraeli Thing." Moynihan had introduced the president to Robert Blake's biography cf the British prime minister and then encouraged the notion (as Nixon put it) that "Tory men and Liberal policies are what have changed the world." Moynihan appealed to Nixon's place in history; great presidents dream and act grandly. You can have vision and not be a great president, but you can't be a great president without vision. Pat Moynihan proposed the Family Assistance Plan. Arthur Burns proposed caution. Burns was a wise man and his analysis may well have been correct. His prescription, however, was not for greatness; Moynihan's was, or so he convinced the president. The date 8 August 1969 concluded the Moynihan/Burns period at the Nixon White House. The president wanted no more intellectual squabbling. Policy was now declared and would be turned over to the implementors.

John Ehrlichman took over as domestic czar. Moynihan's staff was scattered. (I became national chairman of the White House Conference on Children and Youth.) Pat was elevated to cabinet rank, but without a formal portfolio. This was okay with him. He always had planned to return to Harvard when his two-year leave was over. And Pat never lacked for interesting things to do, especially if a White House address could help to get them done. Some of his energy moved into the international sphere. He had early urged the government's diplomatic channels to respond vigorously to counter "the French connection" in the processing of heroin.[16] Also, on the fortieth anniversary of NATO in April, the president had proposed creating a NATO Committee on the Challenges of Modern Life, a sort of Urban Affairs Council for Europe. Each nation was to sponsor projects to solve technological problems. Pat assumed a lead role in this effort.

As a "federal executive," Moynihan has never been an executive in the sense of running an enterprise. We are a nation with no shortage of managers. Rather, Moynihan is the political man of ideas. Some are his own, some he borrows, some are cosmic, others more modest—our generation's greatest spotter of ideas that might make our society somehow better. This is a remarkable talent. But what turns it into a national treasure is a finely attuned antenna for knowing when an idea is ready for the public arena, the skill to be in positions to make his ideas matter, and the flair to make others notice. It is a harnessing of intellectual energy and political smarts that is so rare that when such a person is also blessed with long life, we must create opportunities to celebrate.

NOTES

1. See Stephen Hess, *America's Political Dynasties* (New Brunswick, N.J.: Transaction Publishers, 1997), 451–54.

2. It needs to be noted, however, that Goldberg and Moynihan were importantly responsible for Executive Order 10988, promulgated by President Kennedy in January 1962, which resulted from a "special task force" chaired by Goldberg with Moynihan as staff director. Executive Order 10988 conferred legitimacy on union organizing of public employees where previously there had been little or none.

3. See Louis W. Koenig, *The Chief Executive*, rev. ed. (New York: Harcourt, Brace, and World, 1968), 11.

4. Tom Wicker, "President Sets Up Highest Civil Honor," *New York Times*, 23 February 1963, A4; also see John F. Kennedy, *Public Papers of the Presidents, 1963* (Washington, D.C.: GPO, 1964), 209–10.

5. Daniel Patrick Moynihan, letter to author, 20 December 1996.

6. When Labor Secretary Goldberg proposed an arbitration award of a small raise in the salaries of New York's Metropolitan Opera orchestra musicians, he included a suggestion, drafted by Moynihan, of government subsidies for all performing arts. Many believe that this led, in due course, to the creation of the National Endowment for the Arts. See Marjorie Hunter, "Goldberg Urges U.S. to Subsidize Performing Arts," *New York Times*, 15 December 1961, A1.

7. Daniel P. Moynihan, *The Politics of a Guaranteed Income: The Nixon Administration and the Family Assistance Plan* (New York: Vintage Books Edition, 1973), 108.

8. Larry Van Dyne, "Up with Pat," *Washingtonian*, July 1996, 45.

9. Robert L. Kunzig, Administrator, General Services Administration, "Memorandum for the Council for Urban Affairs. Subject: Socio-Economic Impact of Federal Construction Program," 2 December 1969, and "Internal Revenue Service Presentation [to the Urban Affairs Council], Fresno Site Selection," unsigned and undated.

10. Martin Fischbein, "Memorandum for Daniel P. Moynihan and Stephen Hess," The White House, 11 September 1969.

11. See William Safire, *Before the Fall: An Inside View of the Pre-Watergate White House* (Garden City, N.Y.: Doubleday, 1975), 497.

12. Moynihan, *The Politics of a Guaranteed Income*, 144.

13. Quoted in Douglas Schoen, *Pat: A Biography of Daniel Patrick Moynihan* (New York: Harper & Row, 1979), 162.

14. Richard M. Nixon, *Public Papers of the Presidents, 1969* (Washington, D.C.: GPO, 1971), 640.

15. Adam Yarmolinsky, "The Prophet Daniel," *Washington Monthly* (December 1996), 60.

16. Moynihan's thoughts on heroin traffic are contained in a memorandum he sent to Attorney General John Mitchell on 11 February 1969, a copy of which was sent by the president to Secretary of State William Rogers for comment on 7 April 1969.

CHAPTER EIGHT

THE AMERICAN AMBASSADOR

SUZANNE R. GARMENT

Of the various titles Daniel P. Moynihan acquired during his years in the executive branch, "ambassador" may be the one he held for the briefest time. Yet, Moynihan's ambassadorial career was long enough to teach us something about modern American diplomacy. In particular, his performance in India and at the United Nations helps us understand why it is hard to be a superior diplomat nowadays without possessing a distinctly undiplomatic mind.

The term "modern American ambassador" comes near to being a double oxymoron. First, the very word "ambassador" calls to mind the diplomacy of Cardinal Richelieu, a system that today's foreign service officers can only long for nostalgically. This traditional type of diplomacy rests squarely on the twin pillars of secrecy and inequality.

The inequality of nations is, as classic diplomacy sees it, not a mere principle but a massively obvious fact of life. Its corollary is that powerful states, when pursuing their aims, cannot possibly do so by dealing with their less powerful neighbors as equals. Instead, great nations must treat feebler ones with a combination of manipulation when possible and threats when necessary.

In this same view, inequality among individuals is just as obvious a fact as inequality among nations. Thus, in foreign affairs, only professional initiates can be trusted to practice the diplomatic arts.

Secrecy is deemed necessary by traditional diplomacy, not just because nations have enemies but because most people should not be allowed to hear what the professionals know. Relations between states are stable only when based on nations' enduring self-interest, and this self-interest is the sort of base motive that cannot safely be displayed in public.

It is no surprise that such a well-ordered view should provoke fond backward glances. But it sometimes seems that every aspect of human history since World War I has cooperated, in a classic conspiracy of overdetermination, to make the assumptions of traditional diplomacy inoperative.

One of the central tenets of foreign policy as preached by Woodrow Wilson is equality among nations. Equally central is the principle of open covenants, openly arrived at. If the old diplomacy insisted on the gulf between ordinary domestic politics and the highly skilled conduct of foreign relations, the new Wilsonian ethos promulgated at the end of World War I insisted that principles of domestic politics could and must be imported into international affairs. From this idea it was only a short step to asserting that nonprofessionals might have a legitimate role to play in making and implementing foreign policy. The step was not taken soon enough to spare us the more contemptible diplomacy of the 1930s, but eventually it came.

The end of World War II and the start of the Cold War brought a kind of interruption in the weakening of the old diplomacy. For one thing, the Cold War reinforced the old idea of inequality among nations. The largest feature of this struggle was that it had two main participants, each a superpower. Other nations were subordinate actors in the drama. The United States and the Soviet Union might work at garnering majorities in the United Nations; but no one could escape the fact that in the new nuclear world, some nations were distinctly more equal than others.

The Cold War also lent a second wind to the principle of secrecy. If ever a nation had an implacable enemy, so the argument went, it was the United States faced with a hostile Soviet Union. And if ever an era was marked by international ugliness too horrible for civilian consumption, this was it.

Yet, in spite of these characteristics, the Cold War, too, weakened the hold of the old diplomacy. Because the struggle was so heavily ideological, both sides were forced to pay heavy, sustained attention to public arguments, which had to be couched in the language of ideas rather than interests. These ideas had their own independent potential for inspiring, inflaming, and destabilizing. They were yet another cross for the old diplomacy to bear.

The transition from traditional diplomacy to a more heterogeneous one provided an apt demonstration of the familiar dictum that God protects little children, drunkards, and the United States of America. Circumstances made the United States better equipped than a European nation would have been to operate in the more freewheeling world of a newer diplomacy.

In part, we had an advantage at the newer game simply because we—the Wilsonian "we"—invented it. We were also advantaged because of the appeal of our diverse, improvisational culture, though this strength was not apparent until rather late in the game.

But the United States was also prepared for success by virtue of its prior failure. We had succeeded much less fully than Europe in professionalizing our foreign service, and so we had less to unlearn.

As the republic aged, U.S. diplomacy naturally grew more professional. To take one indicator, during the early years, many diplomats were former members of Congress. Through 1800 the figure was almost 50 percent. Through 1879, the proportion was nearly a third. But by 1890, it had dropped to less than 15 percent, and today it is negligible.[1] To look at it in another, perhaps more invidious way, during the first decade of our nation's life, 50 percent of U.S. ambassadors were published authors of some sort; by the 1970s, the figure had dropped to 3 percent.[2]

Still, the drive toward professionalism could never quite suppress the tendency of American domestic politics—sometimes high, sometimes low, always messy—to intrude into the selection of diplomatic personnel.

This was not just a matter of rich, crude presidential campaign contributors demanding cushy ambassadorial appointments. One remembers the counterexample of New Dealer Adolf Berle, who was named U.S. ambassador to Brazil in 1945 as a kind of consolation prize—and who promptly proceeded, largely on his own initiative, to help foment the ouster of the then-reigning dictator.

U.S. foreign policy professionals have never had thorough control of their domain. This has, on the whole, been a piece of good luck. For every ambassador who has committed terrible errors, cozying up to the wrong dictator or mispronouncing the native tongue so as to address Her Royal Highness as a camel's ass, there has been an infusion of talent that could never have emerged from inside the foreign policy bureaucracy or, indeed, any bureaucracy.

In this great American tradition of no tradition stands Daniel P. Moynihan. In the 1970s he received and carried out two ambassadorial assignments. From 1973 to 1975, he served as U.S. ambassador to India; from 1975 to 1976, he was U.S. permanent representative to the United Nations, heading an American team of several diplomats with ambassadorial rank. Both tours of duty demonstrated that it is the major winds sweeping through the world, rather than particular diplomatic arrangements, that now play the larger role in determining our relations with other countries. If the winds are adverse, the most that diplomatic skill can do is limit their damage; if the winds are right, this country had better have someone on the scene who is capable of raising the nation's sails to take advantage of them.

In India from 1972 through 1974, Moynihan was an ambassador as the foreign service would understand the term, though he brought to the job intellectual resources and political experience that few professional ambassadors could have mustered. When he arrived in New Delhi, U.S. relations with India were at one of the lowest of their several low points during the Cold War. The 1971 war between India and Pakistan had just taken place, including the famous U.S. "tilt" toward Pakistan. This source of mutual mistrust was part of a broader tension, caused by a recently signed Soviet-Indian cooperation treaty and the beginnings of a U.S.-Pakistani-Chinese axis. In turn, all the juggling and rearranging of alliances reflected a still deeper problem—the endlessly provocative moralizing of India's prime minister, Indira Gandhi, spokesperson for the misnamed nonaligned nations and self-appointed minister to the morally challenged Americans.

At the time of Moynihan's appointment, anti-American sentiment in India was such that Moynihan's predecessor, Ambassador Kenneth Keating, was assigned a twenty-four-hour bodyguard. On the drive from the airport in New Delhi to the American ambassador's residence, the most prominent architectural feature of the landscape was the red neon hammer and sickle shining over the entrance to the Soviet embassy compound.

Moynihan's arrival as ambassador was actually delayed in order to express U.S. government displeasure with some particularly grating pronouncement by Mrs. Gandhi. Once in New Delhi, Moynihan was warned by American security personnel that when he traveled from place to place in his official limousine, he should, for safety's sake, omit the usual practice of flying a small American flag from one of the car's fenders. Naturally, he did not take this advice, causing a certain nervousness among visitors, like me, who had occasion to share the car with him on one journey or another.

As ambassador to India, Moynihan did some unusual things. One was to institute a program, through the United States Information Agency, that brought prominent U.S. intellectuals to India to speak to Indian audiences. Some of these new visitors were, as chance would have it, friends of

Moynihan's. The range of their views was considerably wider than that of the usual American academic travelers to India. This novelty led to interesting exchanges—or nonexchanges, such as the one that occurred when I tried, in my capacity as a political scientist, to explain to some of my Indian counterparts why American policymakers had come to feel that the country needed less government regulation of its economy.

Still, despite such activities, the deed for which Moynihan's ambassadorship is most remembered in India—the renegotiation of the rupee debt—was in the classic diplomatic tradition.

In the 1950s and 1960s, the United States had sold India large quantities of food. This food was paid for in Indian rupees, but the rupees were nonconvertible. So they sat in Indian banks, growing like the proverbial mushroom. When Moynihan arrived in India, they had increased to the equivalent of about $3 billion and threatened to become a significant, distorting percentage of India's total money supply.

The Indians, not surprisingly, wanted the United States to write off the entire rupee debt. But the Nixon administration could not do so, because Congress would not hear of it.

Moynihan, in prolonged negotiations, forged a compromise. A third of the rupee debt, a billion dollars' worth, would be paid back to the United States in the form of rupees given to the U.S. embassy in India for the embassy's operating expenses. The other two-thirds of the debt would be written off—with the understanding that the Indian government would spend an equivalent amount on development programs.

Even here, Moynihan brought something more than diplomatic skill to the enterprise: He succeeded in selling the rupee compromise to Congress, a feat that a less politically well-connected diplomat would have found hard to accomplish. Yet, this was in some ways a textbook case of diplomacy at work. The Indian government, in its 1974 survey of foreign policy, judged that relations with the United States "have steadily improved." It pointed to the rupee debt settlement as a "positive sign" and specifically praised Moynihan's work.[3]

A month later, unfortunately, the Indians surprised America and the world by launching what it called a "peaceful nuclear explosion" in the Rajasthan desert. The roller coaster of U.S.-Indian relations plunged downward once more; it then sank still lower, when Mrs. Gandhi declared a national emergency and suspended basic civil liberties. Matters did not improve until the Indian electorate turned her out of office.

The possibilities of diplomacy have always been limited by the demands of great power politics; in the modern world, they are constrained as well by a proliferation of nations with their own distinct interests and by the growing importance of ideas like democracy and human rights. A diplomat can do only so much, and Moynihan did it.

By contrast, when the winds blow right, an American of sufficient resources who is thrust into a fluid diplomatic situation can do a great deal. Such was the case when Moynihan was named ambassador to the United Nations.

By now, the story of Moynihan's ambassadorship to the UN has been told more than once.[4] He first startled the UN community and the U.S. public by denouncing Idi Amin, president of Uganda, for the latter's attack in the General Assembly on America and its alleged Zionist manipulators. Moynihan denounced the UN majority for its hypocrisy on the issue of Israel and its callousness toward issues of human rights. He vexed Secretary of State Henry Kissinger with his style and independence. Kissinger responded by pushing him to the edge; Moynihan then resigned his UN post, returned to Harvard, then ran for the U.S. Senate and won.

There is still room for a few personal observations, by someone—me—who served as Moynihan's special assistant throughout his tenure at the UN.

Moynihan went to the UN knowing that a major theme of his would be human rights. He knew that in order to pursue this theme, he might have to lock horns with the State Department; but he did not arrive at Turtle Bay itching for confrontation with the UN or its majority. On his previous diplomatic tour, as ambassador to an India fully capable of provoking a desire for confrontation, he nevertheless tried to conciliate.

Moynihan's first major effort at the UN was to try to bring the United States and the UN majority into agreement on the perennially divisive issue of world economic development, to which the General Assembly was devoting its Seventh Special Session just as he was taking up his post. The United States was willing to give the Third World a certain amount of economic aid for this purpose but insisted that a better life for the world's population could and should come only through growth in the world's economy. The Third World's most vociferous spokespeople argued the opposite: Their countries would be just fine if they could only get their hands on a piece of the material wealth that the West had created and already held.

The two positions would not seem easily reconcilable, but Moynihan determined to squeeze, shave, and shade them into alignment. The General Assembly had before it an anti-Western tract of a resolution; he rewrote the screed ever so subtly, using his rhetorician's sleight-of-hand to turn a redistributionist call to international class warfare into a moderate prescription for economic growth.

I watched this process with some alarm. I had served as what in olden days was called a section man for a course that Moynihan taught at Harvard. I then signed up for a tour of duty at the UN with Moynihan the neocon—only to see there, in his UN office, a liberal at work, trying assiduously to gain the nonaligned nations' goodwill. When the General Assembly passed Moynihan's version of the economic development resolution, he thought he might actually have succeeded in opening an era of good feelings. It was not his predilection but events that turned him confrontational.

Yet, one can say that as the direction of events changed, no one was quicker than Moynihan to get the drift. When he did, it was easier for him to start making policy at the U.S. mission to the UN (USUN) than it would have been at some other embassy.

True, he had to put up with a great deal of unsolicited attention from Washington. New York is so close to the nation's capital that it is much harder for an ambassador to keep control of his subordinates at USUN than it is at more remote posts. Even in this era of modern communications, it is easier to phone Washington from New York than from New Delhi.

Moreover, foreign service personnel at USUN tend to have been at their posts for a relatively long time, which means they have learned how to use the system. Moynihan's fellow ambassadors and some of USUN's foreign service officers kept myriad back channels to Washington humming, and the buzz was a constant source of obstacles to Moynihan's efforts.

He treated these interferences as nothing more than what was to be expected. On one occasion, White House speechwriters asked USUN for a draft paragraph on the UN to be inserted into a presidential speech. Moynihan and I wrote a pretty good passage and sent it to the White House—which turned it into a pretty bad passage and sent it back to us. "Why?" I asked, anguished. "You must understand," said Moynihan patiently. "These are White House speechwriters. No one treats them with respect. Therefore it never occurs to them to treat anyone else with respect either."

Still, in those of his allies who, like me, were unaccustomed to the day-to-day practice of treachery, the repeated attempts to sabotage Moynihan occasioned virtually homicidal rage.

It must be admitted that this almost reflexive undermining of Moynihan was far outweighed by the special resources that a UN permanent representative can bring to bear on policy-making. Of all the embassies, it is said, USUN is the most frantic. Other embassies can be involved in more important issues or handle vastly more business in areas such as trade. But because the UN is the world's preeminent multilateral body, the sheer number of issues before it is unmatched. On a great number of these issues, each nation has an interest and a potential input. And many of these issues come complete with their own action-forcing deadlines.

At USUN, in other words, there are always a dozen things going on at once. These matters will distract the attention of most people there, especially people who take the UN's agenda as their own. Also, the UN's many deadlines often require U.S. action even if there has been no time to consult thoroughly with or receive instructions from Washington. Thus a permanent representative who knows how to pick his spots can weave through the maze. Moynihan knew. He also possessed at USUN a photocopy machine that broke down mysteriously and frequently and thus delayed transmission of speech drafts to the State Department. This he perhaps did not know, but I did.

If structure is one factor that makes it hard for the foreign policy bureaucracy to compete with a determined UN ambassador, another factor is the public force that the ambassador can bring to bear on decision making. Moynihan, from his long years in government, was acutely sensitive to the way his various State Department bosses played the insiders' Washington game—through cables and cabals, private communications and selective leaks. But it is probably fair to say that the State Department was more overwhelmed by Moynihan, with his ability to garner public attention, than vice versa. In matters like speech preparation, I was Moynihan's chief apparatchik. If I was driven to murder fantasies by some of my colleagues in the State Department, I can only imagine, looking back, how they must have felt about me.

Perhaps most important, Moynihan succeeded in influencing U.S. politics and policy at the UN because larger movements of public opinion were with him.

When Moynihan denounced Idi Amin's anti-Semitism and pointed out the sheer nerve of this bloody dictator in purporting to lecture us about international morality or, indeed, anything at all, Moynihan got the huge press coverage he did because his message was electrifyingly welcome to American listeners—including journalists. At the time, there was a huge gap between the rhetoric spouted in the conduct of international relations, especially in multilateral bodies, and Americans' convictions about the world and our place in it. Moreover, this gap, as it turned out, was a sign not of American decline, as some said, but of the insubstantiality of the arguments and force arrayed against us.

Yet these facts were not self-effectuating. To have impact, they needed someone to recognize them—and Moynihan, as we know, correctly saw them and placed his bet on them. Other players in Washington made the opposite bet, for which history has already begun to exact a penalty.

One final note: Moynihan's bet was a matter not just of clearheadedness but of nerve. He did what he did at a time when very few public figures would have made such a high-stakes wager. By contrast, beginning in the 1980s with the election of Ronald Reagan, U.S. diplomacy as a whole, and official policy toward UN diplomacy in particular, became much more assertive. It was a deep pleasure to see the U.S. government's new self-confidence at the UN. It should not be forgotten, though, that Moynihan raised his voice at a time when the official foreign policy apparatus did not offer such wholehearted support. With every action he took, there was a nontrivial possibility that some U.S. colleague would openly countermand Moynihan or secretly foment antagonism toward him or try to make him look like a fool. Each gesture had to be calculated, measured for effect, and fought for within the U.S. government labyrinth. The qualities of character needed to carry on under these circumstances are not common criteria in the selection and training of diplomats.

Thus Moynihan turned out to be a very modern American ambassador. In other words, he had capacities very unlike those of a traditional diplomat, and those capacities proved to be utterly necessary for the making of successful U.S. foreign policy.

The foreign service will never be composed of Moynihans—and a good thing, too. The international political system would collapse under the pressure. Still, every so often the debate resumes about whether the foreign service is professionalized enough and whether too many ambassadorial appointments are going to outsiders who do not have "ambassadorial temperament." When we hear this argument, we should remember that making reasonable room for outsiders is necessary if we are to have room for the Moynihans, and that having one Moynihan around at a crucial foreign policy–making juncture makes it worthwhile to put up with entire troops of lesser nonprofessionals in the ambassadorial ranks.

NOTES

1. Elmer Plischke, *U.S. Diplomats and Their Missions: A Profile of Diplomatic Emissaries Since 1978* (New York: Praeger, 1974), 188–89.

2. Ibid., 200–201.

3. Norman D. Palmer, *The United States and India: The Dimensions of Influence* (Washington, D.C.: American Enterprise Institute, 1975), 74.

4. See, for example, his own account: Daniel P. Moynihan (with Suzanne Weaver), *A Dangerous Place* (Boston: Little, Brown, and Company, 1978).

CHAPTER NINE

A RENAISSANCE MAN IN THE SENATE

MICHAEL BARONE

"The State as a Work of Art" Jacob Burckhardt entitled the first chapter of his book on the Renaissance, describing the despots of the thirteenth and fourteenth centuries, the leaders of the republics of Florence and Venice, the Borgia and della Rovere popes who unleashed violence on Italy: each produced a "State as the outcome of reflection and calculation."[1] This chapter could be entitled "The Senate Career as a Work of Art." For when Daniel Patrick Moynihan became a senator in January 1977, he, like Burckhardt's Italians, was entering an almost wholly changed political arena, and like Burckhardt's princes and condottieri, he proceeded through reflection and calculation to make a Senate career congruent with the preoccupations of his mind and quite unlike any other that has been seen for a very long time.

Moynihan has said that he had no thought of running for the Senate before he resigned as ambassador to the UN. He had run for office once before, for president of the city council in New York in 1965, and lost. As a cabinet or sub-cabinet officer in four administrations, two of each party, he had dealt with the Senate, most frustratingly when his Family Assistance Plan died in the Senate Finance Committee. But he had not thought to run for the Senate, though others had urged him to, when he felt obliged to resign as ambassador to the UN in January 1976. His immediate obligation was to return to Harvard. The day his resignation was effective he began campaigning for Henry Jackson for president. Jackson won the New York primary in March 1976, and some New Yorkers urged Moynihan to run for the Senate. They thought that his stirring defense of Israel and opposition to the declaration that Zionism was racism would appeal to Jewish voters, who made up upwards of one-third of New York's Democratic primary electorate.

As it happened, Moynihan was a registered Democrat in New York—not in New York City, but in Delaware County, the location of his farm at Pindars Corners, where he had signed up to vote against West Davenport Town Supervisor Elmer Moore, who had ordered some oak trees alongside the road to be cut down. In June 1976 he declared for the Senate. In the September Democratic primary he barely won, by fewer than 10,000 votes, with 36 percent of the vote, to 35 percent for Bella Abzug. Two other similarly leftish candidates, Ramsey Clark and Paul O'Dwyer, got 10 percent and 9 percent. If they had not run, Moynihan probably would have lost. In the general election he faced the gentlemanly incumbent James Buckley, who had won the seat with a plurality six years before. In 1976 Buckley had to run with the handicap of the association of the Republican Party, which opposed aid to New York City. Moynihan won a solid victory, 56 percent to 44 percent. Since New York began electing U.S. senators in 1914, no Democratic incumbent has been defeated for reelection. (Royal Copeland died in 1938, James Mead ran for governor in 1946, Robert Wagner resigned in 1949, Herbert Lehman retired in 1956, and Robert Kennedy was assassinated in 1968.) Before Moynihan, at age forty-nine, was the prospect of six years and quite likely many more in the Senate.

Harry McPherson, writing about the Senate of the 1950s, described a Senate dominated by "whales" and populated otherwise by "minnows."[2] But the Senate in which Daniel Patrick Moynihan took his seat was quite another place. The three senators after whom the three Senate office buildings were named had all died—Richard Russell in 1971, Everett Dirksen in 1969, Philip Hart in 1976. Sam Ervin had retired in 1974, and William Fulbright was defeated that year. Hubert Humphrey was battling the cancer that killed him in 1978, and his old adversary James Eastland would retire that year. Lyndon Johnson and Robert Taft were long gone. Mike Mansfield had retired, and the new majority leader, Robert Byrd, was regarded as a technician, in an office that carries none of the great powers appertaining to the Speaker of the House. Fully eighteen of the one hundred senators in January 1977 had just been elected for the first time, the largest number since 1958. CBS News had to rent the large room in the Sheraton

Carlton Hotel and repaint it for its "Meet the Senators" program. This was a heavily Democratic Senate, but a Senate without driving Democratic leaders and a Senate that knew little or nothing about its new Democratic president. It was a Senate in which political and policy entrepreneurs could articulate their ideas and advance their causes: not a bad place for a Renaissance man.

"In this Senate, you do your work in committees, not on the floor," Moynihan has said.[3] And so Moynihan's first and perhaps most important decisions were what committees to serve on. He had confronted the question in a debate in the 1976 primary, unsure at first how to answer. His opponents gave predictable answers: labor, said one, because that is where the great urban-aid programs are drawn up; foreign relations, said another, the forum for the great debates on the Vietnam War; another said judiciary, which handled civil rights. Moynihan's answer: "Finance. Because that's where the money is."[4]

Actually, it was the Banking Committee that handled aid to New York City, the great local issue of the day. But in the longer run, Finance, which has jurisdiction over taxes, Social Security, and Medicare, does far more to channel the vast flows of money through the government and through society; and Moynihan went on Finance, the first New York Democrat to serve on the committee since Daniel S. Dickinson in the 1840s and 1850s. Only four years before, in *The Politics of a Guaranteed Income*, Moynihan had written, "The Finance Committee was rarely a positive influence, and now, under the leadership of Russell B. Long of Louisiana, was even less so. . . . [It] had never acquired the individual and group discipline and work habits necessary to mastering a new and difficult subject."[5] But Long was not a vindictive man: he gave Moynihan the chairmanship of the welfare subcommittee and supported an amendment channeling hundreds of millions to New York's welfare program. This was also the beginning of Moynihan's yearly series of reports on New York State and the Federal Fisc, of which the twenty-first is due in July 1998. Characteristically, Moynihan was searching for and lighting upon the few bits of data that reveal an important truth. "As a new Senator I set out to make the case that we were entitled to more federal aid than we were getting, in the sense that we sent much more money to Washington than we got back. This was not clear at the time. Official figures credited us with half the interest on the federal debt, half also of foreign aid outlays; all an artifact of the clearing house banks in Manhattan. After a while we got it straight," and showed that New York has one of the lowest "per capita balance of payments" of the states—information that Moynihan has deployed on dozens of amendments and formula fights.[6]

Moynihan's other committee was Environment and Public Works—an even unlikelier choice, it seemed, for a New Yorker. Yet, it tracked with his long-standing interest in transportation, going back to his work for Governor Averell Harriman in the 1950s, when the New York Thruway was opened, and to his 1950s studies on automobile traffic deaths. It is worth remembering that Moynihan is officially an upstater, not a city resident; if he knows every one of New York's sixty-two county courthouses, he also knows that five are in New York City, four are in suburbs, and fifty-three are upstate. His first project on Energy, with chairman Scoop Jackson's help, was getting the federal government to buy the West Valley nuclear plant in Cattaraugus, which was overstocked with nuclear waste; it was one of the last bills signed by President Carter, in October 1980.

Moynihan did not get a seat on Foreign Relations until 1987; but in the 1970s he made himself a force on foreign affairs. He worked with Scoop Jackson to oppose Jimmy Carter's nomination of Paul Warnke as arms control negotiator, and opposed the SALT II Treaty, which was never ratified by the Senate. But he was an original thinker tied to no particular camp. At a time when most politicians were still arguing about the Vietnam War, Moynihan called it a regrettable mistake, but said little more about it and moved on to other things. One was the assertion of America's moral superiority over tyrannies, at the UN and then in the Senate; the world, he insisted, was "a dangerous place."

Earlier than most others to sense the perils of détente, Moynihan was earlier than almost anyone else to sense the weaknesses of our great adversary. With the help of service on another committee, the Select Committee on Intelligence, starting in 1979, "I had quite changed my mind. I had grown convinced that the danger from the Soviet Union would come not from its expansion, but its disintegration. Watching the economy decline, seeing the ethnic tensions rise, I came to the judgment . . . that the Soviet Union was about to break up."[7] So he wrote in *Newsweek* in 1979; on the Senate floor on the tenth day of the 1980s, he predicted, "The defining event of the decade might well be the break-up of the Soviet Empire."[8] Moynihan was one of only two major public figures—the other was President Ronald Reagan—who so predicted. (Is it only a coincidence that both are of Irish descent?) When Jimmy Carter was declaring that he had first had his eyes opened to the peril of Soviet power, Moynihan had already decided that the Soviet empire was on the verge of falling.

So Moynihan began voting with the foreign policy doves, but for different reasons: They believed that the Soviet Union was dangerous but not evil, that we should mollify it and try to downsize both sides' military forces; Moynihan believed that the Soviet Union was evil but not dangerous, and so the defense buildup of the 1980s was largely unnecessary. In practical politics, this strengthened his position in 1981 and 1982, when politically he was in great peril from both left and right. The left still regretted his 1976 primary victory, and hoped to challenge him in the 1982 primary; the right, encouraged by Ronald Reagan's election as president and Alfonse D'Amato's election to replace Jacob Javits in the Senate, hoped that a Republican could beat him in the general election. Serious challengers were not lacking: Someone on the left might have run in the primary, the Liberal Party was talking about endorsing someone else, and Buffalo-area Congressman Jack Kemp, fresh from seeing his Kemp-Roth tax cut passed into law, was being urged to run in the general. But Moynihan's support of Democratic positions on issues from defense policy to the Equal Rights Amendment removed the threat of a challenge in the Democratic primary. As for the Republicans, Moynihan watched as Westchester Congressman Bruce Caputo geared up to run; then in March 1982 it was revealed that Caputo had falsified his military record. He was out of the race, no serious competitor emerged, and Moynihan was reelected 65 to 34 percent, even as Mario Cuomo beat Lewis Lehrman by the very narrow margin of 51 to 47 percent.

Moynihan had entered a heavily Democratic Senate, probably assuming as everyone else did that the Democrats would keep the majority they had held since the election of 1954. But in 1980 Republicans won control of the Senate, and Moynihan was now in the minority. Nevertheless, he managed to exert great influence. In the spring of 1981, when the Reagan administration proposed cutting future Social Security benefits, Moynihan protested vehemently, and he strode forward with a resolution denouncing any benefit cuts, which was beaten only by a 49-to-48 vote; the Senate promptly adopted a resolution by Bob Dole, which said pretty much the same thing, by 96 to 0. From then on, with the exception of the changes recommended by the bipartisan Greenspan Commission in 1983, Social Security remained untouchable—and a great Democratic political issue—into the 1990s. But this was not without a cost, which Moynihan was among the first to recognize. The architect of Reagan's economic program, Budget Director David Stockman, had once roomed in the Moynihans' house in Cambridge, and Moynihan had noticed how he had moved from one enthusiasm to the other. By 1982, with the Reagan tax cuts passed and previously unthinkably large budget deficits emerging, Moynihan recognized the design behind them: that Stockman and Reagan were hoping to squeeze every existing and potential government program except Social Security and defense and that, in fact, they would have great success in doing so.

How did Moynihan do his work? Not by conferring with fellow members of a Senate club in a capital hideaway with bourbon and branch late in the afternoon; that was not how business was done in the new Senate he entered in 1977. Nor by following detailed memos and reading talking papers prepared by policy entrepreneurs on his staff; many senators are staff-driven, but not this one. Moynihan's staff has been a distinguished one, and the list of alumni is illustrious. They included in the Clinton administration the president's press secretary, the State Department's chief of protocol, the ambassador to Croatia, the director of the Office of Management and Budget. To the list can be added an OMB director and assistant secretary of state in the Reagan administration, an assistant secretary of state and vice president's chief of staff in the Bush administration, and, from Buffalo, the host of *Meet the Press*.

Moynihan is not much for staff meetings; he likes to deal with issues and staffers when he wants to, not the other way around. With Moynihan it is quite clear that it is the senator who has set the priorities, made the decisions, written the prose: His work has an unmistakable imprint. For research he, of course, uses the Library of Congress, whose staff members must be delighted to confront the latest request for arcane information: the details, please, of the 1850s legislation to sell the state of New York to the New York Central Railroad, or the diaries, unconsulted perhaps for years, of Secretary of State (and upstate New Yorker) Robert Lansing. Each summer he returns to his home in Pindars Corners, walks a quarter-mile each morning to his farmhouse, and writes another of his books, on whatever subject has caught his fancy, taking a look at the long growth of society and fastening on the one revealing incident, the one perfectly relevant text which casts old things in new light and shows the way to the future. Only in the afternoon, after lunch and a nap, does he take time to read the day's *New York Times*.

Moynihan's chief political aide has been his wife, Elizabeth Moynihan, a Renaissance woman who combines a fine political intelligence with a scholar's knowledge of the Mughal gardens of India, an interest she began when he was ambassador and which she has continued by excavating and documenting her very own garden. She managed his 1976, 1982, and 1988 campaigns with great success; he won in 1988 by 67 to 31 percent, carrying every county but one. Among senators, Moynihan has formed some close friendships, usually with colleagues on committees, but he is also capable of taking umbrage and of silently enduring what he considers political posturing, slipperiness, unsteadiness, and untruths.

Sometimes he is not so silent, especially when he feels he has been lied to by an officer of the executive branch. In April 1984, he resigned as vice chair of the Intelligence Committee because he felt that it had not been properly informed of the CIA's mining of Nicaraguan harbors and charged that CIA Director Bill Casey "was running a disinformation operation against our committee." Two weeks later Casey apologized and Moynihan was persuaded to rejoin the committee. But Moynihan's distrust of the secret agency continued; he has noted that as recently as 1986 the CIA said that East Germany had a higher per capita income than West Germany. By the late 1980s, he was calling for abolition of the agency; in the 1990s, he caused the creation of a special commission on government secrecy.

Through all this preoccupation with international issues Moynihan never forgot that he represented New York. He strongly backed the Free Trade Agreement with Canada, noting that Buffalo is only two hours' drive from Toronto and that Montreal is less than an hour from Plattsburgh.[9] Later, he opposed the North American Free Trade Agreement with Mexico, charging that it has a "Leninist" regime.[10] In 1985, tax reform became a major issue; the Reagan administration and leading members of both parties in Congress sought to eliminate tax preferences and lower tax rates. Moynihan focused on maintaining the deductibility of state and local taxes. It was obviously in the interests of New York voters, whose state and local taxes, and therefore deductions, were the largest in the nation. But more than that, Moynihan insisted, it was a constitutional issue: without deductibility, the federal government would be taxing the revenues of the states. It became obvious that Moynihan's vote on the Finance Committee could not be had without deductibility; so visible did he make the issue in New York that a Long Island Republican on the House Ways and Means Committee told Chairman Dan Rostenkowski that he would support almost any bill as long as it kept state and local tax deductibility. Tax reform passed, with the New Yorkers' votes—and with deductibility.

It was conventional wisdom when Moynihan entered the Senate that he was an idealist and controversialist, a theory-bound professor who enjoyed argument and relished grand gestures in defeat. There is some truth to this, perhaps. But Senator Moynihan has also been a skillful legislative politician, capable of building a consensus around ideas, marshaling support in committee, assembling a coalition, seizing the right moment to take a measure to the floor. So it went on the Welfare Reform Act of 1988 and on the Intermodal Surface Transportation and Efficiency Act of 1991, generally known as ISTEA.

On welfare Moynihan took the occasion of the Godkin Lecture in 1985 to address the issue he had first looked at in the report *The Negro Family* twenty years before. What had happened was that things had gotten much worse. Fatherlessness among African Americans had grown much more common, and welfare rolls had vastly increased. This lecture was published as *Family and Nation*: "We have eliminated poverty for the elderly, only to see it burgeon for children."[11] Moynihan worked to build a consensus for what became the Welfare Reform Act of 1988, which for the first time recognized a father's responsibility to support his children and a mother's responsibility to work; it provided for strict child-support enforcement and encouraged the states to develop workfare programs while providing training, residual aid, and Medicaid for those enrolled.

Moynihan had been thinking about transportation for even longer than welfare. In the 1950s, he was writing about auto safety, years before Ralph Nader; in 1960, he wrote a long critical article about the interstate highway system established by the Federal-Aid Highway Act of 1956. By the early 1990s, he was perfectly positioned to act: He was chair of the subcommittee with jurisdiction over transportation programs, the chair of the full committee was elderly and comparatively inactive, and the highway bill was coming up for reauthorization. Moynihan worked to have the committee develop the group discipline and work habits necessary to master the subject that he had found lacking in the Finance Committee of the early 1970s. The result was the Intermodal Surface Transportation and Efficiency Act, which encouraged states to use federal monies not only on limited-access highways but also on other modes of transportation, including even the Moynihan pet project of maglev (magnetic levitation trains); it also provided for the reimbursement of New York State for the thruway built almost forty years before. It is a fine example of the Renaissance man as legislator.

The Welfare Reform Act of 1988 and ISTEA were passed by a Democratic Congress and signed by a Republican president. In 1992, a Democratic president was elected, and Moynihan succeeded Lloyd Bentsen as chair of the Finance Committee. But presidents and legislators of the same party do not always get along, and it can be argued that there was more tension and distrust between Moynihan and many (though not all) in the Carter and Clinton administrations than between him and many (though again not all) in the Reagan and Bush administrations. It began unhappily with an anonymous Clinton staffer quoted in *Time*, on Moynihan: "He's not one of us. He can't control Finance like Bentsen did. He's cantankerous, but . . . we'll roll right over him if we have to."[12] Then, in her first appearance before the Finance Committee, Health and Human Services Secretary Donna Shalala was upbraided by Moynihan for mentioning welfare reform only in passing.[13] Moynihan did steer the Clinton budget and tax package through the Senate, where it passed by one vote, the vote of Bob Kerrey, committed during a phone conversation with Pat and Liz Moynihan. But the Clinton administration did not follow Moynihan's advice to pass welfare reform and to proceed incrementally on health care finance reform.

That decision has affected mightily the course of the Clinton presidency, the Democratic Party, and public policy. If the course Moynihan urged had been taken, it is likely that the Democratic 103d Congress might have passed a moderate welfare reform, building on Moynihan's 1988 act, plus a moderate incremental health care bill, like the one eventually passed in August 1996. With this record, the Democrats might well have held control of Congress in the 1994 elections and again in 1996. Instead, Republicans won control of Congress and passed a welfare-reform bill ending the federal entitlement to welfare created in the Social Security Act of 1935. Moynihan denounced this in the strongest terms and said that it would put hundreds of thousands of children at grave risk. But President Clinton signed it into law in the weeks before the 1996 Democratic National Convention; if it had come up fourteen weeks after the election rather than fourteen weeks before, Moynihan said, he would have vetoed it.

Moynihan won reelection in 1994, but by the reduced margin of 55 to 42 percent, carrying New York City heavily, but running only about even in the suburban counties and upstate. He was now in the minority again, but remained a powerful and unmanipulable voice, as his former critics in the White House found out once more when he was the first Democratic senator to call for an independent counsel to investigate the Whitewater and Travelgate scandals. He looked forward with relish to the reauthorization of ISTEA, even as he worked with his successor as finance chair, William Roth, to set up the Boskin Commission to assess the consumer price index and then call for a revision of the CPI as one way to move toward a balanced budget and preserve some ability by the federal government to meet new needs and maintain current programs. Then, on the day before St. Patrick's Day in 1998, he presented a plan to reform Social Security by lowering the payroll tax by 2 percent, allowing workers to put that 2 percent in private investment accounts, raising the income on which payroll tax is levied, and adding state and local government employees. Social Security must be reformed, he said, lest it one day be abolished, as federal entitlement to welfare was in August 1996. Moynihan's proposal, politicians of both parties said, made it much more likely that reform would come. And he held hearings on that usually hush-hush subject, government secrecy. He sees secrecy as a form of regulation, one that, while often not successful in hiding things from the public, often serves to reduce rather than increase understanding by those in government.

While he and others grappled with front-page issues, Moynihan has set himself up as a one-man Senate to preserve and nurture islands of intellectual and artistic excellence in our society. (It has caught his attention that those islands are especially numerous in New York.) One of the prerogatives of a senator is the selection of federal judges, and no other state's federal bench is as important as New York's. From 1977, when Moynihan first set up a panel of experts to select top-flight judges, he has agreed with his Republican colleagues Jacob Javits and Alfonse D'Amato that the senator whose party holds the White House will choose three of every four judges and the other senator will choose the fourth. He is especially concerned about maintaining the very high level of trial judges in the Southern District of New York, which sits in lower Manhattan. "I want every serious lawyer who wants to litigate a difficult case to bring that case in the Southern District of New York," he has said, and to a very considerable extent they do. While California has a federal bench overloaded with ideologues of left and right and the federal bench in Chicago has more than its share of political appointees, the federal bench in New York is by general consent excellent—a worthy successor to the tradition set by judges like Learned Hand and Simon Rifkind and Edward Weinfeld.

Moynihan has also worked to nurture other great institutions. In return for his support of the Clinton tax increase of 1993, he insisted on maintaining the deductibility of gifts of appreciated property to nonprofit institutions such as universities and museums. Arguments of tax equity say that such incentives are inefficient. But Moynihan saw that they are a vital ingredient of the unplanned flowering of learning and culture in a huge and diverse society. In the great health care debate of 1993 and 1994, Moynihan almost alone was vitally concerned with maintaining the place of teaching hospitals, which have institutionalized so much learning and contributed so much original research to our society. It would be a "sin against the Holy Ghost," he insisted, to allow these institutions to wither, a crime akin to the burning of the library of Alexandria. Others argued that teaching hospitals were in the short run expensive or inefficient; Moynihan looked to the very long run and insisted they were essential.

And he looked at buildings. Franklin Roosevelt superintended the design of the Jefferson Memorial, which every president sees every day across the lawn of the White House; but it is hard to think of any other political officeholder who has given much thought to how buildings look and cities work. Moynihan has. During the Kennedy administration, when the new Labor Department building was being planned, he recommended the redevelopment of Pennsylvania Avenue, which now has been splendidly accomplished, with the Moynihans ensconced in an apartment across the avenue from the National Archives. He is the father of the Thurgood Marshall Judiciary Building, which speaks respectfully but attractively to Union Station next door. He caused a new color to be developed, an almost rusty red, for the Hell Gate railroad bridge, the one you see from the Triborough (at whose dedication in 1936 Moynihan was present), which had not been painted for fifty-some years. His latest project is to convert New York's old Beaux Arts Post Office into a new Pennsylvania Station: The funds are tucked into some transportation bill.

But it is not surprising that a man who has made his Senate career a work of art has also sponsored works of art in his Senate career. Daniel Patrick Moynihan is the nation's best thinker among politicians since Lincoln and its best politician among thinkers since Jefferson. Like the state of Burckhardt's Renaissance Italians, the Senate career of this Renaissance man from Hell's Kitchen and Pindars Corners has been the outcome of reflection and calculation—the disciplined product of an original thinker whose ideas dazzle and a political operator whose skills are hidden like strong walls overpainted with a Renaissance fresco.

NOTES

1. Jacob Burckhardt, *The Civilization of the Renaissance in Italy* (New York: Harper, 1958), vol. 1, 22.

2. Harry McPherson, *A Political Education* (Boston: Houghton Mifflin, 1988), 48–49.

3. Daniel Patrick Moynihan, interview with the author, 5 February 1997.

4. Ibid.

5. Daniel P. Moynihan, *The Politics of a Guaranteed Income* (New York: Random House, 1973), 455.

6. See, for example, Daniel Patrick Moynihan, introduction to *NY State and the Federal Fisc: XVII/ Fiscal Year 1992* (29 June 1993), x–xi.

7. Daniel Patrick Moynihan, *Pandaemonium* (New York: Oxford University Press, 1993), 41.

8. Ibid., 42.

9. Daniel P. Moynihan, interview.

10. Daniel P. Moynihan, "Free Trade with an Unfree Society," *National Interest* (summer 1995).

11. Daniel P. Moynihan, *Family and Nation* (New York: Harcourt Brace Jovanovich, 1986).

12. Quoted in Michael Barone and Grant Ujifusa, *The Almanac of American Politics 1994* (Washington, D.C.: National Journal, 1993), 860.

13. Ibid., 861.

CHAPTER TEN

THE THIRD BRANCH

RICHARD K. EATON

Much of what has come to be Senator Moynihan's work in the Congress reflects those matters that were his interests, some might say his preoccupations, prior to his arrival in the Senate. Family policy, traffic safety, public architecture—each of these had found its place in Senator Moynihan's earlier careers as professor of government or public servant, often in both.

PROSECUTORS AND JUDGES

But what has become one of the most sustained efforts of his Senate career can be traced to lunch on 14 January 1977—after the senator had been sworn in for his first term, but six days before Jimmy Carter's inauguration. The senator's lunchtime companion was Leonard Garment, a distinguished lawyer and longtime friend, and by the time coffee was poured, Senator Moynihan had decided, with Len's help, that New York's incumbent U.S. attorneys should be invited to serve out their full four-year terms and that a bipartisan panel should screen candidates on the basis of merit for vacancies on the U.S. District Court and for future U.S. attorney vacancies.

These decisions were, in fact, revolutionary—but that they were requires some explanation. By long tradition, a state's senior senator, belonging to the same political party as an incoming president, would recommend the replacement of all incumbent U.S. attorneys of the party previously in office. By equally long-established tradition, the incoming president would ask for the incumbents' resignations and appoint those recommended by the senior senator of his party.

In like manner, it was—and is—the prerogative of that senator to propose the names of federal district court judges who are then almost invariably nominated. This tradition of senatorial courtesy is as old as the Constitution and has resulted in a certain amount of contention. In 1881, both New York senators resigned after President Garfield appointed a collector for the Port of New York who was not to Senator Roscoe Conkling's liking. But Senator Moynihan knew that deciding who should prosecute federal crimes and who should make up the third branch of the national government were matters of large and serious import. And, as a result of his election coinciding with a change in the party controlling the White House, Senator Moynihan was in a position to do something about it. He announced his plans soon thereafter, to the consternation of some party regulars[1] but to near-universal praise elsewhere. The *New York Times* editorialized:

> In his first major act, Senator Moynihan broke with crusty tradition, enraged some of his warmest political supporters and set a worthy precedent for his colleagues in the Congress. He recommended that the Carter administration retain [the then-incumbent Republican U.S. attorneys] for the Eastern, Southern, and Northern Districts of New York. . . . It is a courageous break with hoary political practice.[2]

In the long history of the United States, as far as the historian of the Senate could discover, this was the first time U.S. attorneys were not changed with a change of administration and party.[3] Senator Moynihan also broke with tradition by inviting his then-colleague, Senator Jacob Javits, to recommend a candidate for every fourth district court opening, saying, "it seemed to me that no political party should have a monopoly on judicial appointments such that the party out of power might come to believe that the judiciary's impartiality is compromised."[4] After President Reagan's election, Senator Alfonse D'Amato decided to continue this precedent with regard to both U.S. attorneys and district judges, and with President Clinton's election the system has continued.[5]

Indeed, following President Clinton's election, Southern District U.S. Attorney Otto Obermaier told reporters that he expected to stay until the end of his term because that was the "tradition"[6] in New York. Senator Moynihan was extraordinarily pleased by this comment because it demonstrated that what had been abnormal in 1977 was now the norm. And he had made it the norm.

These new traditions have by all accounts been successful. With his panel's help Senator Moynihan has now proposed thirty district court judges who have been confirmed by the Senate, and seven U.S. attorneys (Table 10.1). And there are more to come. The panel itself is now twenty years old and during its lifetime has had members who are lawyers from big and small firms, academics, businessmen and businesswomen, and even two reporters (Table 10.2). They have made their selections on merit and with predictable results. New York University Law School Professor Stephen Gillers has written:

> In most places, lawyers who count, who want to be judges become politically active. In New York, lawyers who want to be Federal trial judges complete a twelve-page questionnaire containing thirty-seven questions. An eleven-member panel screens applicants and recommends nominees. . . .
>
> Who have been Moynihan's nominees? . . . They are a first-rate group, as might be expected from the process that produced them.[7]

Or, as Paul Hoffman has written, the Moynihan Committee has

> tabbed an impressive array of legal talent for the bench—from both large and small firms, government and academe. Since much of America's commercial litigation is argued in New York's Southern District, the panel's action had national implications.[8]

Table 10.1 Recommendations of Senator Daniel Patrick Moynihan to Federal District Court Judgeships

	District	Term Began
Eugene H. Nickerson	Eastern	1977
Charles P. Sifton	Eastern	1977
Pierre N. Laval	Southern	1977
Leonard B. Sand	Southern	1978
Mary Johnson Lowe	Southern	1978
Abraham D. Sofaer	Southern	1979
Neal P. McCurn	Northern	1979
John E. Sprizzo	Southern	1981

Table 10.1 (*continued*)

	District	Term Began
Israel Leo Glasser	Eastern	1981
William Hellerstein	Southern	Recommended 1984[1]
Edward R. Korman	Eastern	1985
Miriam Goldman Cedarbaum	Southern	1986
Peter Strauss	Southern	Recommended 1987[2]
Robert P. Patterson Jr.	Southern	1988
John Carro	Southern	Recommended 1989[3]
John S. Martin Jr.	Southern	1990
Sonia Sotomayor	Southern	1992
David G. Trager	Eastern	1993
Thomas M. Whalen III	Northern	Recommended 1993[4]
Deborah A. Batts	Southern	1994
Denise Cote	Southern	1994
Harold Baer Jr.	Southern	1994
Denny Chin	Southern	1994
Lewis A. Kaplan	Southern	1994
John G. Koeltl	Southern	1994
Barrington D. Parker Jr.	Southern	1994
Rosemary S. Pooler	Northern	1994
Shira A. Scheindlin	Southern	1994
Frederic Block	Eastern	1994
John Gleeson	Eastern	1994
Allyne R. Ross	Eastern	1994
Clarence Sundram	Northern	Recommended 1995[5]
Barbara S. Jones	Southern	1995
Jed S. Rakoff	Southern	1996
Nina Gershon	Eastern	1996

[1]Recommendation never acted upon by Justice Department. Hellerstein was, at the time of the senator's recommendation, the attorney-in-charge, Criminal Bureau of the Legal Aid Society. Hellerstein withdrew his name in 1985. It is noteworthy that in July 1993, Hellerstein, then a professor at Brooklyn Law School, was one of six candidates nominated by the State Commission on Judicial Nomination for a vacancy on the New York Court of Appeals, the state's highest court.

[2]Recommendation never acted upon by Justice Department. Strauss was, at the time of the senator's recommendation, a member of the faculty of the Columbia University School of Law. Strauss withdrew his name in 1987.

[3]Recommendation never acted upon by Justice Department. Carro was, at the time of the senator's recommendation, a justice of the Appellate Division of the Supreme Court of the State of New York. Judge Carro withdrew his name in January 1991.

[4]Recommendation never acted upon by the Justice Department. Whalen was, at the time of the senator's recommendation, the mayor of Albany, New York. Mayor Whalen withdrew his name in December 1994.

[5]Sundram is chair of the New York State Commission on Quality of Care for the Mentally Disabled. In September 1995, President Clinton sent his nomination to the U.S. Senate. His nomination was not acted upon by the 104th Congress. In January 1997, President Clinton again nominated Sundram.

Table 10.1 U.S. Attorney Recommendations by Senator Daniel Patrick Moynihan (*continued*)

	District	Term Began
George B. Lowe	Northern	1978
Edward R. Korman	Eastern	1978
John S. Martin Jr.	Southern	1980
Leslie G. Foschio	Western	Nominated by President Carter on July 20, 1980; not acted upon by Senate Judiciary Committee before adjournment of Ninety-sixth Congress.
Patrick Henry NeMoyer	Western	1993
Zachary W. Carter	Eastern	1993
Mary Jo White	Southern	1993
Thomas J. Maroney	Northern	1993

Table 10.2 Senator Daniel Patrick Moynihan's Committee on Judicial and U.S. Attorney Appointments

Current Members	Former Members
Edith Evans Asbury	Honorable Lawrence H. Cooke
Richard K. Eaton, Chairman	Honorable Charles Desmond (deceased)
Carolyn Gentile	Leonard Garment
Judah Gribetz	Suzanne Garment
Kenneth Gross	Bernard R. Gifford
David L. Hoffberg	Nathan Glazer
Robert Katzmann	Charles V. Hamilton
Joel W. Motley	Robert Kasanof (deceased)
Herbert Rubin	Diane Ravitch
Betsy Seidman	Chester Straub
John Trubin	James Q. Wilson

JURISDICTION STRIPPING

So, I think, began Senator Moynihan's interest in the courts and their deliberations. His interest has not ended with prosecutors and judges. He has become something of a protector of what Alexander Hamilton called the "least dangerous branch" because he knows that by custom it is unable to speak for itself.

The senator has seen to it that the courts, and those who administer them, are properly housed both here in Washington and in New York, and he has not been free of criticism for having done so. He has been sympathetic to the judges' concerns about their pay. And he has tried to do something of much greater importance: He has defended the ability of the courts to do their work—which is to say, to hear cases and to do so in an independent fashion.

In some ways I think that Senator Moynihan's interest in and deep respect for the courts result from his being—in the curious term used by members of the bar—a nonlawyer. He brings to his reading of cases—and he does read cases—a fresh understanding, and he carries the professor of government's reverence for the Constitution with him always.

And the third branch has been the beneficiary. In the late 1970s and early 1980s, it became popular for members of Congress who disagreed with various federal court rulings to seek to prevent future onerous decisions by denying the courts the power to decide certain types of cases.[9] Most commonly these cases dealt with school busing, school prayer, and abortion. These proposals became known as jurisdiction strippers. In the Ninety-seventh Congress alone, over thirty of these bills were introduced.[10] Between 1979 and 1984, a majority of the Senate voted eight times to approve one or another of them. Senator Moynihan did not vote with the majority on these occasions, and indeed, he regularly participated in the extended debates that stopped them from becoming law.

While these filibusters served this purpose, they also served as some of the few occasions in modern times where something like an actual debate has been heard on the Senate floor. As C-SPAN viewers know, most of what goes on in the Senate is the reading of speeches—set pieces that can be used to great effect—as with Senator Bill Bradley's speeches on race and race relations. But real debate is seldom heard. Consideration of jurisdiction-stripping measures, though, often became a debate, with one side represented by such senators as Jesse Helms of North Carolina or Bennett Johnston of Louisiana asserting that the Supreme Court case of *Ex Parte McCardle*[11] surely stood for the proposition that the Congress had the power to restrict the Court's jurisdiction. And Senator Moynihan or Senator Lowell Weicker of Connecticut, representing the other side, would say that surely a clear reading of *McCardle* did not lead to the conclusion that the Supreme Court's jurisdiction could be restricted by Congress. And, of course, there was always the argument that even if Congress did have the power to restrict a court's jurisdiction, it was not necessarily a good idea to exercise that power. In all of this, Senator Moynihan's grasp of the issues and precedents equaled any on the floor.

One of these debates occurred on 20 September 1982. Senator Jesse Helms of North Carolina proposed an amendment that would have stripped the Supreme Court of its power to hear cases relating to voluntary school prayer. During the course of the debate Senator Moynihan said:

> If you can strip from the Supreme Court the right to hear one question, you can strip from it the right to hear any question. There is no right in the Constitution that would not be placed in jeopardy.
>
> The great fear of the Founding Fathers was that we should have a tyranny of the majority. They spoke over and over again of a tyranny of the majority and they devised the Court as the institution in which minority rights would be protected.
>
> Those rights are embodied in the Constitution and . . . as Justice Marshall [wrote], it is emphatically the province of the Court to declare what the law is. It is not for us to do. We may have our views, we make the laws, but we make them in the context of a higher law, the Constitution, and the Court compares.[12]

In time the enthusiasm for these jurisdiction-stripping measures waned, then in 1995 Senator Moynihan again found himself on the Senate floor trying to keep the Congress from stripping the courts of their jurisdiction. This time he lost.

HABEAS CORPUS

Since 1867, federal courts have had the power to review state criminal convictions. This review was conducted by means of a writ of habeas corpus—the Great Writ of English judges requiring the warden to produce the body of a prisoner. After months of consideration, last year as part of—but unrelated to—the antiterrorism bill, the Congress passed, and President Clinton signed, a measure that binds federal judges to state court rulings when determining the fairness of a criminal trial. Only when those findings are unreasonable or flatly contradict clearly stated Supreme Court rulings can the federal court overturn them. This notion troubled Senator Moynihan so profoundly that he was moved to say:

> If I had to choose between living in a country with habeas corpus but without free elections, or a country with free elections but without habeas corpus, I would choose habeas corpus every time.[13]

And at the conclusion of the debate, the man who had seen so many of these jurisdiction-stripping measures stated:

> Mr. President, we need to deal resolutely with terrorism. And we will. But if, in the guise of combating terrorism, we diminish the fundamental civil liberties that Americans have enjoyed for two centuries, then the terrorists will have won.[14]

Not bad for a nonlawyer. It should be noted that on 21 January 1997—some twenty years and a week after his lunch with Len Garment—Senator Moynihan introduced a first-day bill that would restore the Great Writ. Twenty years is a long time, but the true administration of justice is not a job for the short-winded.

NOTES

1. "Moynihan Backs 3 G.O.P. Officials," *New York Times*, 19 January 1977, A1.
2. Editorial, "Our Freshman's Splendid Debut," *New York Times*, 20 January 1977, A36.
3. Leonard Garment, *Report of the Committee on Judicial and United States Attorney Appointments 1977–1982*, 27 September 1982, 1.
4. "Sen. Moynihan to Resume Lead in Recommending Federal Judges and U.S. Attorneys," press release, 5 November 1992.
5. Ibid.
6. Ibid.
7. Steven Gillers, "Judgeships on the Merits," *The Nation* 229, no. 8 (1979): 242–43.
8. Paul Hoffman, *Lions of the Eighties: The Inside Story of the Powerhouse Law Firms* (Garden City, N.Y.: Doubleday & Company, 1982), 64.
9. See, e.g., Daniel Patrick Moynihan, "Constitutional Crisis," *The Catholic Lawyer* 27, no. 4 (1992): 271.
10. See, e.g., the following bills dealing with school busing: S. 1147, 97th Cong., 1st sess. (1981); S. 528, 97th Cong., 1st sess. (1981); H.R. 2047, 97th Cong., 1st sess. (1981); H.R. 761, 97th Cong., 1st sess. (1981).

11. *Ex Parte McCardle*, 74 U.S. (7 Wall.) 506 (1869). The Supreme Court upheld a law that repealed an earlier statute to the extent that the earlier one authorized appeals to the Supreme Court from denials of habeas corpus by circuit courts. Congress had sought to prevent such appeals in order to avert a Supreme Court ruling on the constitutionality of the Military Reconstruction Act, which placed ten defeated southern states under military rule. Congress feared that the Court would use the then-pending case of William H. McCardle as an occasion to strike down the act. McCardle was a southern newspaper editor who had been arrested on charges of disturbing the peace, inciting to insurrection and disorder, impeding reconstruction, and libel. Having been arrested and held by military order under the Military Reconstruction Act, McCardle was appealing a circuit court's denial of habeas corpus. When the Supreme Court finally decided the case, it declared that it would not inquire into the motives of Congress and that the Constitution expressly grants Congress the power to make exceptions to the Court's jurisdiction. It is worth noting that the case was decided prior to the adoption of the Fourteenth Amendment.

12. *Congressional Record*, 97th Cong., 2d sess., 20 September 1982, 128, no. 18.

13. *Congressional Record*, 104th Cong., 2d sess., 17 April 1996, 142, no. 49.

14. Ibid., S. 3441.

PART THREE

THE MAN

CHAPTER ELEVEN

WIT AND WISDOM

MOYNIHAN AND *MEET THE PRESS*

TIM RUSSERT

One of my first and most important realizations after arriving in Washington was just how much you could learn from Senator Moynihan.

A case in point.

The senator's administrative staff had sifted through hundreds of resumes from applicants interested in being the Moynihan office liaison to the Environment and Public Works Committee and the Intelligence Committee. We recommended the senator interview two distinguished men—Dr. Abe Shulsky and Dr. Jared Cohen.

We scheduled them for private appointments with Senator Moynihan. Unfortunately, when Dr. Shulsky entered the office he was introduced as the "candidate for the Environment and Public Works" position. Senator Moynihan promptly asked Dr. Shulsky the difference between fission and fusion. Shulsky gave a detailed explanation.

Moynihan opened the door and said "Hire the man!" "Senator," I stammered, "we made a mistake. Shulsky is the candidate for the Intelligence Committee slot."

He answered, "No matter. He got the answer right. No substitute for a good mind!"

And so it began. The world according to Moynihan.

Senator Daniel Patrick Moynihan celebrates his seventieth birthday the same year that *Meet the Press* marks its fiftieth anniversary. Senator Moynihan is a historic figure in the annals of *Meet the Press.* He has been a guest

Lawrence Spivak, left, moderator of *Meet the Press*, 12 December 1965, and Daniel Patrick Moynihan

Tim Russert, left, moderator of *Meet the Press*, 26 November 1995, and Daniel Patrick Moynihan

an extraordinary twenty-four times, and his appearances span thirty-one years. For more than three decades, he has played a central role in our nation's history and has been at center stage on *Meet the Press.*

1965 ON THE BLACK FAMILY

Mr. Spivak: One of the major conclusions you come to in your report is that the Negro family has deteriorated. How is that generalization justified in view of the great growth of the Negro middle class?

Mr. Moynihan: That is an important point. It seems to me that there are a great many Negro Americans, perhaps half the population which is securely in the middle class, doing very well, taking care of itself, needing no help from anybody, thank you very much. But the slums are also filling up with a lower-class people, unemployed, ill-educated, ill-housed, for whom the cycle of no jobs and bad education and bad housing just reproduces itself and takes its most poignant, personal form in the great tragedy of the family lives of these men and women and of their children.

1969 ON THE FAMILY ASSISTANCE PLAN

Mr. Spivak: Mr. Moynihan, how will the president's Family Assistance Plan help a city like New York City, for example, which is spending over $1.5 billion on welfare? Will it cut the welfare rolls of New York City; will it cut its welfare expenditures? Just how will it help?

Mr. Moynihan: Let me first say, when I was on *Meet the Press* four years ago, we were just beginning to see the emergence of this situation. There were about 420,000 people on welfare then. Today there are 1,050,000. It is this extraordinary, corrosive growth that has led the president to say: We can't just improve this system, just fix it up; we have got to get rid of it and replace it.

The emphasis on job training, the emphasis on day-care centers, day-care provisions for the first five years of life—the president is going to provide in this proposal 150,000 training slots, training opportunities for welfare mothers, and provision for 450,000 day-care opportunities to take care of their children while they are working. No mother with children under six would ever be required to do this, but she could if she wished. The point is we want to move people out of welfare, not to improve welfare. It has turned out to be destructive to the people, corrosive to the society. We want to get them into work, and the president has provided unprecedented amounts of money to do just this.

1971 ON J. EDGAR HOOVER

Mr. Moynihan: I think the FBI is endangering its essential role in this country by a very casual and clumsy attitude to[ward] such things as this. I think the Justice Department is not nearly as sensitive as it ought to be to the feeling in the country that civil liberties are not as respected as they ought be. I think that the sooner Mr. Hoover retires, the better the FBI will be. It has become a cankered bureaucracy preserving the unnecessary vanities of a man who has been too long in office. When I came to work with President Kennedy, among the first things I found was the FBI up in arms because of an article I had written for *The Reporter* about organized crime, saying that one of the things the FBI did was to stay away from organized crime, and my goodness, they swarmed all over the Labor Department and obviously expected Arthur Goldberg to fire me, because I had said something mildly unflattering about them. Well, Arthur Goldberg wasn't about to be pushed around by that, and they didn't know what to do once he didn't, but there has been too much of that.

1977 ON THE CARTER WHITE HOUSE

Mr. Emory: Senator, you have been critical of a number of the president's programs and timings of some others, like the delay in introducing welfare. As a result, there have been some leaks out of the White House, particularly on the staff side, to the effect that the president and his top advisers don't like you and resent you. What do you think of those criticisms?

Senator Moynihan: I think what the president thinks, who said the other day that if he finds the SOB who is responsible, he will find another job for him fast.

Mr. Emory: Has he fired him yet?

Senator Moynihan: He hasn't found him.

1986 ON IRAN-CONTRA

Mr. Hunt: Senator Moynihan, you were a longtime member of the Senate Intelligence Committee and, therefore, have intimate knowledge of the way the CIA functions. Is it conceivable to you that this operation could have taken place, the funneling of money to the Contras, without Director William Casey knowing about it?

Senator Moynihan: It is conceivable that a rogue National Security Council staff, avoiding the law, found itself in cahoots with agents inside the agency who helped it avoid the law. The law has been broken by people with no sense of their constitutional responsibility here, and we are going to find that these intrigues [are] everywhere. This you can have—you could see it coming as they began that secret move to overthrow the Nicaraguans without ever telling themselves even fully what they were doing.

1986 MOYNIHAN AND SENATOR PHIL GRAMM

Senator Gramm: To show you what miracles there are in Gramm-Rudman, we have on one side here one of the strongest supporters of national defense in the country and one of the weakest. And yet—

Senator Moynihan: Oh, wait, wait, wait. Come on, friend. Name a bill—name a bill.

Senator Gramm: And yet now, suddenly, we're having all of the Democrats who have not supported the president on defense, who are saying, My God, Gramm-Rudman is going to decimate defense. Well, it's not going to decimate defense. We're not going to have the across-the-board cuts; we're going to make hard choices, because we're not going to have any alternative.

Mr. Kalb: But Senator, are you going to allow—are you going to allow the president to have a 3 percent increase—

Senator Moynihan: Marvin, I'm not going to allow my voting record to be misrepresented. You're one year in the Senate, fella; you don't do that to another senator. I have voted with one exception for every defense appropriation bill since I've come to the Senate. And, this year, under Gramm-Rudman, for the first time in fifteen years, the dollar amount for defense spending is going down, first time in fifteen years, under your bill. I would not misrepresent you; you don't misrepresent me.

1988 ON THE UNITED NATIONS

Mr. Kaiser: Senator Moynihan, what about the UN's future? Does it have one?

Senator Moynihan: Well, if we pay our dues, it might have one.

1990 ON CARDINALS

Mr. Utley: You're being very diplomatic here, senator. Is the cardinal off base?

Senator Moynihan: Cardinals are never off base: I was taught that very early by the sisters. They are frequently ill-advised.

1993 ON PRESIDENT CLINTON

Mr. Russert: You just heard Treasury Secretary Bentsen say that there will be a spirit of cooperation. Let me talk to you about the *Time* magazine article, which will appear tomorrow, a top administration official saying that they are in fact going to roll over you, that you were for Bob Kerrey, not Bill Clinton, and that they can handle the Finance Committee without you.

Senator Moynihan: Oh, the president doesn't think that; I mean, he put me on his television advertisements in New York in the primary that won him the nomination. On the issue of Social Security flat tax, which would eliminate the Social Security trust fund, I said don't do that. And he won New York, and that's why he's president today.

1993 ON TAXES AND DEATH

Mr. Russert: Is the energy tax a fight until death, or are you willing to compromise a little bit with Senator Boren, modify it a bit—

Senator Moynihan: Fight until death over taxes? Oh no. Women, country, God, things like that. Taxes? No.

1993 TAXES (PART II)

Ms. Myers: Let's talk about the specifics of the differences between the House and Senate—

Senator Moynihan: Sure. Sure.

Ms. Myers:—deficit reduction packages. The big difference, really, is the energy tax. For weeks now, the BTU tax has been sitting there like a corpse in the living room. Everyone knows it's dead, but they're waiting for someone in a position of authority to make the pronouncement. Are you willing to say today that the BTU tax is dead?

Senator Moynihan: Mr. Rostenkowski, my colleague and friend and senior, has said that he could see a combination of a gasoline tax and maybe a utility tax, which is kind of a way of saying, yeah, would somebody call an undertaker, please?

Ms. Myers: So is it dead?

Senator Moynihan: You said it.

Ms. Myers: All right. But so you agreed, correct?

Senator Moynihan: Yes.

1994 ON NORTH KOREA

Mr. Russert: Some say that while we were talking about a potential summit and talking about potential sanctions, the North Koreans are buying time, winning time, and that by the next two years, they'll have ten nuclear weapons. One, should we continue to press for sanctions while there is talk of a summit? Two, should we be beefing up our military troops in Korea in the event of a war?

Senator Moynihan: Oh, no, neither. We should make clear to the North Koreans that they can—there's a reward for abiding by their treaties, and if they go ahead with what they have been doing, in defiance of the world and the clear understanding of what is going on, you bomb them.

Mr. Russert: You bomb them?

Senator Moynihan: Bomb them.

1995 ON DOLE AND D'AMATO

Mr. Russert: Senator Gregg, before we go, a parochial question: Will you help Bob Dole win the New Hampshire primary?

Senator Gregg: Well, I think Bob Dole is a great guy and a wonderful leader of the Senate. I haven't made a formal commitment to any of the candidates. We've got a real strong field out there, and New Hampshire is pretty exciting.

Mr. Russert: So you're not endorsing Bob Dole?

Senator Gregg: Not at this time.

Senator Moynihan: All right. I'll endorse Bob Dole in New Hampshire for the Republican nomination. That's all.

Mr. Russert: One last parochial question: Is Senator D'Amato, your colleague, really in love?

Senator Moynihan: Oh, yeah. Oh, yeah. I'm pretty old, but I can still recognize the signs.

1996 ON WELFARE REPEAL

Mr. Russert: Senator Moynihan, why did President Clinton sign the bill if he wants to change the bill?

Senator Moynihan: Why don't you get him on and ask him?

CONCLUSION

Senator Moynihan taught the nation and me that politics is much more than a competitive sport, that ideas do matter, that elections have consequences, and that it is your duty and your honor, if elected, to influence, shape, and make public policy. As it turns out, it's also a pretty good blueprint for re-election—and future appearances on *Meet the Press.*

CHAPTER TWELVE

A COLLEAGUE'S PERSPECTIVE

BILL BRADLEY

I served with Pat Moynihan for eighteen years. We are from neighboring states, and we are fellow Democrats with eclectic interests. In my first visit with him, I as a candidate and he as a newly elected senator, he told me that the most important accomplishment in his first term would be getting on the Senate Finance Committee, which confirmed my own hunch. After all, as he observed during a critical moment in a debate in the campaign of 1976, "that's where the money is."

My first major piece of Finance Committee activity was the Tokyo Round Multilateral Trade Talks. As I walked into the committee and took my place as the junior member, far at the end—even with a temporary desk—I listened to talk of antidumping, most favored nation status, subsidy codes, safeguards, countervailing duties, dispute settlements, and I understood absolutely nothing. I was totally bewildered. Senators who spoke did so with great knowledge and became giants in my mind. Pat Moynihan was comfortable with the arcane language of trade law and interspersed his comments with historical references to past trade talks, to the history of free trade, and to the advisability of free trade. Only with the passage of time and much hard work did I nod in agreement with what Ham Lewis, the Democratic whip in the 1930s, told Harry Truman in his first term: "Harry," he said, "the first six months you're here you'll wonder how the hell you got here. And after that, you'll wonder how the hell the rest of us got here." That assessment applied to most everyone I knew in the U.S. Senate with one very real exception, and that is Senator Moynihan. He has always remained a giant to me.

In a blurb for his book *Miles to Go,* I wrote, "To explore the lessons of the recent past with a colleague who has so consistently foreseen the near future is a journey full of revelation and insight. Pat Moynihan sees great truths where others are lost in a fog of politics, and he sees mothers and children, and people struggling for meaning in their lives, where others see only abstract policy choices. His contribution to our understanding of ourselves and our nation, in this book and others, is surpassed only by his dedication and achievement as a public servant."

He "has so consistently foreseen the near future." For example, he sensed that the internal contradictions of Marxism-Leninism were reaching a terminal phase and that the Cold War would soon be over.

He "sees great truths where others are lost in a fog of politics." In the Nixon administration, he made the point that the family is the bedrock of life and that the black family in America was in trouble. I was reminded of that anew as he and I flew with Senator Dole and several other senators to honor our former colleague on the Finance Committee, Senator Danforth, in St. Louis. In a conversation about the latest research on single parenthood, Senator Moynihan pointed out that in 1961, the year I left St. Louis to go to college in New Jersey, 13 percent of the children in St. Louis were born to single parents. In 1994, it was 67 percent of the children; 87 percent among African-American children. Recently, he again spoke the great truth when he looked at urban areas of violence and drugs and said that we are "defining deviancy down."

"He sees mothers and children, and people struggling for meaning in their lives, where others see only abstract policy choices." Welfare reform—Pat Moynihan would have no part of welfare reform that broke the solemn commitment of the federal government to poor children. He stood up and spoke, over and over again. He sought to dissuade the Democratic administration from making the decision that it will spend the next four years trying to make up for. Similar to good Democrats, he also believes that the Declaration of Independence is the primary document of our American government and that the national government is constituted to ensure life, liberty, and the pursuit of happiness for the greatest number of Americans.

PAT MOYNIHAN, THE SENATOR

Pat Moynihan understands two things about the Senate. First, success in the Senate is a function of substance, procedure, and personality, but substance is the most important, not only because when people of substance speak, other people listen, but also because when people of substance speak, often they control the debate. When that person of substance is also the chair, he or she controls the law. Second, Senator Moynihan understands that in the Senate the center is where the action is; extremists don't succeed. They give speeches, shouting from one corner of the chamber to the other corner of the chamber, but they don't write laws. The qualities of a legislator who wants to exercise power are the qualities Senator Moynihan has exhibited throughout his career: the ability to listen, to hear someone of a different point of view, to seek some common ground. His style is rooted in a rational appraisal of the circumstance needed to pass a law—to legislate.

Let me give you some snapshots of Senator Moynihan in the Senate.

Moynihan in Committee

As he says, that's where the work's done. That's where the substance is most important. That's where a loyal and excellent staff is critical. A set of hearings allows you to explore in a wide-ranging and open-ended way, not in a contrived or controlled way, an issue of public importance out of which information will be derived to write the best law.

He also knows that sometimes, in addition to substance, personality is important. Three examples follow. During the Russell Long chairmanship of the Finance Committee, Senator Moynihan and I often remarked that we would have done better on the Finance Committee during Senator Long's tenure if oil had been discovered off the coast of New Jersey or New York. But, alas, that was not the case; therefore, we had to from time to time use whatever tactic we could to achieve whatever advance we could for our states—in the context of a Finance Committee where interests often collided, but ideas not always. And at one point, I recall Senator Moynihan asking for recognition right before a vote was to be taken with Senator Long in the chair and saying, "May I inquire of the chairman which way he is voting—so I can join him—if I can."

The Packwood and Dole chairmanships were fueled by warm personal relations between Senator Moynihan and both chairmen of different parties, and that often produced the following result. A tax bill would be moving, we would be toward the end of the deliberation, and there would be yet one small New York item that had not yet been included in the bill. Senator Moynihan would raise his hand and seek to deliver once more for his constituents in New York. Because of those warm personal relations and because of their mutual respect, he frequently won.

Then there was one moment during the tenure of Senator Lloyd Bentsen of Texas. The issue was the emerging welfare grant that allowed a state to temporarily increase a grant in hardship cases. Well, both New York and New Jersey had used this provision, wisely and creatively. Senator Bentsen began the discussion of the issue by saying that this was the worst thing that he had ever seen. At which point Senator Moynihan, in the back room behind the Senate Finance Committee during the discussion phase of the bill, literally crawled under the table and from under the table said, "I know it's bad, but could you give us a transition year?" And he got it. Senator Moynihan always listened. He reached across the aisle. He would place himself in the center where power rested.

Moynihan on the Floor

I can see him now, dressed in a plaid sport coat and gray slacks and brown moccasins, standing in the back row hitching up his trousers, glancing up at the press ("Yes, the *New York Times* is there")—and beginning, "Mr. President," as if he were addressing an old friend. Whether on Social Security, welfare, human rights, the collapse of communism, the Reagan strategy of precipitating a deficit crisis by granting large tax cuts, Pat—often in an empty chamber—spoke up and spoke on. I have always found him in these moments not only educational but also inspirational. He believed in the process, the bully pulpit, the platform awaiting him on the floor. It was an attitude totally without cynicism. He was building a record, opening eyes to a circumstance, calling attention to a contradiction or muddled thinking because he believed that in the end, substance would triumph over politics, and if not now, at least in the history books.

Moynihan in Caucus

Now the Democratic caucus was not a normal group. It rarely met prior to 1980 when the Republicans took control of the Senate. Evidently Senator Byrd as majority leader preferred to deal with individual senators like spokes in a wheel. There were dangers when you assembled them in one room and had an open discussion. But after 1980, the weekly caucus/luncheon was established. During the first two years, the caucus was dominated by Senator Byrd, who tried to follow a very explicit agenda; Senator Russell Long, who sought to prevent anything from happening in the caucus, thereby enhancing his own power outside the caucus; and Senator Scoop Jackson, who would give us regular reports from his favorite economist, Henry Kaufman, about where the economy was headed and about what the state of play in Russia might be that week. Then Scoop died.

Pat began to rise more frequently, and when he rose he would explain how two seemingly unrelated facts were intricately tied together and how seeing them as such presented a new insight. But even insights need a common language. Now some of the people in the caucus did not serve with him on committees. I remember one case where he began and spoke for four or five minutes, at the end of which a southern senator reached over to me and said, "What'd he say?" I explained to him the substantive point that Senator Moynihan was making, and he replied, "No, I don't mean that. I mean, I couldn't understand him—his accent."

Moynihan and Presidents

On the whole I would say the relationship has been respectful, but candid. It was with Carter, it was with Bush. Reagan rarely talked to any senator, including Senator Moynihan. In fact, that Moynihan and Reagan are Irish is only a testimony to Irish diversity, from my perspective. I remember one discussion with Senator Moynihan in which we agreed we would define a successful Senate career as having passed a major piece of reform at least once every four or five years. You had to introduce the bill; the public had to get used to it; the interest groups had to examine it; they then had to make their contribution; you then had to adjust it; you then had to figure out your legislative strategy; you then had to marshal the forces that would implement the legislative strategy; and then, maybe then, you had a chance at big reform.

So it was with some trepidation that both he and I received the president's health care plan in 1993. And when we were told that this complicated plan would be passed by the 4 July recess, we raised our skeptical eyebrows, and then we were told, again, at least by the August recess. We knew that things might not turn out the way they were supposed to in the White House. Senator Moynihan as chairman did his level best to tell people in the White House that things needed to be changed a little here and there, but to no avail. The relationship deteriorated on the edges. That reminds me of the story of Walter George of Georgia, who in the 1930s was a thorn in the side of FDR. In 1938, FDR was so angry at Senator George, chairman of the Finance Committee, that he put his own candidate in the Democratic primary in Georgia. But Senator George naturally won and returned to the Senate as chairman of the Finance Committee. The president realized he had a problem. So he sent a young emissary up to see Senator George. He walked into his office, and he tried to find just the right words that would mollify the Senate power, and he said, "Oh, Mr. Chairman, the president, the president, sometimes he's his own worst enemy." To which Walter George replied, "No, he isn't."

President Clinton, unlike FDR, has never sent the right emissary to Senator Moynihan.

Moynihan and Sports

His interests are architecture, foreign policy, social policy, history, ideas, Disraeli—*not* sports. Robert Byrd once admitted at a Democratic luncheon, "I've attended three baseball games in my life, two of them were a doubleheader on one afternoon." He went on, "And one football game. I went at half-time to crown the West Virginia queen when we played at the University of Maryland. I don't watch many games on TV because I figure when you've seen one, you've seen 'em all." Senator Byrd and Senator Moynihan share more than anyone would imagine. They are the only two senators I know who couldn't tell the difference between a field goal in football and a field goal in basketball.

Moynihan and Fund-raising

Once Senator Moynihan observed that under the new campaign finance reform laws, riddled by *Buckley v. Valeo,* things were different. It used to be, he opined, that you raised money in large contributions from twenty people, and you were obligated in spirit to twenty people. Now he said you raise money in thousand-dollar contributions from a whole class of people, and you're obligated in spirit to a whole class of people.

Moynihan and Loyalty

I asked him once, "Are you staying with the labor guys on trade, again?" He said, "Yes." I said, "Why?" He said, "Because they were with me in 1976 when I needed them."

Moynihan and Friendship

I remember when I was running the first time for the U.S. Senate. I asked Senator Moynihan if he would come in to campaign for me in New Jersey—a little fund-raiser, you know. He came in. It was in some suburban New Jersey town, and he arrived at the house. He was there two minutes when he said, "I have to take a walk." He put on his hat and his jacket, and walked around the neighborhood. He was gone for more time than made the first-time candidate comfortable, so I wondered what happened to him (this was a safe neighborhood). I found him and brought him back, not knowing what he would say at this gathering. And, of course, what he said was that I would make a good senator. And he recalled a passage from Woodrow Wilson, a student of the presidency. Observing the physical strains on presidential nominees, Wilson—Moynihan recounted—said that if this should continue, we would be reduced to choosing our chief executive from "among wise and prudent athletes: a small class."

So, how would I sum up Moynihan's Senate years? I would say they are characterized by absolute integrity, by wide-ranging intelligence, by pride in America and its traditions, by genuine compassion for those who are fighting against the odds, and finally, by one other quality, his capacity for friendship (often seated with Liz around a dinner table in the Moynihan house). And it is for this last quality that I am most grateful.

CHAPTER THIRTEEN

PAT

JAMES Q. WILSON

This symposium on the works of Daniel Patrick Moynihan has only scratched the surface. There is scarcely any man in public life, and no other in politics, about whom a daylong symposium could be held that would deal, as this one did, with ethnicity, poverty, families, schools, traffic, crime, drugs, architecture, transportation, international law, and the United Nations.

But some important matters were left out. Let me mention three of them. First is Pat the Edwardian athlete. When Pat and I were colleagues as professors of government at Harvard, we once attended the annual social event of that distinguished department, the summer picnic and softball game. Pat, being new to the department, was assigned to right field, where all novices must begin. The first batter lifted a high fly ball to—of course—right field. As I looked out from my position at second base, I noticed that Pat was wearing a fielder's glove on his right hand. Since he is right-handed, this is the wrong place for a glove. As the ball drifted down, he threw off the useless glove. It, and the ball, untouched, hit the ground. I ran out to retrieve a ball for what was now going to be a home run and to ask him why he didn't catch it. He said: "I had no glove." I replied: "But

---

This tribute is based on after-dinner remarks offered at the conclusion of the Moynihan festschrift.

you did have a glove, on the wrong hand. Why did you wear that?" He stared at me with the contempt an Edwardian aristocrat has for a defunct colonist: "A proper fielder must always wear a glove."

Then there is Pat the naturalist. Late one night after much food and wine at his farm in Delaware County, Pat and I walked along the dirt road connecting the farmhouse to his small study. An animal appeared on the road in front of us. "Pat," I said, "I think that is a skunk." "Nonsense," he replied, "that's a woodchuck." Ten minutes later we stood on his front porch, removing our clothes in the vain hope that Liz and Roberta would not notice that we smelled like polecats.

Finally, there is Pat the mechanical genius. Last summer, after another wonderful stay with Liz and Pat at their farm, Roberta and I wondered what gift we could send to a couple that already owned next to nothing. We decided on the world's finest corkscrew. It was sent, but to no response. Finally, Liz called to say that Pat could not operate it. A bit later, Pat himself wrote me, on stationery borrowed from a prominent Washington law firm, one that generally represents only Democratic causes, to complain that I had in fact sent him, not a corkscrew, but a device to extract rings from the pistons of Volvo engines. By claiming it was a corkscrew and not a ring-puller, and by failing to include a label that said, "Not to be used on Château Lafitte Rothschild," I was guilty of false advertising that would get me in trouble with several federal agencies.

As these examples suggest, it is not easy to describe Pat Moynihan. No two of his traits seem to fit together. He is a liberal, but belongs to few, if any, liberal causes and spends at least as much time decrying fellow liberals as opposing dedicated conservatives. His first national office was in the Kennedy administration, his second in the Nixon one, despite the fact that Kennedy and Nixon had been bitter rivals in 1960. In all, he served in two Democratic and two Republican administrations, not because he had no views but because he persuaded the presidents in each case that their views should move toward his. He has spent much of his life in public office but hates the ways by which the protectors of those in office glorify their leader by minimizing his contact with ordinary people. He has written many books, but few when he was a professor and several when he was a politician. He has the height and stature of a forward on a basketball team and the hand-eye coordination of a four-year-old. He looks formidable, but Liz has to drive their car if he is not to wreck it. Everyone has heard of his days as a young boy shining shoes in the Hell's Kitchen area of New York City, but he was born in Tulsa, Oklahoma. He believes in the two-parent family, but was largely the product of a one-parent family. For thirty years he has worried deeply over the growth in illegitimacy, but he is the first to admit he does not know what to do about it. By my estimate he has been one of the most liberal members of the Senate from 1981 through 1992 and one of the less liberal senators from 1977 through 1980 and from 1992 until today. In short, he is very Democratic unless there is a Democrat in the White House.

Pat, to the great consternation of many of his friends, turns out to be exactly what he always said he was—a Democrat. Unlike many of his colleagues, he refused to make the failures of government policy a reason for moving from the Democratic Party, which often makes poor policy, to the Republican Party, which often does precisely the same.

But he remains a Democrat who greatly worries other Democrats. For thirty years, he told them that the family was getting weaker. He was denounced. For almost as long, he pointed out that you cannot improve education simply—if at all—by spending more money on it. He was ignored. Thirty years ago he told liberals that "their essential interest is in the stability of the social order," an interest that should induce them to make effective alliances with conservatives. I was not at the Americans for Democratic Action meeting when he said that, but I doubt that he was cheered to the ceiling.

Early on, he and Nat Glazer published a book that denied that being a proletariat was the most important political thing in one's life. As the Students for a Democratic Society issued its announcements about participatory democracy for the poor, Nat and Pat pointed out that race and ethnicity were at least as important (Friedrich Engels had agreed with them). If you looked at how ethnic groups organized their lives, you would find a lot of participatory democracy. It was called "politics." The facts were on their side; ambition was on the side of their critics. When trendy leftism became fashionable in the 1960s and 1970s, the presidents of several Ivy League colleges were caught up by it. Pat, like the president of the AFL-CIO, wouldn't touch it.

He told liberals that treaties designed to reduce strategic nuclear weapons were actually authorizing increases in them. Now people began to mutter about his drinking problem. As George Will was to say later, such folk should be treated as Abraham Lincoln treated critics of General Ulysses S. Grant: Find out what he's drinking and pass the bottle around.

Pat is a Democrat, I think, for the same reason as are most people who had the Great Depression and the Second World War as their defining experiences. If you see one-fourth of a nation unemployed, you take the provision of jobs quite seriously. If you watch the elderly expect nothing but uncertain charity, you become preoccupied with ways of systematically supplying a retirement benefit. If you go to war against fascists who used public disorder as their route to power, you worry about college students who pretend that their adolescent version of revolution will have happy consequences. If you become an adult when black families are largely intact and then watch as they, and to a lesser degree their white counterparts, turn into poor, unmarried young mothers, you would have to be blind not to think that something very wrong has happened.

The impress of these monumental events will be clearly felt by any intelligent mind. One can argue, as some of his friends have done, that there are better ways to meet these problems. Perhaps Social Security taxes should be invested in the stock market. Perhaps new initiatives will re-create families that have been destroyed by profound social forces. Perhaps the circle will be squared and night turned into day. That is to say: Perhaps man in the future will be smarter than man in the past. But until somebody can show us that the new man will be smarter than the old one, it is very hard for a thoughtful person to embrace untested changes. And Pat is a thoughtful person.

But he is not always a prudent one. I recall our first meeting; I was a junior faculty member at Harvard and Pat was in the Kennedy administration. He arrived at the Joint Center for Urban Studies to talk about the FBI. He roundly, and rightly, denounced it for not taking seriously organized crime. I was fascinated by the Mafia and aware of the FBI. I thought to myself, "Here is a remarkable man. While holding a presidential appointment, he attacks the one agency in Washington that could destroy him. I must meet him." And, of course, the FBI did counterattack: It took Pat off its list of people who got bureau Christmas cards. Most men in Washington trembled at that threat. Pat did not.

One of my next conversations with him occurred within the year. Somebody had shot President Kennedy. At Harvard it was widely assumed that the "somebody" was a right-wing nut. After all, it happened in Dallas. (Harvard folk know less about Dallas than they do about Sweden.) Pat called. Unlike everybody else I spoke to, he did not speculate on who might have killed Kennedy. Instead he said, with chilling foresight, that "we must get Oswald out of Dallas." Nobody listened; Oswald was not moved, and within hours he was dead. And so the fanciful conspiracy theorists live on, and Oliver Stone has a topic for a movie.

Though Pat has spent many more years in public than in academic life, he retains the good sense of a social scientist. By this I do not mean the ability to calculate a chi-square test or to estimate a regression equation, but rather the knowledge that the best social science can do for public policy, beyond occasional bits of description, is to evaluate what government has done. Social science can tell you whether efforts at criminal rehabilitation have rehabilitated anyone, whether supported work programs for unemployed youth actually produce work, whether spending more money on schools makes students learn more, and whether a negative income tax makes families more or less stable. Pat has been a faithful student and ardent supporter of such research, even when it leads him in directions he would prefer not to go. He would like criminals to be rehabilitated, worker-training programs to produce employment, more money to make better schools, and the negative income tax to strengthen families, but most of these efforts have failed, and the few that have helped have produced, at best, modest effects. To me, Pat is the ideal public servant, not because we always agree but because he will follow the facts and even pay, in public money and dashed hopes, to get the facts. If the Senate had a hundred Moynihans, two things would happen: speeches would be a lot better, and the government would be driven by hard facts rather than by empty ideology.

Pat understands social science and knows how different it is from the art of making laws and judging events. Because many social scientists are more eager to make laws or judge events than to evaluate effects, Pat is properly skeptical of many claims made by ardent professors. But when he thinks the law has got the facts wrong, he will write extraordinary criticisms of misguided judges. Only a minority of senators ever supported his effort to produce tuition tax credits for parochial as well as public schools. The courts insisted that public money going to parochial high schools was wrong, but then allowed public money to go to parochial as well as public colleges. Pat knows nonsense when he sees it. He produced at least two masterful essays that absolutely demolished the Supreme Court's view of this matter. They are a bracing reminder of what the Founders meant when they gave us a Bill of Rights. Their influence on Court and Senate opinion was, of course, zero.

Of course, speaking about just Pat being thoughtful is a mistake, because there is not just Pat: There is Pat and Liz or, better yet, Liz and Pat. They are a remarkable pair, each supplying what the other may lack. Pat is in love with ideas; Liz knows how to get him elected. Pat understands government; Liz knows who in government is nuts. Pat rarely offends those with whom he disagrees; Liz will not go to their parties and, with the slightest urging, will tell them to get lost. Pat has written about automobiles; Liz knows how to drive one. Pat alone would be a talented professor trying to get a grant to pay his expenses; Liz alone would be a brilliant politician trying to find a candidate worth electing.

Pat has the gift of all great writers: He not only can tell a fascinating story and make an important point but also can coin a phrase by which the argument is forever remembered. Our acceptance of rising crimes rates is now known as "defining deviancy down." The tendency of bureaucratic organizations to copy the agencies against which they struggle is the "iron law of emulation." The overeager participation of people in a community action program is "maximum feasible misunderstanding."

But it is much more than phrase-making. Consider Pat's tenacious loyalty to the least-defended cause in the world—the law of nations. Over and over again he has argued that there is an international legal order to which the United States ought to appeal. Some critics of this view think he is being tenderhearted in a coldhearted world. They don't understand his point. There is a law; we ordinarily act on the side blessed by this law. When we face an international crisis, we should get the International Court of Justice—an entity that lacks work, and hence would respond quickly—to assert our being on the right side of the law, and then we should bomb those on the wrong side of the law. Instead, when Iran seized our diplomats, we sent someone to discuss the matter with them. You may approve or not of Pat's view on international law, but you cannot call it tenderhearted or think it is irrelevant to the philosophy on which this regime was founded.

Pat's attachment to international law in an age that has either ignored or denounced it is more than quaint antiquarianism. Consider what he did for eight months as U.S. ambassador to the United Nations. With power and wit, he defended the rule of law and a decent respect for human rights against a totalitarian attack waged by Soviet allies and Arab money against the state of Israel. The attack was simple: Define Zionism as equal to racism. Pat waged a war of words. As Russell Baker was later to write, "Moynihan spoke English, an ancient tongue," and "outraged all humanity by speaking it aloud." By "all humanity," Mr. Baker of course meant a sorry lot of minor tribal kingdoms and trivial autocracies, each of which, in the grand design of American foreign policy, is heavily represented in our own State Department. "All humanity," with its Foggy

Bottom endorsement, succeeded in turning Pat's own government against him. As Mr. Baker concluded, Pat wouldn't stop speaking English or, as I would put it, defending the core precepts of international law—namely, tell the truth, appeal to general principles, and apply each principle to every country.

Lord Palmerston once suggested that politicians have no permanent friends, only permanent interests. He did not know Pat. This world is filled with people who are his permanent friends, even though many of us have interests—or at least beliefs—that differ from his.

Over the years, Pat and I have worked out an eminently satisfactory system for accommodating the fact that, though we agree on many things, we disagree on many others. I don't give him advice he doesn't want to hear, and he doesn't ask questions he doesn't want me to answer. You might think this would reduce a cranky old Republican and a lively old Democrat to absolute silence. Not so. This arrangement leaves us with much to talk about and many opportunities for Liz and Pat and Roberta and me to enjoy one another's company. It leaves us, in short, with what is perhaps the greatest value of life in a free society ruled by a limited government: Politics is not that important, and is infinitely less important than friendship and honor and decency and fun.

Today Saint Patrick is 1,612 years old and Senator Patrick is seventy years old. Saint Pat was, perhaps, the Church's greatest missionary; after all, he subdued the Irish. Senator Pat is also a missionary, and has brought to his task many of the same qualities of his illustrious predecessor: luminous intellect, personal conviction, deep historical knowledge, the eye of an artist and the pen of an angel, and above all, an incorruptible devotion to the common good. If the senator has had less influence than the saint, it is probably because the Irish cared for their souls while most senators care only for reelection.

My toast: To repeat what Michael Barone has said, Pat is the finest thinker among politicians since Abraham Lincoln and the finest politician among thinkers since Thomas Jefferson. Happy birthday, Pat.

APPENDICES

APPENDIX A

BIOGRAPHICAL FACTS SENATOR DANIEL PATRICK MOYNIHAN

Daniel Patrick Moynihan is the senior U.S. senator from New York. He was elected in 1976 and reelected in 1982, 1988, and 1994.

Senator Moynihan is the ranking minority member of the Senate Committee on Finance. He is also the second-ranking minority member of the Committee on Environment and Public Works and serves on the Committee on Rules and Administration.

A member of the cabinet or sub-cabinet of Presidents Kennedy, Johnson, Nixon, and Ford, Senator Moynihan is the only person in American history to serve in the cabinet or sub-cabinet in four successive administrations. He was the U.S. ambassador to India from 1973 to 1975 and U.S. representative to the United Nations from 1975 to 1976. In February 1976 he represented the United States as president of the UN Security Council.

Senator Moynihan was born on March 16, 1927. He attended public and parochial schools in New York City and graduated from Benjamin Franklin High School in East Harlem. He attended the City College of New York for one year before enlisting in the U.S. Navy, where he served on active duty from 1944 to 1947. In 1966, he completed twenty years in the Naval Reserve and was retired. Senator Moynihan received his bachelor's degree cum laude from Tufts University and his M.A. and Ph.D. from the Fletcher School of Law and Diplomacy.

He was a member of Averell Harriman's staff in the campaign for governor of New York in 1954 and served on the governor's staff in Albany until 1958. He was an alternate Kennedy delegate at the 1960 Democratic Convention. Beginning in 1961, he served in the U.S. Department of Labor, first as an assistant to the secretary and later as assistant secretary of labor for policy planning.

In 1966, he became director of the Joint Center for Urban Studies at the Massachusetts Institute of Technology and Harvard University. He has been a professor of government at Harvard University and assistant professor of government at Syracuse University, a fellow at the Center for Advanced Study at Wesleyan University, and has taught in the extension programs of Russell Sage College and the Cornell University School of Industrial and Labor Relations. Senator Moynihan is the author or editor of sixteen books and the recipient of sixty-one honorary degrees.

He has served as a member of the President's Science Advisory Committee (1971–73), a member of the board of directors of the American Association for the Advancement of Science (1969–76) and vice president of the American Association for the Advancement of Science (1972), and as a member of the board of trustees (1969–76) and vice chairman (1971–76) of the Woodrow Wilson International Center for Scholars. He was the founding chair of the board of trustees of the Hirshhorn Museum and Sculpture Garden (1971–85), and currently serves as a regent of the Smithsonian Institution, having been appointed in 1987 and again in 1995.

In 1992, Senator Moynihan was the recipient of the Laetare Medal of the University of Notre Dame. He received the Seal Medallion of the Central Intelligence Agency (1986) and the Britannica Medal for the Dissemination of Learning (1986).

He has also received the Arthur S. Flemming Award as "an architect of the Nation's program to eradicate poverty" (1965); the International League of Human Rights Award (1975); the John LaFarge Award for Interracial Justice (1980); the Thomas Jefferson Award for Public Architecture from the American Institute of Architects (1992); and the Thomas Jefferson Medal for Distinguished Achievement in the Arts or Humanities from the American Philosophical Society (1993). In 1994, he received the Gold Medal Award "honoring services to humanity" from the National Institute of Social Sciences.

In 1984, Senator Moynihan received the State University of New York at Albany's Medallion of the University in recognition of his "extraordinary public service and leadership in the field of education." In 1983, he was the first recipient of the American Political Science Association's Hubert H. Humphrey Award for "notable public service by a political scientist."

His wife of forty-three years, Elizabeth Brennan Moynihan, is an architectural historian with a special interest in sixteenth-century Mughal architecture in India. She is the author of *Paradise as a Garden: In Persia and Mughal India* (1979) and numerous articles. Mrs. Moynihan serves on the Visiting Committee of the Freer Gallery of Art of the Smithsonian Institution, the board of the National Building Museum, the Trustees Council of the Preservation League of New York State, and is former chair of the board and a board member of the American Schools of Oriental Research and a member of the Indo-U.S. Subcommission on Education and Culture.

The Moynihans live near Pindars Corners in Delaware County, New York, and in Washington, D.C. They have three children, Timothy Patrick, Maura Russell, and John McCloskey, and two grandchildren, Michael Patrick Avedon and Zora Olea Moynihan.

PERSONAL

Born: March 16, 1927, Tulsa, Oklahoma
Resident of New York since 1928

PUBLIC SERVICE

Staff, Governor Averell Harriman of New York, State Capitol, Albany, 1955–58: assistant to secretary to the governor Jonathan Bingham; assistant secretary for reports, 1956; acting secretary to the governor, 1958
Special assistant to the secretary of labor, U.S. Department of Labor, 1961–62
Executive assistant to the secretary of labor, 1962–63
Assistant secretary of labor for policy planning and research, 1963–65
Assistant to the president for urban affairs, The White House, 1969–70
Counselor to the president, member of cabinet, 1969–70
Consultant to the president, 1971–73
Member, U.S. delegation to the Twenty-sixth General Assembly of the United Nations, 1971
U.S. ambassador to India, New Delhi, 1973–75
Permanent representative to the United Nations, New York, 1975–76

ELECTED OFFICE

Candidate for New York City Council president, 1965
U.S. senator from New York, 1977–

SENATE COMMITTEES

Committee on Finance—Ranking Minority Member. Subcommittees: a) International Trade; b) Social Security and Family Policy; c) Taxation and IRS Oversight

Chair, Senate Committee on Finance, 1993–94

Committee on Environment and Public Works—Second-ranking Minority Member. Subcommittees: a) Superfund, Waste Control, and Risk Assessment; b) Transportation and Infrastructure

Chair, Senate Committee on Environment and Public Works, 1992

Committee on Rules and Administration

Joint Committee on the Library

Joint Committee on Taxation

Foreign Relations Committee, member, 1987–95

Budget Committee, member, 1979–87

Select Committee on Intelligence, member, 1977–85; vice chair, 1981–85

LEGISLATIVE ACHIEVEMENTS

West Valley Demonstration Project Act of 1980

Sponsor. Authorized U.S. Department of Energy to clean up and remove 600,000 gallons of nuclear waste stored at West Valley, New York. Committed federal government to convert liquid wastes into solid glasslike logs.

They are then to be moved from the West Valley site to a permanent and secure federal repository.

The Acid Precipitation Act (Became Title VII of the Energy Security Act of 1980)

First federal legislation dealing with the problem of acid rain. Established a ten-year program for research on the causes and effects of acid rain and possible control strategies.

Clean Air Act Reauthorization of 1982

Mandated an eight-million-ton reduction in annual sulfur dioxide emission in the eastern United States by 1 January 1995.

Social Security Act Amendments of 1983

Chief Democratic sponsor of amendments guaranteeing solvency of the Social Security system well into the twenty-first century.

Water Resources Development Act of 1986

Authorized $1.1 billion for thirty-three New York water projects. Obtained funding for the Erie Canal, Olcott Harbor, and Coney Island.

Superfund Reauthorization Act of 1985

Principal cosponsor. Provided $8.5 billion over five years to clean up toxic waste.

Tax Reform Act of 1986

One of six principal drafters of the law. Successfully opposed attempts to eliminate the deduction for state and local income and property taxes. Played a critical role in formulation of legislation that took millions of working poor off the tax rolls, lowered rates, and closed down tax shelters and other loopholes.

Family Support Act of 1988

Began process of transforming the Aid to Families with Dependent Children (AFDC) program from an income-security program to one that helps individuals secure permanent employment.

Clean Air Act Amendments of 1990

Original cosponsor. First revision of the Clean Air Act since 1977. The acid rain control provisions resulted in part from the first federal legislation to address acid rain: Moynihan's Acid Precipitation Act of 1980.

Intermodal Surface Transportation Efficiency Act of 1991 (ISTEA)

Chief sponsor of bill, known as ISTEA, which redirected federal surface transportation policy to include more spending for non-highway-related projects. Also greatly increased the amount of Federal Highway Trust Fund money going to New York. New York received $12 billion in highway and transit funds over six years, and will be paid back $5 billion for the New York State Thruway over fifteen years.

1994 Crime Bill—Ban on "Cop-Killer" Bullets

Introduced and obtained Senate passage of legislation to protect police officers from a new class of armor-piercing ammunition. The bill extends the 1986 Law Enforcement Officers Protection Act, also sponsored by Senator Moynihan, to prohibit this new type of "cop-killer" bullet.

Tax on Black Talon Bullet—1994

Introduced legislation to impose a 10,000 percent tax on the Black Talon bullet, which expands on impact into six razor-sharp points. Nineteen days after the legislation was introduced, the manufacturer withdrew the Black Talon from sale to the general public.

TEACHING AND ACADEMIC POSITIONS

Assistant in government, Fletcher School of Law and Diplomacy, Tufts University, 1949–50

Lecturer, Russell Sage College, 1957–58
Lecturer, NYS School of Industrial Relations, Cornell University, 1959
Assistant professor of political science, Maxwell Graduate School of Citizenship and Public Affairs, Syracuse University, 1960–61
Fellow, Center for Advanced Studies, Wesleyan University, 1965–66
Director, Joint Center for Urban Studies, MIT and Harvard University, 1966–69
Professor of education and urban politics, Harvard University, 1969–73
Professor of government, Harvard University, 1973–77

COURSES TAUGHT

Harvard University

1971–72
Administration and Social Policy x-154: Social Science and Social Policy
A review of the rise of social science influence in the formulation of social policy with respect to other than predominately economic issues and an examination of changing perceptions of the political orientation of social science findings. Class work concentrated on case studies drawn from recent American experience.

Administration and Social Policy x-227: Federal Policy toward Higher Education
A consideration of the emergence of federal policy toward higher education in the context of historical programs and the social policies they reflect, in order to define the choices implicit in the adoption of a formal national policy.

Administration and Social Policy x-256: Social Science and Educational Policy
An exploration of recent and prospective influences on educational policies of social science theory and research; includes consideration of the policy-making processes within the educational system and various modes of response to social science findings.

1972–73
Government 251: Ethnicity in American Politics
A historical inquiry into the role of ethnic group identity as an organizing factor in American politics.

1976–77

Social Science 115: Social Science and Social Policy

An examination of the influence of various social science disciplines on the formulation of social policy.

1976–77

Government 216: Ethnicity in Politics

A historical and theoretical inquiry into the role of ethnicity as an organizing principle in modern politics.

FELLOWSHIPS

1969	Honorary Fellow, London School of Economics and Political Science
1976	Chubb Fellow, Yale University

LECTURESHIPS

1985	Feingold Lecturer, Columbia University
1985	Feinstone Lecturer, U.S. Military Academy at West Point
1986	Godkin Lecturer, Harvard University
1986	Marnold Lecturer, New York University
1987	Gannon Lecturer, Fordham University
1991	Cyril Foster Lecturer, Oxford University
1997	Marver H. Bernstein Lecturer, Georgetown University

HONORARY DEGREES

LL.D.	LaSalle College, 1966
LL.D.	Seton Hall College, 1966
D.P.A.	Providence College, 1967
D.H.L.	University of Akron, 1967
LL.D.	Catholic University, 1968
D.S.W.	Dusquesne University, 1968
D.H.L.	Hamilton College, 1968
LL.D.	Illinois Institute of Technology, 1968
LL.D.	New School for Social Research, 1968
LL.D.	St. Louis University, 1968

LL.D.	Tufts University, 1968
D.S.S.	Villanova University, 1968
LL.D.	University of California, 1969
LL.D.	University of Notre Dame, 1969
LL.D.	Fordham University, 1970
H.H.D.	Bridgewater State College, 1972
D.S.	Michigan Technological University, 1972
LL.D.	St. Bonaventure University, 1972
LL.D.	Indiana University, 1975
LL.D.	Boston College, 1976
Ph.D.	Hebrew University, 1976
LL.D.	Hofstra University, 1976
LL.D.	Ohio State University, 1976
LL.D.	St. Anselm's College, 1976
D.H.L.	Baruch College, 1977
LL.D.	Canisius College, 1977
D.C.L.	Colgate University, 1977
LL.D.	LeMoyne College, 1977
LL.D.	New York Law School, 1977
LL.D.	Salem College, 1977
LL.D.	Brooklyn Law School, 1978
LL.D.	College of St. Rose, 1978
LL.D.	Hartwick College, 1978
LL.D.	Ithaca College, 1978
D.H.L.	Rabbinical College of America, 1978
LL.D.	Skidmore College, 1978
LL.D.	Yeshiva University, 1978
D.H.L.	Marist College, 1979
LL.D.	Pace University Law School, 1979
LL.D.	St. John Fisher College, 1980
LL.D.	Dowling College, 1981
LL.D.	Bar-Ilan University, 1982
LL.D.	New York Medical College, 1982
LL.D.	Pratt Institute, 1982
LL.D.	Rensselaer Polytechnic Institute, 1983
D.C.L.	Union College, 1983
D.S.I.	Defense Intelligence College, 1984
D.H.L.	New York University, 1984
LL.D.	Syracuse University School of Law, 1984

D.H.L.	Bard College, 1985
D.H.L.	Hebrew Union College, 1986
LL.D.	Marymount Manhattan College, 1986
LL.D.	Columbia University, 1987
LL.D.	Touro College, 1991
D.H.L.	Hobart and William Smith College, 1992
D.H.L.	University of San Francisco, 1992
D.C.L.	St. Francis College, 1993
LL.D.	University of Rochester, 1994
LL.D.	Union College, 1995

OTHER POSITIONS

Budget assistant, United States Air Force base, Ruislip, England, 1951–53

Director of public relations, International Rescue Committee (IRC), New York—Human Rights Organization: assisted refugees forced to leave their own countries through persecution, 1954

Director, New York State Government Research Project, Syracuse University, 1959–61

COMMISSIONS AND COMMITTEES

Member, New York State Tenure Commission, 1958–60

Member, President's Council on Pennsylvania Avenue, 1962

Vice Chair, President's Temporary Commission on Pennsylvania Avenue, 1965–74

Member, Advisory Committee on Traffic Safety, Department of Health, Education, and Welfare, 1966–68

Member, President's Science Advisory Committee, 1971–73

DEMOCRATIC POLITICS

Volunteer, New York City mayoral campaign of Robert Wagner, 1953

Secretary, Public Affairs Committee of the New York State Democratic Party, 1958–60

Member, New York state delegation to the Democratic National Convention, 1960, 1976

Wrote position papers for John F. Kennedy's presidential campaign, 1960

EDUCATION

Graduated from Benjamin Franklin High School, New York, N.Y., 1943
One year at City College of New York (1943–44), followed by naval service
B.N.S., Tufts University, 1946
B.A., Tufts University (cum laude), 1948
M.A., Fletcher School of Law and Diplomacy, Tufts University, 1949
Fulbright Scholarship, London School of Economics, 1950
Ph.D., Fletcher School of Law and Diplomacy, 1961 (thesis on the International Labor Organization)

NAVAL SERVICE

V-12 Naval Officer training program, Middlebury, Vt., 1944–45
ROTC Tufts University, 1945/B.N.S., 1946
Communications and gunnery officer, USS *Quirinus*, 1947

MEDALS

American Campaign Medal—Given to those in service between 1941 and 1946; recipient must have served outside the United States for thirty days or within the United States for one year.
Naval Reserve Medal—Given to those who have given ten years of honorable service to the Naval Reserve.
World War II Victory Medal—For service in the armed forces, 1941–46.

HONORS AND AWARDS

Meritorious Service Award of the U.S. Department of Labor (1963)
For exceptional service as staff director of the President's Task Force on Employee-Management Relations, and for outstanding contributions to development of the policy of employee-management cooperation in the federal service.

Arthur S. Flemming Award as an "Architect of the Nation's War on Poverty" (1965)
Given to ten most outstanding young men and women in the federal service; selected by an independent panel of judges.

International League of Human Rights Award (1975)

For extraordinary commitment in the area of international human rights; oldest human rights award in the nation.

John LaFarge Award for Interracial Justice (1980)

Given by the Catholic Interracial Council (New York) for commitment and leadership in fighting racism and discrimination.

Medallion of the University, State University of New York at Albany (1984)

For extraordinary service to the university and to education. The highest award for distinguished service the university bestows.

Henry Medal of the Smithsonian Institution (1985)

For outstanding service to the Smithsonian Institution, presented by the board of regents.

Seal Medallion of the Central Intelligence Agency (1986)

In recognition of outstanding accomplishments as vice chair of the Senate Select Committee on Intelligence from February 1977 to January 1985.

Britannica Medal for the Dissemination of Learning and the Enrichment of Life (1986)

Presented by Encyclopedia Britannica; first winner of the award.

Memorial Sloan-Kettering Cancer Center Medal (1986)

For distinguished service and outstanding achievement in the cancer field.

Gold Medal, American-Irish Historical Society (1986)

In appreciation of significant service rendered to the cause of Ireland.

Nathan Sharansky Humanitarian Award, Rockland Committee for Soviet Jewry (1987)

For distinguished achievements on behalf of human rights and noble efforts in support of Soviet Jewry and the Jewish people throughout the world.

Honor Award, National Building Museum (1989)

For fostering excellence in the built environment; received the 1989 award for championing the resurrection of Pennsylvania Avenue, for promoting quality in federal building programs, and for spearheading an effort to rebuild the nation's deteriorating infrastructure.

Wolfgang Friedmann Award, Columbia University School of Law (1991)
For outstanding contributions to the field of international law; given by Columbia Law School's *Journal of Transnational Law.*

President's Medal, Municipal Art Society of New York (1992)
Presented to an individual whose accomplishments have made an enduring contribution to urban life in America, and especially to New York City.

Thomas Jefferson Award for Public Architecture, American Institute of Architects (1992)
For advocacy furthering the public's awareness and/or appreciation of design excellence.

Laetare Medal, University of Notre Dame (1992)
The university's highest honor, given to those who have "ennobled the arts and sciences, illustrated the ideals of the Church, and enriched the heritage of humanity"; regarded as the most significant annual award conferred upon Catholics in the United States; winner is selected by a committee headed by the president of the University of Notre Dame.

Thomas Jefferson Medal, American Philosophical Society (1993)
The society's most prestigious medal in recognition of distinguished achievement in the arts, humanities, or social sciences.

Distinguished Leadership Award, American Ireland Fund (1994)
In recognition of the senator's long-time interest in and concern for Irish issues.

The Gold Medal Award for Distinguished Service to Humanity (1994)
Presented by the National Institute of Social Sciences.

United Jerusalem Award, Union of Orthodox Jewish Congregations (1994)
For being the single most consistent, thoughtful, and articulate champion of a united Jerusalem in the U.S. Congress.

Profiles in Courage Award, American Jewish Congress (1996)

For significant and courageous contributions to the cause of democracy and human freedom at home and abroad.

Award for Public Service Excellence (1996)

Presented by the Association of American Medical Colleges for "visionary leadership in the U.S. Senate as a champion for the education, research, and patient care missions of our nation's medical schools and teaching hospitals."

Cartwright Prize, Columbia University

Moynihan was awarded the prestigious Cartwright Prize of the College of Physicians and Surgeons of Columbia University. The prize is given to individuals in recognition of their outstanding contribution to medicine. Senator Moynihan is the first person outside the biological sciences to be awarded the Cartwright honor in its 116-year history.

CURRENT MEMBERSHIPS

Aleph Society, New York, N.Y.
American Academy of Arts and Sciences, Cambridge, Mass.
American Antiquarian Society, Worcester, Mass.
American Heritage Dictionary, Usage Panel
American Philosophical Society, Philadelphia, Pa.
Bedford-Stuyvesant Development and Service Corporation, New York, N.Y.
Century Association, New York, N.Y.
Committee on the Constitutional System, Washington, D.C.
Corporation for Maintaining Editorial Diversity in America, Washington, D.C.
Fletcher School of Law and Diplomacy (Board of Trustees), Medford, Mass.
Franklin and Eleanor Roosevelt Institute, Hyde Park, N.Y.
The Harry S. Truman Research for the Advancement of Peace, New York, N.Y.
Harvard Club, New York, N.Y.
Irish Georgian Society, New York, N.Y.
Jacob K. Javits Foundation, Inc. (Board of Trustees), New York, N.Y.

Jerome Levy Economic Institute at Bard College (Board of Trustees), Annandale-on-Hudson, N.Y.
The Maxwell School of Citizenship and Public Affairs (Board of Trustees), Syracuse, N.Y.
National Academy of Social Insurance, Washington, D.C.
National Democratic Institute for International Affairs, Washington, D.C.
New York Landmarks Conservancy, New York, N.Y.
Project on Ethnic Relations, Princeton, N.J.
The Public Interest/National Affairs, Inc., Washington, D.C.
Smithsonian Institution, Washington, D.C., Regent, (appointed 1987 and 1995)

PAST MEMBERSHIPS

President's Science Advisory Committee (1971–73)
American Association for the Advancement of Science, Vice President (1972), Board of Directors (1969–76)
Woodrow Wilson International Center for Scholars, Board of Trustees (1969–76), Vice Chair (1971–76)
Hirshhorn Museum and Sculpture Garden, Founding Chair, Board of Trustees (1971–85)

APPENDIX B

A SELECTED ANNOTATED BIBLIOGRAPHY OF THE WRITINGS OF DANIEL PATRICK MOYNIHAN

MICHAEL J. LACEY

The purpose of this bibliography is to provide a starting point for students and researchers with an interest in the career and opinions of Daniel Patrick Moynihan. Researchers should note the existence of a large collection of Moynihan papers (188 linear feet containing some 164,000 items) in the Manuscript Division of the Library of Congress. The papers were deposited in the library in 1978, and several additions have been made since that time. Access to the collection is restricted, and permission of the donor is required. A register of the papers, prepared in 1992 by Connie L. Cartledge with the assistance of Allyson H. Jackson, Patrick Kerwin, and Margaret Martin, is available in the Manuscript Division.

A few points must be made in connection with the following list of Senator Moynihan's writings. It is selective. No attempt has been made to establish a comprehensive bibliography, far too formidable a task, given that the subject has been very active and productive as an author and journalist, political commentator, policy analyst and historian, educator, diplomat, presidential cabinet member, and senator for over forty years now. But while the listing is not comprehensive, it *is* intended to show the range and continuity of Moynihan's interests, and the articles include, so the author hopes, his most important and influential shorter pieces. There is a bit of overlap involving some of the articles and the contents of a few of the books, but since a process of editing and cutting down sometimes occurred between the appearance in one format and the other, and since many students will prefer the texts that appeared originally in the periodicals, these redundancies have not been noted except in a few cases. Finally, in the interest of providing a rounded picture of the senator's work, the listing also contains references to sometimes obscure government reports in which his hand was especially important. The annotations accompanying items in the list are telegraphic in style and are intended to do no more than give a sense of the contents.

The author wishes to thank Robert A. Katzmann, the project's organizer and the volume's editor, and Richard Bland, deputy chief of staff to Senator Moynihan, for their help in getting copies of cited materials.

BOOKS

1. Nathan Glazer and Daniel P. Moynihan, *Beyond the Melting Pot: The Negroes, Puerto Ricans, Jews, Italians, and Irish in New York City* (Cambridge: MIT Press, 1963). Classic study of ethnic group life in American society and politics. Questioned contemporary conception of America as a homogeneous society in which group differences were fading with the passage of time. Relevant, also, to historical and analytical writing on the Irish in America and the bearings of Irish-American Catholicism on American culture more generally.

2. Daniel P. Moynihan, ed., *The Defenses of Freedom: The Public Papers of Arthur J. Goldberg* (New York: Harper & Row, 1966). A selection of the papers of the Supreme Court justice and American ambassador to the United Nations.

3. Daniel P. Moynihan, *Maximum Feasible Misunderstanding: Community Action in the War on Poverty* (New York: Free Press, 1969). The role of community action in the war on poverty, and why the Johnson administration's poverty program did not live up to expectations. This book, too, merits the designation "classic." There is nothing more difficult than "coordinating" separate bureaucratic agencies and programs, and coordination and encouraging participation were the twin goals of the 1960s reforms under study. Focus is on what became of legislative requirements for "maximum feasible participation" by the poor in community development projects. Moynihan is especially alert to the emergence of a new style of professionalized reform, utopian in character, developed by liberal, middle-class whites and blacks, which proved incapable of living with the agencies and institutions of established, representative democracy, particularly local governments. Lays out the different understandings of the meaning of participation that resulted in the maximum feasible misunderstanding of the title. Concludes that the key failing was one of intellect and leadership within the upper levels of the national government. "This is the essential fact: *The government did not know what it was doing.* It had a

theory. Or, rather, a set of theories. Nothing more. The U.S. Government at this time was no more in possession of confident knowledge as to how to prevent delinquency, cure anomie, or overcome the midmorning sense of powerlessness, than it was the possessor of a dependable formula for motivating Vietnamese villagers to fight Communism."

4. Daniel P. Moynihan, ed., *On Understanding Poverty* (New York: Basic Books, 1969). A collection of essays by leading academics and experts in the field of poverty studies.

5. Daniel P. Moynihan, ed., *Toward a National Urban Policy* (New York: Basic Books, 1970). Essays by academics and urban experts on a range of subjects related to urban affairs: housing, urban planning, transportation, crime, health, and race, among other concerns.

6. Daniel P. Moynihan, *Coping: Essays on the Practice of Government* (New York: Random House, 1973). Essays on a range of subjects encountered during Moynihan's years of government service: welfare, political reform, race relations, traffic safety, education, urban affairs, and other issues. Argues for the importance of what the trained social scientist can contribute to the practices of government.

7. Daniel P. Moynihan, *The Politics of a Guaranteed Income: The Nixon Administration and the Family Assistance Plan* (New York: Random House, 1973). An explanation of the Family Assistance Plan, a program that guaranteed a minimum income to families with children, and the politics that brought left and right together to defeat the proposal. The plan was devised by Moynihan and proposed by the Nixon administration.

8. Nathan Glazer and Daniel P. Moynihan, eds., *Ethnicity: Theory and Experience* (Cambridge: Harvard University Press, 1975). A still important, even cutting-edge, collection of essays by academics and social commentators exploring the meaning and significance of ethnicity in modern society.

9. Daniel P. Moynihan (with Suzanne Weaver), *A Dangerous Place* (Boston: Little, Brown, & Company, 1978). Based on his journals and commonplace books, provides an account of Moynihan's term as ambassador to the UN. Recounts battle against UN resolution to equate Zionism with racism.

10. Daniel P. Moynihan, *Counting Our Blessings: Reflections on the Future of America* (Boston: Little, Brown, & Company, 1980). A collection of essays on foreign policy, the judicial system, domestic and regional economic policy, arms control, and other issues. Argues in favor of public aid to nonpublic schools, and the nation's role in stressing human rights in the world forum.

11. Daniel P. Moynihan, *Family and Nation* (New York: Harcourt Brace Jovanovich, 1986). Delivered as the Godkin Lecture at Harvard University in 1985. On the disintegration of the American family. Argues for the establishment of a national policy designed specifically to support and enhance the viability of families. Reflects "the continued hope that as a polity we might a little better learn the uses of social science. Such uses are limited. There isn't a great deal *of* social science. Some argue there is none. I don't. To the contrary, I have contended that there are 'modes of

anticipation,' including social science, that can be helpful and should be attended to. Social policy must flow from social values; social science never creates such values. Yet if attended to, it can help somewhat, at some times, to secure them. My purpose in narrating certain events is to point to moments when we might have done this, and did not." Contains the author's criticisms of the conservative, antistate, social science of Charles Murray, so prominent in Republican Party thinking about dismantling the welfare state. Included also is an observation especially pertinent to Moynihan's own sense of a properly grounded statecraft: "The central conservative truth is that it is culture, not politics, that determines the success of society. The central liberal truth is that politics can change a culture and save it from itself."

12. Daniel P. Moynihan, *Loyalties* (New York: Harcourt Brace Jovanovich, 1986). On the history and meaning of the arms race, respect for international law, and the Communist theory of racism applied to those who opposed Soviet totalitarianism. The book argues for loyalty to principles of law, rights, and humanity.

13. Daniel P. Moynihan, *Came the Revolution: Argument in the Reagan Era* (New York: Harcourt Brace Jovanovich, 1988). A collection of speeches, essays, and other thoughts from 1981 to 1986.

14. Daniel P. Moynihan, *On the Law of Nations* (Cambridge: Harvard University Press, 1990). An examination of international law and the history of American internationalism in the twentieth century.

15. Daniel P. Moynihan, *Pandaemonium: Ethnicity in International Politics* (New York: Oxford University Press, 1993). An account of how ethnicity has been and will continue to be an elemental force in international politics. How the power of ethnicity defied both the liberal myth of the melting pot and the Marxist ideal of proletarian internationalism.

16. Daniel P. Moynihan, *Miles to Go: A Personal History of Social Policy* (Cambridge: Harvard University Press, 1996). Analysis of the changing welfare state and the nation's social strategies over the last sixty years. Topics include welfare, family disintegration, health care, deviance, and addiction along with larger concerns about civil rights and the fate of capitalism. Trenchant criticisms of the fiscal policies of the Reagan era and the GOP's "Contract with America" of 1994. The last chapter of the volume, a "prologue to the era of social policy which may now be in prospect," is a gloomy forecast of a postmodern cultural order that neither social science nor national government is prepared to deal with, one in which worsening problems of poverty and inequality are rooted not so much in circumstances that might be changed by government policy as in values seemingly beyond the reach of public agency.

ARTICLES AND REPORTS

1. Daniel P. Moynihan, "Epidemic on the Highways," *The Reporter* 20, no. 9 (30 April 1959): 16–23. Something more than urging people to stop killing each other

must be done by commentators and officials. Outlines new, pre–Ralph Nader perspective on possibilities of policy to increase safety by looking at automobile traffic fatalities in same fashion as medical epidemics, rather than as simple failures of judgment or bad luck on the part of individual drivers.

2. Clark D. Ahlberg and Daniel P. Moynihan, "Changing Governors—and Policies," *Public Administration Review* 20, no. 4 (fall 1960): 195–204. Joint paper presented at a symposium on the transition of administrations at the level of state government. Theme is difficulty of change at state level, obstacles of public finance, legislative disarray, and some of the shortcomings of an increasingly professionalized civil service unresponsive to electoral change.

3. Daniel P. Moynihan, "New Roads and Urban Chaos," *The Reporter,* 14 April 1960, 13–20. An early critique of the disruptive, harmful effects on communities and land use of the 1956 Federal Aid Highway Act and the voracious interest-group politics that kept it going under the guise of democratic planning. An account also of the history of federal government involvement in transportation planning, an area in which Moynihan had expert knowledge beginning in the late 1950s. Points to damage to earlier planning traditions and futility of carrying on a number of federal urban development programs completely independent of each other.

4. Daniel P. Moynihan, "The United States and the International Labor Organization, 1889–1934" (Ph.D. diss., Fletcher School of Law and Diplomacy, Tufts University, 1960). Moynihan's Ph.D. dissertation, this is a major work of archival research conducted over a decade in four nations on the role of the United States in the establishment following World War I of the International Labor Organization and the steps by which America eventually came to join the organization in 1934.

5. Daniel P. Moynihan, "How Catholics Feel about Federal School Aid," *The Reporter,* 25 May 1961, 34–37. If there are to be new kinds of federal aid to primary and secondary education, as appeared likely with the activism of the Kennedy administration, Catholics wanted in, a problem for secular liberals, who "come to a screeching halt at the word parochial." Calls for dialogue on fears harbored by both sides prior to discussion of constitutionality of issue.

6. Daniel P. Moynihan, "When the Irish Ran New York," *The Reporter,* 8 June 1961, 32–34. Point here is that "more has been written against Tammany Hall than about it." Key to the Irish era in New York from the 1880s onward was the ethnic structure of the Democratic Party bureaucracy, a massive organization "which rivaled the medieval Catholic Church in the proportion of the citizenry involved." Analysis of how boss rule worked.

7. Daniel P. Moynihan, "'Bosses' and 'Reformers': A Profile of the New York Democrats," *Commentary* 31, no. 6 (June 1961): 461–70. Moynihan's first appearance in *Commentary.* Discussion of class, ethnicity, and religion—most important, the wariness and suspicion between Catholics and Jews—in relation to the internal troubles of the New York Democrats. Heavy emphasis on reasons why predominance of Catholics in party means reformers in minority.

8. U.S. House Committee on Public Works, *Report to the President by the Ad Hoc Committee on Federal Office Space,* 87th Cong, 2d sess., 1 June 1962. Portions written by Moynihan include "Guiding Principles of Federal Architecture," 11–12, and "The Redevelopment of Pennsylvania Avenue," 12–15. The architectural guidelines came to apply to new federal office buildings, and have shaped two generations of federal building design. In addition to reflecting criteria of efficiency and economy, the guidelines insist that such buildings "must provide visual testimony to the dignity, enterprise, vigor, and stability of American government." Principles include the need to attend to regional traditions of art and architecture and to incorporate the work of living American artists in design qualities. The second element of the *Report,* on the need for planning to focus on the redevelopment of Pennsylvania Avenue so as to round out and complement the planning of the nation's capital that began with George Washington and Maj. Charles Pierre L'Enfant, commenced a large urban-renewal enterprise, just now coming to a conclusion.

9. Daniel P. Moynihan, "The Question of the States: Some New Horizons," *The Commonweal* 77, no. 3 (12 October 1962): 65–68. In an age of growing centralization of federal power, what future is there for state governments? Will the outcome of the Supreme Court's reapportionment decisions be accompanied by a revival of interest in state government, which, since the New Deal, has "declined amidst neglect, indifference, and worse, disdain"? Argues revival is likely because post–New Deal federal programs require new levels of competence in states. Most pressing issue is ethno-religious conflict over future of education. In new "post-Protestant" era, states may be able to experiment with new forms of support for education in ways not possible at federal level.

10. President's Task Force on Manpower Conservation, *One-Third of a Nation: A Report on Young Men Found Unqualified for Military Service* (Washington, D.C.: GPO, 1964). In July 1963, Moynihan proposed to the White House that a study be made of the rejection rates of males called up under the Selective Service Act. At the time, about one-half of such men failed the physical or mental examination or both. Closer analysis showed that if the whole age cohort was examined, the rejection rate would be one-third. Great variation appeared along regional and racial lines, arguing the case that social provision was equally varied. Presented to President Johnson in January 1964, *One-Third of a Nation* became the principal database for the planners of the Johnson antipoverty program.

11. Daniel P. Moynihan and James Q. Wilson, "Patronage in New York State, 1955–1959," *American Political Science Review* 58, no. 2 (June 1964): 286–301. Analysis of the efforts of the Harriman administration to discover and apply guidelines for patronage decisions that would optimize the attainment of two conflicting goals—staffing the government with competent administrators and consolidating power over the party apparatus. Prominence of ethnicity and class considerations in both.

12. U.S. Department of Labor, Office of Policy Planning and Research, *The Negro Family: The Case for National Action* (Washington, D.C.: GPO, 1965). The famous "Moynihan Report," which brought together the data, historical and social scientific, to back the assertion that "The United States is approaching a new crisis in race relations," a crisis that would follow upon the provision of full civil rights for African-Americans. "Being Americans, they will now expect that in the near future equal opportunities for them as a group will produce roughly equal results, as compared with other groups. This is not going to happen. Nor will it happen for generations unless a new and special effort is made." The report cited two reasons for this prediction. "The racist virus in the American blood stream still afflicts us: Negroes will encounter serious personal prejudice for at least another generation." Second was a fundamental problem new to social policy. Argues that after "three centuries of sometimes unimaginable mistreatment" a heavy toll had been taken. "The fundamental problem . . . is that of family structure. The evidence—not final but powerfully persuasive—is that the Negro family in the urban ghettos is crumbling. A middle class group has managed to save itself, but for vast numbers of the unskilled, poorly educated, city working class, the fabric of conventional social relationships has all but disintegrated. . . . So long as this situation persists, the cycle of poverty and disadvantage will continue to repeat itself." The thesis of the report was that this situation confronted the nation with "a new kind of problem. Measures that have worked in the past, or would work for most groups in the present, will not work here. A national effort is required that will give a unity of purpose to the many activities of the Federal government in this area, directed to a new kind of national goal: the establishment of a stable Negro family structure."

13. Daniel P. Moynihan, "Breakthrough at Ljubljana," *National Jewish Monthly* (September 1965), 15–17. Ethno-religious factors at the international level. At conference of UN Commission on Human Rights, Soviets agree to right of groups and individuals to associate with one another "across borders."

14. Daniel P. Moynihan, "Employment, Income, and the Ordeal of the Negro Family," *Daedalus, Journal of the American Academy of Arts and Sciences* (fall 1965), 745–70. Argues most pressing problem in American social policy is need to "provide such a measure of full employment for Negro workers that the impact of unemployment on family structure is removed." Assumes relationship between employment and family structure, "not an inconsiderable assumption. No one knows whether it is justified or not. The relationship between economic phenomena, such as employment, and social phenomena, such as family structure, has hardly begun to be traced in the United States."

15. Daniel P. Moynihan, "The Professionalization of Reform," *Public Interest* (fall 1965), 6–16. An influential article that contrasted the reforms of the New Deal, rooted in party concerns, in the exegencies of crisis, and in long-standing views of constituencies, with the reforms of the early 1960s, rooted not in strong ties either to party or to groups on the ground but rather to the arguments of social scientists

in the bureaucracy and academe, and adopted in part because of an embarrassment of riches—the government's surplus revenues, which relentlessly increased at the time despite tax cuts and new experiments in revenue sharing.

16. Daniel P. Moynihan, "The War against the Automobile," *The Public Interest,* no. 3 (spring 1966): 10–26. Discussion of the dimensions and ramifications of the problem of automobile safety. Three reasons for size of the problem: the venality of the auto industry, the psychological role of the automobile (a symbol of potency and power), and the failure of government to think and act seriously about the matter.

17. Daniel P. Moynihan, "Who Gets in the Army?" *The New Republic,* 5 November 1966, 19–22. The American armed services, having become a potent instrument for education and occupational mobility, have been systematically excluding the least-educated, least-mobile young men—African American males—a situation that amounts to "perhaps the largest single area of de facto job discrimination."

18. Daniel P. Moynihan, "The President & the Negro: The Moment Lost," *Commentary* (February 1967), 31–45. Argues that Republican gains in the 1966 elections indicated an electorate fed up with demonstrations and riots and in the midst of withdrawal of sentiment from the African American cause. Elections herald beginnings, manifest in "the popularity of Ronald Reagan's disquisitions on welfare mothers," of long-term GOP drive to assume control of national government. The moment lost was the failure to follow up on Lyndon Johnson's Howard University speech of 4 June 1965, with a then-possible total (as opposed to partial) commitment to the cause of African American equality. Foreshadows a theme of lost moments that would be elaborated in detail as related to Nixon's policy proposals in *The Politics of a Guaranteed Income.* One reason claimed for the loss was the "frenzy of arrogance and nihilism" generated by civil rights militants, black and white, in reaction to Moynihan's Department of Labor report *The Negro Family: The Case for National Action.*

19. Daniel P. Moynihan, "Urban Conditions: General," *Annals of the American Academy of Political and Social Science* 371 (May 1967): 159–77. Solving urban problems is an increasingly important concern for American government, and social scientists can make a contribution by providing useful social indicators. Spells out factors that go into making such indicators useful and interpreting them in a useful fashion.

20. Daniel P. Moynihan, "Sources of Resistance to the Coleman Report," *Harvard Educational Review* 38, no.1 (1968): 23–36. Moynihan's first effort to figure out why those one might have expected to be friends of the kind of social research that both he and Coleman were identified with (data in Coleman's work on equality of educational opportunity were strongly convergent with data developed by Moynihan on the African American family) were in fact quite hostile toward it. Analyzes responses to Coleman Report of three interested groups: the educational establishment, the reform establishment, and the research establishment.

21. Daniel P. Moynihan, "Toward a National Urban Policy," *The Public Interest* (fall 1969), 3–20. Lead chapter in the edited volume of the same title, a major state-

ment on the need for greater coherence in fragmented federal policies aimed at cities. Based on the observation that "there is a certain nonlinearity in the relationship between the number of categorical aid programs issuing forth from Washington and the degree of social satisfaction that ensues." Calls for a national urban policy not burdened by "institutional naïvete" and suggests a "primary mark of competence in a federal official should be the ability to see the interconnections between programs immediately at hand, and the urban problems that pervade the larger society." Sets out ten fundamentals to be kept in mind in confronting urban affairs, among them the need to acknowledge "hidden policies" as well as manifest ones and the need to make federalism work in the interests of more satisfying local communities. Washington alone cannot make a difference. There is need to step back "from the worship of the nation state with its barbarous modernity and impotent might."

22. Daniel P. Moynihan, "Politics as the Art of the Impossible," *The American Scholar* (fall 1969), 573–83. A commencement address at University of Notre Dame. Argues that "much of the intense difficulty of our time is in nature conceptual, and that it arises from a massive misstatement of our problems." Takes up the hostility, disorder, and generalized rejection of authority on campuses at the time, suggesting "diffusion of violence to our intellectual life is likely to lead to even greater failure to state our problems correctly than has been the case to date." Argues that "crisis of the time is not political, it is in essence religious," involving large numbers of "intensely moral, even godly, people who no longer hope for God." Rather, they transmute "the quest for divinity" into "secular form, but with an intensity of conviction that is genuinely new to our politics." Result is "the great disease of the committed intellectual of our time" and pursuit of the impossible through politics. Among the things government cannot provide: "it cannot provide values to persons who have none, or who have lost those they had. It cannot provide a meaning to life. It cannot provide inner peace."

23. Daniel P. Moynihan, "The Presidency & the Press," *Commentary* 51, no. 3 (March 1971): 41–52. Reviews deteriorating relationship and its cultural background in the deceits and secrecy deployed for policy purposes during the Vietnam War. "The result was a contradiction impossible to resolve. The public interest was at once served and disserved by secrecy; at once disserved and served by openness. Whatever the case, distrust of government grew." Outlines five basic circumstances at work to undermine the historic balance between the presidency and the media. "It is the thesis here that if this balance should tip too far in the direction of the press, our capacity for effective democratic government will be seriously and dangerously weakened."

24. Daniel P. Moynihan, "Equalizing Education: In Whose Benefit?" *The Public Interest*, no. 29 (fall 1972): 69–89. Discussion of an "autogamous mode of government growth: big government ordering itself to become bigger" via court rulings on the equalization of per-pupil expenditure. Review of evidence in sociology of

education on limits of effect from rulings of this type, and argument that poor could suffer rather than benefit from changes. New expenditures have not induced "strong perception of unmet needs being met." Points to dramatic expansion of public sector under way, driven in part by work of new middle class in "the helping professions." Outlines cycle "anyone who has worked for social legislation will be familiar with. As government responds to a problem and the situation commences to change, those who initiated the response, and who benefit from it one way or another, seek to ensure continued response by charging that the situation either has not improved, or has worsened, or has always been worse than originally asserted." Argues case for judicial restraint, particularly need to take social scientific evidence seriously.

25. Daniel P. Moynihan, "An Address to the Entering Class at Harvard College, 1972," *Commentary* (December 1972), 55–60. Discussion of the work of Joseph Schumpeter and Lionel Trilling as prophets and critics of liberal capitalism who predict rise of extremist ideological politics. Argues, "the ideological initiative at Harvard has been yielded to the extremists. Many ignore their views, but few contest them."

26. Daniel P. Moynihan, "Presenting the American Case," *The American Scholar* (fall 1975), 564–83. Lecture at the University of Chicago takes up the international history of the twentieth century and the rivalry of communism, socialism, and the liberal tradition. Spells out the sense in which world politics is becoming collectivist. "To write of this phenomenon with ill temper or ridicule is unworthy," but the American case for a combination in liberalism of the claims of both liberty and equality must be presented. Suggests social democrats of America, given their historic relations with the labor unions, make up the sector that should be heard in international circles.

27. Daniel P. Moynihan, "Aid for Parochial Schools," *Catholic Mind* (September 1977), 51–60. Commencement address at LeMoyne College. Reviews history of church-state separation from the standpoint of the history of the American Catholic subculture and critiques recent Supreme Court rulings in area. Argues for constitutionality of a tax credit scheme that would provide federal aid to Catholic schools, and makes case for pluralism rather than uniformity as a proper end for federal policy-making.

28. Daniel P. Moynihan, "The Politics and Economics of Regional Growth," *Public Interest*, no. 51 (spring 1978): 3–21. Takes up the question of the federal government and regionalism in American history, arguing that the West and South have benefited excessively while the Northeast has declined. Observes, "we must not politicize the question of relative regional growth, or, for that matter, regional decline." Insists that it is "contrary to the spirit of the Constitution" for federal government to try to prevent natural movements of capital and people from one state or region to another, and in any case is too complex a set of problems for it to handle. But while "government should not promise to do what it can't do," nonetheless "government must do what it can." Identifies with tradition of "activist national

liberalism" of the New Deal, a tradition given birth in the Northeast. Calls for federal assistance in saving the city of New York and for new research efforts in connection with the social and economic dynamics of regional movements.

29. Daniel P. Moynihan, "The Case for Tuition Tax Credits," *Phi Delta Kappan* (December 1978), 274–76. The issue is not the future of public schools, but whether public education will soon have a monopoly in the United States. Argues that "the public sector is slowly but steadily vanquishing the private."

30. Daniel P. Moynihan, "Social Science and the Courts," *The Public Interest,* no. 54 (winter 1979): 12–31. Deals with relations between social science and jurisprudence from the time of Pound, Cardozo, and Holmes to present. Expresses "wonder at the legal realists' seeming perception of 'natural law' as pre-scientific. It may have been for them, but it was nothing of the sort to the framers of the Constitution, for whom natural law, as we think of it, and scientific law were parts of an integrated understanding of the behavior of both physical objects and human beings." Discusses both utility and limits of social science for the duties of the courts.

31. Daniel Patrick Moynihan, "Patterns of Ethnic Succession: Blacks and Hispanics in New York City," *Political Science Quarterly* 94, no. 1 (spring 1979): 1–14. Reviews data on education, occupation, and income of blacks and Hispanics in connection with theory of ethnic succession. Politics of ethnic succession had brought considerable progress, which must not be undone by government. New forms of economic planning are necessary. "The social programs of the 1960s, overpraised at the time . . . , are now generally overcriticized."

32. Daniel P. Moynihan, "What Do You Do When the Supreme Court Is Wrong?" *Public Interest,* no. 57 (fall 1979): 3–24. Takes up once again Court thinking on separation of church and state. Reviews reasons why even an original intent position would show "the state, at any level, is allowed to cooperate with religious groups in a nondiscriminatory manner in the furtherance of acceptably secular purposes." Commends public debate and legislative action as techniques for turning the Court around.

33. Daniel P. Moynihan, "Rescuing the Family," *America,* 26 July 1980, 26–27. Citing the authority of John LaFarge, S.J., on the Catholic doctrine of race relations ("the right to economic security attaches *primarily* to the family, as the primary unit of society, and to the individual in his relation to the family"), Moynihan recalls that the Family Assistance Plan of the Nixon administration, designed to aid children and families, eventually provided financial assistance for everyone *but* children and families. The subject has now disappeared from the national agenda. Claiming to know less than he did a quarter-century before, Moynihan gives this estimate of the way things are with respect to race relations and policy: "The condition of minorities in the United States, especially urban minorities, has both vastly improved and significantly deteriorated in recent years." The improvements for the one group are highly visible and associated with the benefits of government social policy. "By contrast, the other group is more and more hidden from public view, less and less understood either with respect to its conditions or its periodic convulsions. The re-

sult is increasing bitterness and the conviction on the part of those for whom social policy has brought little that little or even less was intended."

34. Daniel P. Moynihan, "Remembering John Dollard," *New York Times Book Review*, 9 November 1980, 7, 35–36. An appreciation for the work of John Dollard, published a few weeks after his death on 8 October, speaks of his 1937 classic *Caste and Class in a Southern Town* as "the finest study of group relations ever done." Treats as his greatest achievement the development of the "frustration-aggression" thesis, which displaced earlier, utilitarian views of behavior.

35. Daniel P. Moynihan, "One-Third of a Nation," *New Republic*, 9 June 1982, 18–21. Argues need to maintain "single most important federal program dealing with children, Aid to Families with Dependent Children (AFDC)" against "the most radical change the Reagan Administration has proposed," which would abolish Title IV of the Social Security Act and, under the guise of "the new federalism," return the care of dependent children "to those states that give a damn—and to those states that don't." Argues for more thoroughgoing nationalism in this case, with AFDC and Medicaid programs federally financed and providing uniform benefits. "What is not needed . . . is a response to the dilemma of welfare dependency that repeals the social insurance programs of the New Deal." Same argument would be made fourteen years later in opposition to the Clinton administration's welfare-reform proposals.

36. Daniel P. Moynihan, "The Paranoid Style in American Politics Revisited," *Public Interest*, no. 81 (fall 1985): 107–27. Discussion of the themes of Hofstadter's classic book as related to the suspicions regarding government and the media harbored by the Reagan-era new right.

37. Daniel P. Moynihan, "The Family and the Nation, 1965–1986," *America*, 22 March 1986, 221–23. The issue reprinted the seminal article the not-yet senator wrote for the magazine twenty-one years previously ("Family Policy for the Nation," 18 September 1965), which argued that the formulation of a national policy concerning the quality and stability of family life could be the cornerstone for a new era of U.S. social legislation, together with his up-to-date assessment of changes in social and political conditions since that time. The editors found his 1965 piece to have been "eerily prophetic and still woefully timely after a full generation."

38. Daniel P. Moynihan, "Constitutional Dimensions of State and Local Tax," *Publius: The Journal of Federalism* (summer 1986), 3–9. Argues that "Federalism is not a form of decentralization with which large corporations occasionally experiment when things get clogged at the top," but rather an American expression of what political scientist Daniel Elezar had treated as the "idea of covenant." Suggests separate jurisdictions are not rigid, but rather "all membranes of the federal system are permeable, but they are not to be ripped"—as they would be, he suggests, by proposed Reagan administration tax reforms that would eliminate deductibility of state and local taxation.

39. Daniel P. Moynihan, "The 'New Science of Politics' and the Old Art of Government," *Public Interest*, no. 86 (winter 1987): 22–35. Reflections on founders' belief, particularly Madison's, that government could be established on scientific prin-

ciples and that a "new science of politics" was possible. Comparison of Marx and Madison. Develops thesis that whereas the aim of Madisonian politics was to see that government would leave the citizens alone, "the problem now is that the citizens won't leave the government alone. They now plunder the State as the State was once thought to plunder them."

40. Daniel P. Moynihan, "The Modern Role of Congress in Foreign Affairs," *Cardozo Law Review* 9, no. 5 (April 1988): 1489–500. Discusses friction in legislative executive relations rooted in overuse of secrecy and national security argument. Excoriates executive branch disregard for international law rooted in the attitude of the Reagan administration: "Put plainly: it's for wimps, sissies, liberals, and anticommunists."

41. Daniel Patrick Moynihan, "Toward a Post-Industrial Social Policy," *Public Interest*, no. 96 (summer 1989): 16–27. Discussion relevant to the basic categories used in social analysis and policy. "If one sees the 1960s and early 1970s as the culmination of a long effort, beginning in the Progesssive era, to eliminate the particular kinds of poverty and distress associated with industrialism, they were hugely successful years. The effort could not, however, deal successfully with an emergent form of dependency: the kind associated with *post*-industrial society." Discusses rise of the "post-marital" family and the problems it presents for theories of socialization. Suggests family structure may now be principal determinant of class structure. Argues that new family arrangements mean we have "entered a new social condition."

42. Daniel P. Moynihan, "How to Lose: The Story of Maglev," *Scientific American* (November 1989), 130. Reports story of a contest no one was watching—development of a new mode of rail transportation invented in the United States but developed in Japan, Germany, and Great Britain rather than the United States because of the incompetence of American government. Reflections on the history of government transportation policy.

43. Daniel P. Moynihan, "Family and Nation Revisited," *Social Thought* 16, no. 2 (1990): 49–60. Contrary to the promise of the 1960s, the condition of families and children in the United States has deteriorated, and ideas of family policy must be readdressed, including culturally sensitive questions of family structure, poverty, drugs, and race. The relations between fiscal policy and family issues must be examined, and, in general, the findings of social science must be taken more seriously. "It is not the social science that has failed; it has been the inability of the larger society to understand and make use of the social science. A considerable essay could be written as to the institutions and individuals who rejected the information, distorted it, and defamed those associated with the work." Invokes the importance of religious tradition for understanding of social science, and places on "record the view of the author that, curious as it will seem to some, almost alone, the Catholic tradition in American social policy had the least difficulty accepting and interpreting the social science findings of those years. At a time of near panic in the 'policy classes,' somehow this religious tradition showed no fear of reason."

44. Daniel P. Moynihan, "Educational Goals and Political Plans," *Public Interest,* no. 102 (winter 1991): 32–48. Stresses the lack of fit between political pronouncements about educational goals and a now historically deep and consistent body of data from the sociology of education on educational performance and the variables that account for differences with respect to the same, a prominent theme in Moynihan's thought. Discussion of the findings and reception of the Coleman Report on equality of educational opportunity. Points out how little the educational innovations of the past generation have changed the basic situation. "Yet to leave the matter there would miss the point, for Coleman did more than put in place a new way of thinking about education. He also put in place a potentially powerful mode of accountability. His outputs, measured by specialists, can still be grasped by the general public. If, as forecast, the year 2000 arrives and the United States is nowhere near meeting the educational goals set out in 1990, the potential will nonetheless exist for serious debate as to why what was basically a political plan went wrong. We might even consider how it might have turned out better."

45. Daniel P. Moynihan, "Social Justice in the *Next* Century," *America* 165, no. 6 (14 September 1991): 132–37. Reflections on Pope John Paul II's encyclical on social justice, *Centesimus Annus,* and on the tradition of Catholic social thought beginning in the late nineteenth century and based on natural law thinking and the extension of "the concept of rights to the marketplace. Labor, it was decreed, was not a commodity." Questions the emphasis in *Centesimus* on failures of "the Social Assistance State" and suggests that this part of "the papal pronouncement has American fingerprints all over it. It would be well for those involved to come forward, and it would help if Rome let it be understood that to do so would be not only acceptable but necessary. How so? Because the argument must proceed from evidence." Inferences from natural law are not enough; Catholic social thought must take the findings of history and social science seriously.

46. Daniel P. Moynihan, "Senator Daniel P. Moynihan Spoofs Abstractionist Art at a Dedication Ceremony," in *Lend Me Your Ears: Great Speeches in History,* selected and introduced by William Safire (New York: W.W. Norton and Company, 1992), 208. As chairman of the board of the Hirshhorn Museum and Sculpture Garden at the Smithsonian Institution, Moynihan was asked for dedicatory remarks on the receipt of the massive abstract sculpture *Isis* by the artist Mark di Suvero. "*Isis* achieves an aesthetic transubstantiation of that which is at once elusive yet ineluctable in the modern sensibility," he observed. "Transcending socialist realism with an unequalled abstractionist range, Mr. di Suvero brings to the theme of recycling both the hard-edge reality of the modern world and the transcendent fecundity of the universe itself; a lasting assertion both of the fleetingness of the living, and the permanence of life; a consummation before which we stand in consistorial witness. It will be with us a long time."

47. Daniel P. Moynihan, "How the Great Society 'Destroyed the American Family,'" *Public Interest,* no. 108 (summer 1992): 53–64. Points out that the presidential-

election campaign then under way "marks the first in American history in which the issue of welfare dependency has been raised to the level of presidential politics." Reviews arguments about dependency and policy from days of Moynihan Report onward. Of the report, while insisting on the accuracy of its forecasts, remarks, "the report should have been published, but the thesis ought never to have been raised to the level of presidential pronouncement." On the legacy of the Great Society and the argument of 1990s conservatives that dependency was caused and encouraged by welfare policies, points out "this is absurd. The breakdown was there in the data before the Great Society." Concedes there is one sense in which conservative argument has a point: "For a brief time, the Great Society gave great influence in social policy to viewpoints that rejected the proposition that family structure might be a social issue."

48. Daniel P. Moynihan, "Defining Deviancy Down," *The American Scholar* (winter 1993), 17–30. Discussion of the concept of deviancy in the work of Emile Durkheim and Kai T. Erikson. While "social scientists are said to be on the lookout for poor fellows getting a bum rap," Erikson's theory of deviancy "clearly implies that there are circumstances in which society will choose *not* to notice the behavior that would be otherwise controlled, or disapproved, or even punished." Against this background, develops the "thesis that over the past generation . . . the amount of deviant behavior in American society has increased beyond the levels the community can 'afford to recognize,' and that, accordingly, we have been redefining the deviancy so as to exempt much conduct previously stigmatized, and also quietly raising the 'normal' level in categories where behavior is now abnormal by any earlier standard. This redefining has evoked fierce resistance from defenders of 'old' standards, and accounts for much of the present 'cultural war' such as proclaimed by many at the 1992 Republican National Convention." Proceeds to define and elaborate three categories of redefinition along these lines: "the *altruistic*, the *opportunistic*, and the *normalizing*."

49. Daniel P. Moynihan, "The Professionalization of Reform II," *Public Interest*, no. 121 (fall 1995): 23–41. This is a revisit to the themes first spelled out in Moynihan's classic 1965 piece on this subject, which appeared as the first article of the first issue of *The Public Interest.* That piece stressed the idea that the major government reforms of the time did not issue from the bottom up and with the benefit of long political deliberation and testing, but rather from the schemes of professional social scientists in the bureaucracy and academe, which has been the source for new energy in the executive. Excess revenues in the period, even after substantial tax cuts, required new initiatives for reasons of economic management. Out of this historic mix of circumstances a deep-seated "pattern emerges. Great undertakings are proposed in political campaigns, often crafted by professional techniques such as polling and focus groups. If the campaign succeeds, the undertaking is taken as validated. Experts are set to work and the bill emerges." Treats the handling of the Clinton health care plan as the prime recent example of this style of reform. As the

"deficit came to be the central fact of central government, whatever professionals might think best, it could not be paid for." The political costs of failure to link expertise with genuine democracy weighed heavily on the fortunes of the Democrats, as the Republicans devised new forms of populist rhetoric aimed at the social controls of modern government established by the professionals.

50. Daniel P. Moynihan, "Moved by the Data, Not Doctrine," *New York Times Magazine,* 31 December 1995, 25. Moynihan's obituary appreciation for the work of his friend James S. Coleman, "the foremost mathematical sociologist of his age." Stresses the degree to which the "Coleman Report" on equality of educational opportunity of 1966 had isolated family structure as the most important variable in explaining differences in educational achievement. Points out that in the furor over busing and desegregation that followed in the wake of the report, "Coleman became one of the first of the politically incorrect scholars of our time. It was the singular fate of postwar American liberalism that at its peak moment of social optimism, the mid 1960s, a number of studies appeared that argued that social change was going to be far more difficult than anyone had thought. This information was received with equanimity in some liberal quarters but with denial in most. Coleman was viciously attacked in the mode that Hannah Arendt had observed among the totalitarian elites in Europe—the ability to immediately dissolve every statement of fact into a question of motive. Liberalism faltered when it turned out it could not cope with truth. Even the tentative truths of social science."

51. Daniel P. Moynihan and Taubman Center for State and Local Government, "The Federal Budget and the States: Fiscal Year 1997" (John F. Kennedy School of Government, Harvard University and Office of Senator Daniel P. Moynihan, 1996). This is the twentieth edition in an annual series of "Fisc reports" begun by Moynihan in 1976. Initially confined to New York State and its federal relations, the series in the 1990s became nationwide in coverage. The data provide details on the "balance of payments" as between the states and Washington. Moynihan is author of the introduction, "A Culture of Waste," a phrase used in a charge against him by the speaker of the House of Representatives, Newt Gingrich. Gingrich had asserted, "Moynihan has a terrible problem. He has got to go to the country and defend an extraordinarily expensive government in the state of New York, and extraordinarily expensive government in New York City, absurd union work rules and a culture of waste for which they expect us to send them a check." In response, Moynihan observes, "summoning balance of payments figures from previous Fisc reports, I stated, 'New York has been subsidizing Georgia for the last 60 years. End of subject.'"

52. Daniel P. Moynihan, "When Principle Is at Issue," *Washington Post,* 4 August 1996, C7. Excerpted from a speech on the Senate floor in opposition to the passage of the Welfare Reform Act of 1996, argues the "premise of this legislation is that the behavior of adults can be changed by making the lives of their children as wretched as possible. This is a fearsome assumption, and certainly not a conservative one." Points out that welfare-to-work elements of the bill require for success a "large scale

public jobs program, and that would require a great deal of money." Stresses long-term negative impact on state and local governments. On idea that historic bill represents a defeat for the liberals, argues "this is nonsense. It is conservatives who have lost. For the best part of two years now, I have pointed out that the principal—and most principled—opponents of this legislation were conservative social scientists who for years have argued against liberal nostrums for changing society." Points also to opposition of Catholic bishops to legislation. "All honor to them. They have kept to their principles. Honor on high as well to the Catholic bishops, who admittedly have an easier task with matters of this sort. When principles are at issue, they simply look them up. Too many liberals, alas, simply make them up."

53. Report of the Commission on Protecting and Reducing Government Secrecy, *Secrecy,* S. Doc. 105-2, 103d Cong. (Washington, D.C.: GPO, 1997). Moynihan served as chairman of the commission (only the second government inquiry in this field in forty years), and the author of a lengthy "Chairman's Foreword," which reviews the history of the problem and government policy in this field, together with some of the major writings by social scientists and others bearing upon what has come to be called "the culture of secrecy." The report argues for "a new way of thinking about secrecy," and suggests such a way in observing "secrecy is a form of government regulation." Growth and expansion of the culture of secrecy has "degraded the public service" and undermined public trust in the statements of officials. Concedes that "some secrecy is vital to save lives, bring miscreants to justice, protect national security, and engage in effective diplomacy," yet calls for much greater openness and points out that "the classification system, for example, is used too often to deny the public an understanding of the policymaking process, rather than for the necessary protection of intelligence activities and other sensitive matters." Declassification and tighter restrictions on classification in the future "by allowing for a fuller understanding of the past" will provide "opportunities to learn lessons from what has gone before—making it easier to resolve issues concerning the Government's past actions and helping prepare for the future."

54. Daniel P. Moynihan, "Not Bad for a Century's Work," *Washington Post,* 23 November 1997, C7. Lays out in considerable detail the twentieth-century history and achievements of urban planning in the nation's capital from the work of the McMillan Commission of 1901 through the reconstruction of Pennsylvania Avenue between Capitol Hill and the White House, "the defining symbol of separate but connected legislative and executive branches of government," a process of development with which he was closely associated from the 1960s onward, culminating in the opening of the Ronald Reagan Building in 1997.

55. Daniel P. Moynihan et al., "Memorandum of Points and Authorities of Senators Robert C. Byrd, Daniel Patrick Moynihan, and Carl Levin as Amici Curiae in Support of Plaintiffs' Motions to Declare Line Item Veto Act Unconstitutional," in the case *The City of New York v. Clinton* (26 November 1997). A section of the brief drafted by Senator Moynihan argues that the Line Item Veto Act interferes with the

process of trade-offs and compromise envisioned by the framers and used by Congress throughout American history to build coalitions and obtain a majority of votes to pass legislation. The provision for the vice president's deciding vote when the Senate is equally divided recognizes the process by which coalitions are formed. The brief contends that the act unconstitutionally empowers the president to repeal a provision or provisions whose inclusion in the legislation may have been essential to its passage. "Absent that provision," according to the brief, "a Senator (or Representative) might have voted 'nay,' and the bill would have failed. Under the Line Item Veto Act, the President can strike that provision and create a 'truncated version' of law which would not have passed the Congress."

56. Daniel P. Moynihan, "On the Commodification of Medicine," 10 December 1997. "Health insurance is important, but health is more important. It comes out of discovery, and we are in a great age of discovery." He continued that "the existence of public goods provides a rationale for the government to intervene in markets and either directly provide the public good—as it does with national defense—or to support the provision of the public good through indirect payments." To that end, Moynihan noted that as chairman of the Finance Committee, he had offered the first proposal creating a medical education trust fund that recognizes medical education as a public good—one that should be supported by dedicated, stable, long-term funding. That proposal has yet to pass. "Expect matters to grow more difficult in the near future. . . . But be of good cheer. Some things take a long time, as Lewis Thomas attested. Most importantly, may a layman urge that you [medical school educators] be importunate."

ABOUT THE CONTRIBUTORS

Michael Barone is a senior staff editor of *Reader's Digest.* A journalist with a law degree, he has been an editorial writer and columnist for the *Washington Post* and a senior writer for *U.S. News & World Report.* He is the author of *Our Country: The Shaping of America from Roosevelt to Reagan* and the coauthor of *The Almanac of American Politics.*

Charles Blitzer was the director of the Woodrow Wilson International Center for Scholars from 1988 to 1997. Prior to assuming that position, he was president and director of the National Humanities Center from 1983 to 1988. He held two posts at the Smithsonian Institution from 1965 to 1983: director of education and training and assistant secretary for history and art. He taught political science at Yale University and has been a lecturer and visiting professor at other institutions. He coauthored *The Age of Power* (with C. J. Friedrich) and has written three books: *An Immortal Commonwealth, The Commonwealth of England,* and *The Age of Kings.* Over the years, he has collaborated with Daniel Patrick Moynihan on a variety of projects.

Bill Bradley, U.S. senator from New Jersey (1979–97) was a colleague of Daniel Patrick Moynihan's. His areas of expertise include tax reform, international trade, pension reform, community building, and race relations. Among his legislative achievements are the 1992 Freedom Exchange Act and the Omnibus Water Bill of 1992. He is the author of *Life on the Run* (about his decade with the New York Knicks basketball team), *The Fair Tax* (which helped popularize ideas that eventually became the Tax Reform Act of 1986), and *Time Present, Time Past* (a memoir based largely on his experience as a senator and his travels around the country). Since leaving the Senate, he has divided his time among the University of Maryland, Stanford University, the National Civic League, the Advertising Council's Advisory Committee on Public Issues, CBS-TV Evening News, and J.P. Morgan and Co.

Richard K. Eaton is the managing partner in the Washington, D.C., office of the New York law firm of Stroock & Stroock & Lavan LLP. Prior to that, he worked for Senator Moynihan for eight of the first eighteen years of Senator Moynihan's congressional career, including two stints as the senator's chief of staff. He has been associated with the senator's Judicial Screening Panel since its inception in 1977 either as a member of the senator's staff or as a member of the panel itself. He is now chair of the Judicial Screening Panel.

Nicholas N. Eberstadt is a researcher at the American Enterprise Institute and the Harvard Center for Population and Development Studies. He is the author of numerous studies on demographics, economic development, and public policy. His most recent book is *The Tyranny of Numbers: Mismeasurement and Misrule.* He was a teaching fellow in Professor Moynihan's course "Social Science and Social Policy" (Social Science 115).

Suzanne R. Garment is a resident scholar at the American Enterprise Institute, where her research includes media coverage of politics, ethics in government, and government-business relations. Her most recent book is *Scandal: The Culture of Mistrust in American Politics.* She worked with Ambassador Moynihan at the United Nations and on the book *A Dangerous Place.*

Nathan Glazer is professor of sociology and education emeritus, Harvard University, and coeditor of the journal of public affairs *The Public Interest.* He is the author and editor of numerous books on American ethnicity, race relations, and social policy. His most recent book is *We Are All Multiculturalists Now.* With Daniel P. Moynihan, he wrote *Beyond the Melting Pot* and edited *Ethnicity: Theory and Experience.*

Stephen Hess has been a senior fellow in governmental studies at the Brookings Institution since January 1972. He is the author of fifteen books, including *International News & Foreign Correspondents, News & Newsmaking, Presidents & the Presidency, Live from Capitol Hill! Studies of Congress and the Media, The Presidential Campaign, Organizing the*

Presidency, The Washington Reporters, The Government/Press Connection, and *The Ultimate Insiders: U.S. Senators in the National Media.* He has served the nation in a variety of positions in government, and worked closely with Daniel Patrick Moynihan as deputy assistant for urban affairs to President Nixon.

Robert A. Katzmann is Walsh professor of government, professor of law, and professor of public policy at Georgetown University; president of the Governance Institute; and acting director of the government studies program at the Brookings Institution. A lawyer and political scientist, he most recently published *Courts and Congress.* He was head teaching fellow in Professor Moynihan's course "Social Science and Social Policy" (Social Science 115), has been a member of Senator Moynihan's judicial screening panel, and served as special counsel in the Supreme Court confirmation of Justice Ruth Bader Ginsburg.

Michael J. Lacey is a historian and director of the division of U.S. studies for the Woodrow Wilson International Center for Scholars. He is the author of numerous articles and the editor of several books, including *A Culture of Rights: The Bill of Rights in Philosophy, Politics, and Law 1791 and 1991* (with Knud Haakonssen); *Religion and Twentieth-Century American Intellectual Life; Government and Environmental Politics: Essays on Historical Development since World War II; The Truman Presidency;* and *The State and Social Investigation in Britain and the United States* (with Mary Furner).

Seymour Martin Lipset is the Hazel professor of public policy at the Institute of Public Policy, George Mason University; a senior fellow at the Hoover Institution at Stanford University; and a senior scholar at the Woodrow Wilson International Center for Scholars and at the Progressive Policy Institute. His major work is in the fields of political sociology, Canadian and American societies, trade union organizations, social stratification, public opinion, the American Jewish community, the sociology of intellectual life, and the conditions for democracy in comparative perspective. Among his many works are *Political Man, The First New Nation, The Politics of Unreason,* and most recently, *American Exceptionalism: A Double-Edged Sword* (1996). He is the only person to have been president of the American Sociological Association (1992–1993) and the American Political Science Association (1979–1980). Professor Lipset was a colleague of Daniel Patrick Moynihan's at Harvard University, where he was the George D. Markham professor of government and sociology.

T. P. Moynihan has been a cartoonist for most of his life, but he was not published until he was fourteen. His work has appeared in a range of places, from *Playboy* to *American Spectator.* A native of Albany, New York, Moynihan lives in Brooklyn with his wife and daughter. He is Senator Moynihan's eldest child and a longtime fan.

Robert A. Peck is commissioner of the Public Buildings Service of the U.S. General Services Administration. In prior public service, he worked at the U.S. Office of Management and Budget, the National Endowment for the Arts, the Carter White House, and the Federal Communications Commission. He was an aide to Senator Moynihan, first as a committee counsel overseeing the Public Buildings Service and then as his chief of staff. A land use and real estate lawyer, Peck was group vice president for government and public affairs of the American Institute of Architects. He has been active in historic preservation and urban design, serving as president of the D.C. Preservation League and as a presidential appointee on the U.S. Commission of Fine Arts, the federal design-review board for the nation's capital.

Tim Russert is moderator of *Meet the Press* and political analyst for *NBC Nightly News* and the *Today* program. He anchors *The Tim Russert Show* and hosts the Fred Friendly Seminars on PBS. Russert also serves as senior vice president and Washington bureau chief of NBC News. Apart from a distinguished career as a broadcast journalist and executive, Russert has held positions of responsibility in government, as special counsel to Senator Daniel Patrick Moynihan (1977–82) and as counselor to New York Governor Mario M. Cuomo (1983–84).

James Q. Wilson is James Collins professor of management emeritus at UCLA. For twenty-six years he was a professor of government at Harvard University, much of that time as the Shattuck professor of government. He is the author or coauthor of fourteen books, the most recent being *Moral Judgment: Does the Abuse Excuse Threaten Our Legal System?* Wilson has served on a number of national commissions concerned with public policy, including the White House Task Force on Crime, which he chaired, and the National Advisory Commission on Drug Abuse Prevention. For five years he was a member of the president's Foreign Intelligence Advisory Board. A former president of the American Political Science Association, he received that organization's highest honor, the James Madison Award for Distinguished Scholarship. He was a colleague of Moynihan's at Harvard, and the two coauthored "Patronage in New York State, 1955–1959," in the June 1964 issue of the *American Political Science Review.*

INDEX